S0-BBS-516

Big Brother NSA

&

Its "Little Brothers"

The
National Security Agency's
Global Surveillance Network

TERRY L. COOK

BIG BROTHER NSA & ITS "LITTLE BROTHERS"

Copyright © 1998
Terry L. Cook
61535 S. Highway 97
Unit 9, Ste. 288
Bend, OR 97702

First Printing — January, 1998

SCM Publishing
61535 S. Highway 97
Unit 9, Ste. 288
Bend, OR 97702

Library of Congress Catalog Card Number 97-062124
ISBN 1-57558-036-5

ALL RIGHTS RESERVED

No part of this publication may be reproduced, stored in a retrieval system, or transmitted in any form or by any means—electronic, mechanical, photocopy, recording, or otherwise—without the express prior permission of Whitaker House (the publisher) and/or Terry L. Cook (the copyright holder), with the exception of brief excerpts in magazine articles and/or reviews.

LUCID 2000™ is a registered trademark of the Advanced Technologies Group, Inc., New Rochelle, New York. Wherever the acronym LUCID or LUCID 2000™ appear in this publication, the trademark provisions of law apply.

Printed in the United States of America

Foreword by Jack Van Impe

The ministry of Terry Cook is a highly specialized one. A former investigator, he delves into his projects with gusto. No one digs as deeply in uncovering facts. His documentation is always awesome and voluminous. This is particularly true in his most recent work, *Big Brother NSA and Its Little Brothers*.

Terry has been a blessing to multiplied ministries—including mine—keeping us informed on latter-day technologies. Anyone reading his books will be mentally and spiritually challenged.

Reverend Terry Cook is undoubtedly the most qualified expert on the subject of the mark of the beast. His documented materials, when presented publicly, will stir hearts in an unprecedented way to either get listeners saved, restored, or revived. I recommend this prophetical specialist to any church for a series of meetings.

— Dr. Jack Van Impe

Contents

About the Author

Terry L. Cook
Second Coming Ministries, Inc.
61535 S. Highway 97
Unit 9, Ste. 288
Bend, OR 97702
Phone: (541) 593-9916
Fax: (541) 593-9917

Terry L. Cook is a fundamentalist Christian researcher and retired Los Angeles Deputy Sheriff, as well as a former State of California fraud investigator/Deputy Real Estate Commissioner. He holds A.A., A.S., B.A. & B.S. degrees. He also holds California State teaching credentials in a variety of subjects and has completed some postgraduate study in Theology. He is a California-licensed real estate broker and an FAA-licensed airline transport jet pilot (commercial) and flight instructor.

For the past six years, Mr. Cook, who is an ordained minister of the gospel, has been investigating current events as they relate to the fulfillment of "last days" or "end times" Bible prophecies, with an emphasis on biometric identification technology, including smart cards and biochip transponder implants. He is accepted widely as an authority in the field. He is much in demand as a speaker in large churches and other lecture forums, including appearances and interviews on radio and television. If your organization is interested in bringing him to your area, you may contact **Second Coming Ministries at 61535 S. Highway 97, Unit 9, Ste. 288, Bend, OR 97702.**

In addition to his speaking ministry, Mr. Cook has produced several educational, informative videos and books on the subject, containing vital documentation of material which heretofore has been difficult—if not impossible—to obtain. Presently, he is making available an excellent package of information on implantable biochip technology and how it relates to the New World Order plan to enslave and control us.

Terry Cook is a man called by God for this particular mission at this particular time. . . to educate and alert the Church, so they won't be caught sleeping or unaware in these last days and overtaken as by a "thief in the night." Remember the admonition in the Word of God, "I would not have you ignorant." Mr. Cook's desire is that you would not be "ignorant" of what is going on around us and the importance of the message it foretells.

Mr. Cook hopes to convey to everyone who reads this book that Jesus is coming soon, and we need to get serious about God and get ready for what's coming!

Big Brother NSA
Big Brother Isn't Coming...
He's Already Here!

Big Brother is planning to enslave you! How? Electronically, via the National Security Agency! It's true. Big Brother, as defined by George Orwell's book, *1984,* is no longer futuristic fiction. Orwell was off in his title—*1984*—by about 20 years (2004 is a more realistic date), however, *the scenario* he described is now closer to truth than fiction. I am convinced that the NSA and its affiliates will be the database source for the functioning of the Big Brother dictatorship, and in this book I shall document the foundation for my convictions.

Big Brother isn't on his way—he's already here! Furthermore, he is on the brink of taking control of the entire world —politically, economically, and theologically. Concurrently, he will enslave everyone electronically in cyberspace, by means of a sophisticated network of global computerization that will operate through an advanced form of the Internet and the National Security Agency, simultaneously.

The hub for this global activity in America will be the NSA Headquarters, located at Ft. Meade, Maryland. Indeed, Big Brother's **technological headquarters** will be located at the **NSA's main facility** at Ft. Meade. Evidence persuades me that ultimately the NSA's headquarters will provide the database into which information from all other information-gathering entities (worldwide) is funneled/downloaded for access by all...sort of like one-stop shopping.

Big Brother—which well could be interpreted *Antichrist*—soon will be "watching" you with ultra sophisticated technology, via thousands of networked "all-seeing-eye" satellites and databases, merging into the worldwide system of the NSA. *NSA techno-tyranny is just over the horizon!*

George Orwell's *1984:* A Big-Brotherly Vision Of the Antichrist

1984—the only thing preventing actual activation of Orwell's Big Brother in 1984 was the lack of sufficient technology to carry out the program, as described in the Book of Revelation (13:16-18). I'm sure that the prayers of the righteous standing in the gap were responsible for the 20-year delay. However, technology has advanced to the degree that keeping track of people, their finances, activities, *et al,* is no longer limited merely to an author's fertile imagination.

What is interesting to me—or perhaps curious is a better word—is 1997's new crop of Fall television programming. Before this year, the name "National Security Agency" was relatively unknown, and its activities even less publicized. Now numerous dramas and science fiction programs have incorporated the activities of the NSA (as well as the FBI and others) into the fabric of their storylines, and without exception, the NSA and its operatives always are portrayed as "the bad guys," with global access to anything through their satellites and other technology. It is depicted as an outfit who operates by "the end justifies the means" method, and invariably the NSA operatives tramp all over civil rights and the Constitution in their efforts to achieve their own ends—just or unjust! Even the first TV movie of the popular mystery program, *Murder, She Wrote!,* featuring "mystery writer Jessica Fletcher," was written around the mystery of the secret being covered up by the NSA about some satellite/computer encryption codes that were flawed, leaving the whole system unprotected, and how they were killing people to prevent the information from becoming public knowledge. By the way, last year's programming already was using GPS locators in its action series.

Without a doubt, George Orwell's *Big Brother* has arrived.
I believe this dictator-type character soon will manifest
himself as the incarnate devil-man of the apocalypse, the
Antichrist, the end-times "beast-man" described in the
Books of Daniel and Revelation. He will be the worst dictator
the world ever has known—he will make Adolf Hitler look
like a choir boy. Orwell's fictional character soon will become
real in the form of the Biblical Antichrist—the "man" whose
number is "666" (Rev. 13:16-18). This scripture declares that
no one will be able to buy or sell (in other words, transact
any business) without the mark of this dictator in either their
right hand or forehead. He will require sophisticated computer
equipment and surveillance technologies to enable him to
monitor and track everyone and everything in the world,
which will mean total enslavement for us. The Antichrist will
control your lives totally. . . Big Brother's NSA will be the
worst nightmare the world ever has known, and it will deliver
the world into the abyss of a new and final Dark Age!

The "666 Beast" Computer System is at the NSA

Contrary to popular belief, especially among Christians,
the "666 Beast Computer System" is not located in Europe.
It's right here in our own back yard, just the proverbial "stone's
throw" from our Capitol. As I pointed out previously, it is
situated on the Ft. Meade Army Base. (Ft. Meade is located
between Baltimore, Maryland, and Washington, DC.)

Soon, You Will Have Zero Privacy!

In order to accomplish their goals, the leaders of the NSA
must—of necessity—confiscate your right to privacy (or
convince you to relinquish it "for the greater good"). The
whole system is a trade-off; we allegedly need the benefits
that such a trade-off enables and must *willingly* give up our
individual freedoms because it is for the *greater good*. Theo-
retically, it will deter kidnapping, terrorism, drug running,
money laundering, bomb threats to airlines and others, crime,

et al, ad infinitum, ad nauseam—very good benefits. . . until they decide that *YOU* are the ones involved (with or without proof—you cease to be "innocent until *proven guilty*" and must, instead, *prove your innocence*). Even if all these benefits were as helpful and benign as they appear in the propaganda, and assuming they actually would work, would you be willing to give up everything, including your privacy, to the control of Big Brother? And the assumption that these "bad things" actually could be stopped by such surveillance and control is highly doubtful, anyway. Let's not be naive in our evaluation of the circumstances. . . when have you ever known the criminals, mafia, *et al*, to be unable to find a way around *any* system? Even if they lack the technology (which I doubt— they have the funds to hire the best, if they do their jobs and don't ask questions), they have no shortage of funds for bribery at the highest echelons. And they always will find someone who wants the additional finances. . . or they can threaten one's family and friends to intimidate them into providing the desired information.

Think **N S A !** Very soon we will have become irreversibly and inextricably trapped electronically via the NSA's computerized, international, Super Information Highway—the Internet, Internet II, and the Next Generation Internet (NGI). Soon, everything will be linked to the National Security Agency—soon, the largest database network on earth, the NSA, will become Big Brother, Incorporated!

NSA Cyber-Slavery: Coming Soon to a Neighborhood Near You

It's horrible, but true! A massive new system of computerized tracking, surveillance, and control is being installed now, right before our eyes. The target date for its completion is the year 2001. It will result in complete electronic enslavement—both of our physical persons and our transactions. Our new high-tech electronic "prison cell" is now under construction in the "Gulags" of cyberspace—*Cyberia*. Cyberia will replace the old Russian Siberia. Cyberia will not be a literal concentration camp in Russia—it will be a new kind of global, electronic concentration camp, located in the Gulags of cyberspace.

Cyberia will consist of thousands of linked databases from everywhere on earth. When fully operational, the system will include the combined "assets" (data) of the Internet, all surveillance and navigational satellites, all biometrically verified ID cards, and literally thousands of linked private, corporate, and government agency computers. Cyberia will become our real-time, computerized, "virtual prison," as it were.

Most of the citizens of this new "global village" won't be locked up in a literal prison, as in the past—that won't be necessary in the New World Order of cyber-slavery. With electronic incarceration—electronic shackles, if you will—Big Brother will know exactly *where we are* and *what we are doing* at all times, via sophisticated electronic surveillance technologies. . . including use of GPS equipment on your person or in your vehicle, television, computer, modem, fax, cellular phone, etc. If we refuse to cooperate totally with Big Brother, our "virtual reality" will be terminated! Indeed, we'll be unable to function in Big Brother's brave new system of global, electronic tyranny. Saying that *"there will be no place left to hide"* is a gross understatement!

Big Brother's Diabolical New World Order

The name of the game is surveillance, control, and enslavement! Soon, Big Brother, the Antichrist, intends to:

- Issue all Americans a national identity card with an international ID number
- Eventually replace these ID cards with an injectable microchip/biochip transponder, implanted permanently in your right hand
- Force you onto the Internet where all aspects of your life can be electronically monitored—tracked, analyzed, profiled, and controlled

- Force you to do all your buying and selling via computers in the coming cashless cyber-society called electronic commerce
- Centralize all government and private databases via Big Brother's National Security Agency at Ft. Meade, Maryland
- Force you into the New World Order, an Antichrist-led system of repackaged global communism, orchestrated through the United Nations

Big Brother According to George Orwell

Let's examine more closely the role of Big Brother in Orwell's book, *1984*, and ultimately, how his surveillance evolved into *total control* and *zero liberty*.

When Orwell wrote this famous (or infamous) novel in 1949, he was depicting society as he visualized it some 35 years into the future. The story is set in an allegedly imaginary, so-called "utopian" future where freedom of thought and action utterly have disappeared, and humans are under the constant scrutiny of an all-powerful, all-enslaving global government, symbolized by **Big Brother**, a male dictator whom the world must both worship and follow. Posters and television screens everywhere warn citizens that "Big Brother is watching you." Children are taken from their parents and raised by the state (and thoroughly indoctrinated or brainwashed with Big-Brotherism).

Love and traditional family relationships are strictly forbidden, and the secret police monitor and control ALL individual thought for "political correctness." (And the liberals of the 1990's thought they invented the concept of "politically correct"! It didn't originate with them—it just came into existence under their manipulation of the equality laws.) In Orwell's scenario, all movement is constantly under surveillance and personal privacy is both *nonexistent and illegal*.

The only important piece of technology missing from Orwell's vision of global control by Big Brother was the Mark-of-the-Beast biochip implant under the skin of everyone's right hand—and if the technology had been available at the time, I'm sure he would not have overlooked such an efficient device for identifying and tracking people. It probably would have been called "the Mark-of-Big-Brother," rather than the Mark-of-the-Beast, but the result would have been the same, without a doubt. One major piece of futuristic technology that he didn't overlook was the interactive televisions—it could look at you as easily as you could look at it. Now with fiber optics cables, *et al*, your television likely will be the place where all transactions—business, entertainment, communications, etc.—will occur. Already, you can order special events programming through your interactive screen, and banks are encouraging you to switch to banking at home on your own system, instead of writing those *old-fashioned paper checks* or requesting that *old-fashioned paper money*. Once the capability exists to use your television to reach into your home or bank account or medical records, how long do you suppose it will be before someone starts abusing the opportunity?

George Orwell, The Socialist

Grolier's 1994 Multimedia Electronic Encyclopedia has some very interesting things to say about George Orwell. "Orwell was a SOCIALIST" (meaning Communist) (emphasis added). Then it defines socialism as:

> A comprehensive set of beliefs or ideas about the nature of human society and ITS FUTURE DESIRABLE STATE [emphasis added].

Grolier's continues the link, by way of Marx and Engels, right down to the Communist Manifesto. The only logical conclusion is that socialism is the initial stage of communism. Can you see this progression in world affairs today?

So, then, in reality, who was George Orwell? Available evidence documents that he was a socialist, i.e., a communist, and his futuristic vision of a totalitarian Big-Brother-led Utopia, as depicted in *1984*, was far more than merely a novel—it was actually his forecast of things to come in an all-encompassing system of tyrannical communism.

The Origin of the Philosophy of Communism

Orwell's thought leaves us with the question of who "invented" the communist philosophy in the first place. It is common knowledge that it was Karl Marx, but what is not common knowledge is the fact that Marx was a *devout satanist*. That's right! The man who invented the most tyrannical form of government in history was a very religious devil worshipper! Satan worship is a religion, you know. Are you beginning to see where this is headed? Read on.

Orwell and The New World Order

Orwell's book seems more like a futuristic snapshot of the coming New World Order of global communism than some outdated novel, doesn't it. In fact, there is nothing outdated about this book; it is just now coming into its own. But could it be that Orwell "borrowed" his Big Brother ideas from Marxist theologies? You see, socialists/communists hate God and Christ (or deny Their existence), and for years have persecuted and exterminated God's people. This has occurred because communism is both a political and theological system. It is important to understand that communism is more than just a political system. It is also a religious system of devout Anti-christism.

From history, we can see clearly that Satan is the real "founder" of communism—not Karl Marx. Marx was simply a tool the devil used to implement his plan. Indeed, the politics of communism is radically religious Satanism. I wonder if Marx ever admitted publicly that "the devil made him do it"?

Not Really a Novel?

Grolier's encyclopedia continues its articles on Orwell with the following eye-opening remarks:

> . . . Although *1984* is sometimes **thought of as science fiction**, it is **actually a notable work of**

Utopian literature that emphasizes what Orwell believed were the dangers inherent in modern, bureaucratic
society [emphasis added].

Could *Grolier's* be saying here that *1984* never was intended
to be a novel, but rather a forecast of things to come in our
modern, technologically advanced world? I believe so! This
amazing admission by *Grolier's* begins to sound like your
typical "paranoid, right-wing extremist" philosophy. Right?
The fact that the opposite philosophical position is true is
what makes this admission so amazing!

Accordingly, when the satanic New World Order achieves
power and authority, what will exist is a slickly repackaged
system of global communism. However, since the word
communism now is regarded as a negative thing throughout
the world, the Big Brother ministers of propaganda will put
a "kinder, gentler" face on it, calling it "global democracy
in a global village." This is just one example of the kinds
of *perestroika* deceptions and Orwellian *newspeak* disinformation (lies) that former Soviet President Mikhail Gorbachev
utilizes as he travels and speaks internationally. His goal is
to have brainwashed everyone thoroughly in the next two
years in preparation for the Second October Communist
Revolution of the world—a New World Order of global communism. The goal is to conquer the world by the year 2001.
At that time, Big Brother NSA's databases can be used by
Satan's communists to control everyone!

Orwell's *1984* Should Have Been Titled *2004!*

As I pointed out previously, Orwell was not off in his predictions, just in the time table. The year *2004* would have been
more accurate. Just before he died, however, Orwell made
the following comment about our probable future:

> I do not believe that the kind of society I describe [in
> *1984*] necessarily will arrive, but I believe . . . that **some-
> thing resembling it could arrive. I believe also that**

totalitarian ideas have taken root in the minds of intellectuals everywhere [emphasis added].

At least he was intellectually honest enough to admit the truth! Orwell's statement pretty much says it all, doesn't it? Is it mere coincidence that globalists everywhere now advocate a similar-sounding New World Order? Is it coincidence that at the same time highly advanced Big-Brother-style surveillance technologies exist that easily could permit a global, tyrannical despot to take full electronic control of the world? Coincidence? *I think not!* Ah, enter Antichrist, the final Big Brother.

George Orwell's *1984* versus Aldous Huxley's *Brave New World [Order]*

In the 1930's—even before Orwell—Aldous Huxley wrote a book titled *Brave New World*. It described how a so-called "fictional," futuristic, totalitarian government might control its populace with modern technology, propaganda, and drugs. Huxley had this to say about such possibilities in 1947, just a few years before the **National Security Agency** was established.

> The theme of *Brave New World* is not the advancement of science as such; it is the **advancement of science as it affects human individuals**. . . . The sciences of matter can be **applied in such a way that they will destroy life** or make the living of it impossibly complex and uncomfortable. . . . **A really efficient totalitarian state would be one in which the all-powerful executive of political bosses [Big-Brother Antichrist] and their army of managers control a population of slaves who do not have to be coerced, because they love their servitude.** To make them love it is the task assigned, in present-day totalitarian states, to the ministries of **propaganda**, newspaper editors, and school teachers. [Emphasis added.]

Huxley's ideas regarding efficiently run dictatorships deserve more investigation and discussion, but I'm sure you get the general picture. Mind-controlling propaganda, news, and education (or as Orwell called it, *newspeak*) will prepare us mentally to *love* the coming New-World-Order tyranny under Big Brother, the devil.

Big Brother's New World Order Under Antichrist

The Bible informs us that in the "last days," just before the return of Jesus Christ to inaugurate His 1000-year millennial reign, the spirit of Lucifer, the Antichrist, Satan-the-Beast, would lead the world for a final, horrible, seven-year period called the **Great Tribulation.** The Bible says this *man,* whose number is **666**, will head a global system of government (presently being called the Ten-Region New World Order), and he will cause the entire world to worship him and receive his **mark** in their **right hands** or foreheads (Rev. 13:16). Scripture says that without this **ID Mark**, no one will be able to buy or sell anything, anywhere! Everyone will be owned and controlled by Big Brother, the Antichrist. And Big Brother's NSA will do the dirty work by identifying and controlling everyone electronically.

Big Brother's Internet-Connected Electronic ID And Money System

Throughout all of recorded history, such an evil system of global computerized control never before has been possible . . . *until now, that is!* Indeed, Satan's evil system of electronic servitude is being installed right before our very eyes, though few see it. This new system has been named by its secular designers "LUCID 2000™." The LUCID 2000™ international identification system will operate through the worldwide Internet Super Information Highway, about which we are hearing so much today. In addition, a new Internet monetary system, called Internet Commerce, soon will permit a digital,

international, cashless society of electronic buying and selling
to emerge fully. And remember to keep in mind, all of this
data will flow either directly or indirectly through the NSA.
The LUCID 2000™ ID system, in conjunction with the
NSA and Internet Commerce, soon will enslave us all electronically. No buying or selling of any kind will be permitted
without first accessing Lucifer's Internet. Of course, use of
the Internet will be restricted to only those who have *positively
identified themselves,* first with an international ID smart card
(probably the LUCID 2000™ "MARC" card), then with a
computer chip implanted in the skin of their right hands (an
RFID biochip transponder). If their projected date stays on
target, after 2001 people will have lost all control over their
freedom, privacy, and money via this new diabolical system
of electronic surveillance and control!

The LUCID 2000™ system is a new, extremely complex
and sophisticated international system of networked, computerized identification databases that will transfer information on us digitally and instantaneously anywhere in the
world. And, as stated above, the global Internet will serve both
as an electronic identification system (the LUCID Net) and
as an entirely new medium through which all electronic
cyber-bartering must pass. The internationally computerized
Internet (via NSA databases) will create the global "electronic
village" that's being touted daily by corporate, government,
and media officials everywhere.

Once in place, all buying and selling will be forced through
this new cyber-system of *Electronic Commerce.* In other words,
the system will function as our new, computerized, electronic
cyber-money—*E-Money.* Soon, cyber-money will be **the
only authorized form of monetary exchange**. Thereafter,
currency and coin will have been illegalized entirely, so that
the mere possession of it will have become a criminal offense
in the New World Economic Order. And without currency,
there will be no way to circumvent this new electronic bartering system. In this way, Big Brother can access information
on everything you do, and ultimately control you. Remember

what Orwell said, *"Big Brother is watching you!"*. . . and he was right.
Contrary to Huxley's opinion that we will "love our servitude" and not have to be "coerced" in to the new system, the Bible tells us that the global dictator, the Antichrist, will force everyone to worship him by means of financial *coercion*. In other words, the world's populace will be told that they first must worship the Beast, then be positively **marked** in their **right hands** by Big Brother's new ID system, an implantable biochip. If they refuse, they'll be unable to transact any business globally. Talk about a new, high-tech kind of ID system, this is it! LUCID 2000™, or something even more advanced, will become Lucifer's ID system for the New World Order. No one will escape its effects, and no sector of our lives will remain untouched. Big Brother's NSA will be watching you! Of course, neither Huxley nor Orwell emphasized that the penalty for refusing to be *coerced* into worshiping the dictator and becoming part of the New World Order system would be *the loss of your head* (read a little further in the Book of Revelation).

The Year 2000—Big Brother's Target Date

In his 1990 book entitled, *The Keys of This Blood: Pope John Paul II versus Russia and the West for Control of the New World Order,* author Malachi Martin, a former Vatican insider and intelligence expert, had this to say about world conditions near the year 2000 under the New-World-Order system of global government.

Willingly or not, ready or not, we are all involved in an all-out, no-holds-barred, three-way global competition. Most of us are not the competitors, however. *We are the stakes.* For the competition is **about who will establish the first one-world system of government that has ever existed** in the society of nations. It is about who will hold and wield the dual power of **authority and control over each of us** as individuals and over

all of us together as a community, over the entire six
billion people expected by demographers to inhabit the
earth by early in the third millennium [around the year
2000]. [Emphasis added.]

Martin continues with some amazing and most astute
remarks.

The competition is all-out because, now that it has
started, **there is no way it can be reversed or called**
off. . . . No holds are barred because, once the competition has been decided, **the world and all that's in it—**
our way of life as individuals and citizens of the nations;
our families and our jobs; our trade and **commerce and**
money; our educational systems and our **religions** and
our cultures; even the badges of our national identity,
which most of us have always taken for granted [Author's
Note: Refer to my book, *America's Identity Crisis and the*
Coming International ID Card]—**all will have been**
powerfully and radically altered forever. No one
can be exempted from its effects. No sector of our
lives will remain untouched. . . . Indeed, the three
rivals [the Pope, Russia, and the West] speak about this
New World Order not as something around some
distant corner of time, but as **something that is immi-**
nent. As a system that will be introduced and **installed**
in our midst by the end of this final decade of the
second millennium [the year 2000]. . . . What these
competitors are talking about, then, is **the most pro-**
found and widespread modification of international,
national, and local life that the world has seen . . .
the millennium end game. . . . The final contender in the
competition for the New World Order *is not a single*
individual leader of a single institution or territory. It is
a group of men [i.e., a conspiracy] **who are united as**
one in power, mind, and will for the purpose of
achieving **a single common goal**: to be victorious in

the competition for *the new global hegemony* [emphasis added].

Malachi Martin concludes these thoughts by quoting Pope John Paul II:

> We are now standing in the face of **the greatest historical confrontation humanity has gone through** ...a test of two thousand years of culture and Christian civilization, with all of its consequences for human dignity, individual rights, and the rights of nations... *wide circles of American society* and *wide circles of the Christian community do not realize this fully* [emphasis added].

Will the LUCID 2000™ Internet-connected, NSA-linked international identification system become the technological means of exerting this "authority and control over each of us"? It certainly appears so.

A New Age Under Big Brother, The Antichrist

Malachi Martin and the Pope have made some very scary, remarkable, profound, and yet enlightened statements here, haven't they? Could they be right? Will this "group of men who are united as one in power, mind, and will" (who desire a New World Order) lead the world, or will they be led by a single individual whom the Bible calls the Antichrist? Undoubtedly, they will be led by the Antichrist. *The Bible says so!* Secular society calls him "Big Brother." Christians call him "Antichrist." Either way, please understand that the secular, socialist, Orwellian concept of such a "fictional" Big-Brother character actually will manifest itself in the incarnation of the Biblical Antichrist. That's why I refer to him as "Big Brother, the Antichrist."

Over the past decade, it seems that the impending loss of our privacy has been recognized by the inquisitive and is receiving much attention from the media. Even secular newspapers and magazines have published articles warning us that Orwell's Big Brother is coming. Due to space constraints, I'll mention only a few of the better-known publications. These articles may be perused at your local libraries, if you don't subscribe to these publications.

Time Magazine
Forbes Magazine
Newsweek Magazine
The Los Angeles Times
San Diego Union-Tribune
The Palm Springs Desert Sun
Automatic Identification News
Electronic Engineering Times Magazine

It is obvious that even the liberal press is trying to tell us something—that an evil surveillance society is just a heartbeat away.

Big Brother's National Security Agency: The Antichrist's Tool for Techno-Tyranny

The following quote by Senator Frank Church regarding the National Security Agency's surveillance capabilities pretty much confirms everyone's fears in this regard.

At the same time, that capability could be turned around on the American people and **no American would have any privacy left,** such [is] the capability to monitor everything: telephone conversations, telegrams, it doesn't matter. **There would be no place to hide.** If this government ever became a tyranny, if a dictator ever took charge in this country, **the technological capacity that the intelligence community has given the government could enable it to impose total tyranny, and there would be no way to fight back,** because the most careful effort to combine together in resistance to the government, no matter how privately it was done, is within reach of the government to know. **Such is the capability of this technology**. . . . I don't want to see this country ever go across the bridge. I know the **capability that is there to make tyranny total in America**, and we must see to it that this agency [NSA] and all agencies [the government intelligence agencies later referred to as "Sister" or "Little Brother" organizations] that possess this technology operate within the law and under proper supervision, so that we **never** cross over that **abyss. THAT IS THE ABYSS FROM WHICH THERE IS NO RETURN.** [Emphasis added.]

Unfortunately, I am convinced we already have crossed that "bridge." Indeed, I believe that we are currently on a fast track toward the Antichrist-led "tyranny of the abyss" feared by Senator Church, George Orwell, and many others, including myself. But should we be surprised by these events? Not at all, if you are schooled in the Bible, even a little. Scripture says the Antichrist will control a global system that will enslave everyone in "the last days." By that time, everyone remaining on earth must have accepted this dictator's 666 Mark in his or her hand to survive. Accordingly, there is absolutely no doubt in my mind that the *sinister National Security Agency,* and its *sister intelligence organizations, such as the Central Intelligence Agency,* will be used by the Beast to accomplish this diabolical plan.

Specifically, regarding the **CIA**, however, David Watters, a telecommunications engineer who several years ago worked with the CIA's communications research and development branch, had this to say:

Tons of electronic surveillance equipment at this moment **are inter-connected within our domestic and international common carrier telecommunications systems**. Much more is under contract for installation. Perhaps this equipment is humming away

in a semi-quiescent state wherein at present "no citizen
is targeted," simply scanned....How soon will it be,
however, before a punched card [or a smart card] will
be quietly dropped into the machine, a card having your
telephone number, my telephone number, or the number
of one of our friends to whom we will be speaking?

Wow! Even one of the engineers who worked on these monster
computers is concerned about their Orwellian capabilities.

Big Brother-NSA Wants to Positively Identify And Control You

Before Big Brother can enslave and control the world
completely, he first must be able to positively identify us.
Without a sophisticated, computerized system of positive
biometrically verifiable identification, he cannot track and
control us. Now, just what organization might you suspect
is behind the entire plan to identify us? You guessed it...
enter the NSA—the National Security Agency in Ft. Meade,
Maryland! In fact, my thorough investigation of NSA's activities
has revealed the following startling information:

- NSA's Biometrics Consortium Division is behind
  all national ID efforts
- NSA has created the entire computer industry
- NSA and IBM created the Lucifer Project
- NSA is directly or indirectly behind virtually
  everything Orwellian
- NSA essentially has become our secret,
  uncontrolled, unelected government

The Bible Says the End of the Age is at Hand

Just as the Bible instructs, there will be only one escape
from this soon-coming nightmare of global satanic bondage.
That escape is Jesus Christ; the Son of God; the Savior of
the world. Only Christ can save us. There is no middle ground.
You must choose either Jesus Christ or Big Brother, Anti-

christ. Yes, doubters, Big Brother will be the Antichrist described in the Book of Revelation. And soon he will reign on earth for a brief seven-year period called the Great Tribulation —the era of The New World Order. The Bible is very clear on this. If you don't belong to Jesus now, you soon will belong to the Antichrist. You'll worship him and take his 666 Mark-of-the-Beast in your right hand or forehead, and subsequently go to hell. At that point, you will have become chattel—cattle in Satan's demonic New World Order. There is no turning back once this decision has been made. You will have condemned yourself to hell for eternity. The choice is clear— *choose Jesus Christ today,* not the Antichrist. For, according to scripture, there is no other name under heaven or on earth by which we can be saved, than the name of Jesus.

> Remember therefore how thou hast received and heard, and hold fast and repent. **If therefore thou shalt not watch,** I will come on thee as a thief, and **thou shalt not know what hour** I will come upon thee (Revelation 3:3).
>
> . . . but the wicked shall do wickedly: and **none of the wicked shall understand; but the wise shall understand** (Daniel 12:10). [Emphasis added.]

This book will inform you about many soon-coming, earth-shaking events that relate specifically to the rise of the Antichrist, satanic deception, and the implementation of the devil's LUCID 2000™ Mark-of-the-Beast system. This book should prove clearly that the Mark-of-the-Beast system will operate through Big Brother-NSA's global computer network, and everyone on earth will be affected by this pervasive, all-enslaving, evil system. Only Christians, however, *will realize that this system will be demonically orchestrated by Satan himself. Only Christians will not worship the devil* nor take his *Mark in their hands.*

We are admonished in the very beginning of the Book of Revelation (chapter one, verse three) to study this book diligently. . . in fact it is the only book in the Bible that promises a blessing for studying it.

> Blessed is he that readeth, and they that hear the words of this prophecy, and keep those things which are written therein: **for the time is at hand** [emphasis added].

Moreover, we find in Revelation 19:10: ". . . for the testimony of **Jesus is the spirit of prophecy**" [emphasis added]. Our Savior, Jesus Christ, is the author of prophetical understanding. Study His prophecies thoroughly so you will not be deceived and be caught as by "a thief in the night." Jesus is the Way, the Truth, and the Life. Trust Him and His written Word unfailingly and you cannot go wrong.

In addition to faithful Bible study, I suggest you also study this book carefully, watching for every opportunity to use it as a powerful and effective witnessing tool for our Lord Jesus Christ during these final moments of human history. Indeed, use it to bring many to Christ quickly, because *the time is at hand!*

Big Brother-NSA: Global Techno-Tyranny Headquarters

Now, let's begin a serious study of Big Brother-NSA's diabolical computer network. Again, it is my well-researched opinion that the NSA's 1000-acre facility in Maryland soon will be used as the Beast's **international techno-tyranny headquarters** for the entire planet. Indeed, the headquarters of Satan's Mark-of-the-Beast system **is not** in Europe, **it's right here in America!** It's Big Brother-NSA.

Appendix to the Introduction

Original Charter of the National Security Agency

Date: Sun, 11 Feb 90 00:03 EST
From: CJS@cwru.bitnet
Subject: FOIA Jewel: Original Charter of the
          National Security Agency

At 12:01 on the morning of November 4, 1952, a new federal agency was born. Unlike other such bureaucratic births, however, this one arrived in silence. No news coverage, no congressional debate, no press announcement, not even the whisper of a rumor. Nor could any mention of the new organization be found in the Government Organization Manual of the Federal Register or the Congressional Record. Equally invisible were the new agency's director, its numerous buildings, and its ten thousand employees.

Eleven days earlier, on October 24, President Harry S. Truman scratched his signature on the bottom of a seven-page presidential memorandum addressed to Secretary of State Dean G. Acheson and Secretary of Defense Robert A. Lovett. Classified top secret and stamped with a code word that was itself classified, the order directed the establishment of an agency to be known as the National Security Agency. It was the birth certificate for America's newest and most secret agency, so secret in fact that only a handful in the government would be permitted to know of its existence. [Quoting James Bamford, *The Puzzle Palace* (1982) at 15.]

The Presidential Memorandum

A 20707 5/4/54/OSO
NSA TS CONTL. NO 73-00405
COPY: D321

Oct 24 1952

MEMORANDUM FOR: The Secretary of State
The Secretary of Defense

SUBJECT: Communications Intelligence Activities

The communications intelligence (COMINT) activities of the United States are a national responsibility. They must be so organized and managed as to exploit to the maximum the available resources in all participating departments and agencies and to satisfy the legitimate intelligence requirements of all such departments and agencies.

I therefore designate the Secretaries of State and Defense as a Special Committee of the National Security Council for COMINT, which Committee shall, with the assistance of the Director of Central Intelligence, establish policies governing COMINT activities and keep me advised of such policies through the Executive Secretary of the National Security Council.

I further designate the Department of Defense as executive agent of the Government, for the production of COMINT information.

I direct this Special Committee to prepare and issue directives which shall include the provisions set forth below and such other provisions as the Special Committee may determine to be necessary.

1. A directive to the United States Communication Intelligence Board (USCIB). This directive will replace the National Security Council Intelligence Directive No. 9, and shall prescribe USCIB's new composition, responsibilities and procedures in the COMINT fields. This directive shall include the following provisions.

1. USCIB shall be reconstituted as a body acting for and under the Special Committee, and shall operate in accordance with the provisions of the new directive. Only those departments or agencies represented in USCIB are authorized to engage in COMINT activities.

2. The Board shall be composed of the following members:

1. The Director of Central Intelligence, who shall be the Chairman of the Board.

2. A representative of the Secretary of State.

3. A representative of the Secretary of Defense.
4. A representative of the Director of the Federal Bureau
   of Investigation.
5. The Director of the National Security Agency.
6. A representative of the Department of the Army.
7. A representative of the Department of the Navy.
8. A representative of the Department of the Air Force.
9. A representative of the Central Intelligence Agency.

3. The Board shall have a staff headed by an executive secretary who shall be appointed by the Chairman with the approval of the majority of the Board.

4. It shall be the duty of the Board to advise and make recommendations to the Secretary of Defense, in accordance with the following procedure, with respect to any matter relating to communications intelligence which falls within the jurisdiction of the Director of the NSA.

1. The Board shall reach its decision by majority vote. Each member of the Board shall have one vote except the representatives of the Secretary of State and of the Central Intelligence Agency who shall each have two votes. The Director of Central Intelligence, as Chairman, will have no vote. In the event that the Board votes and reaches a decision, any dissenting member of the Board may appeal such decision within 7 days to the Special Committee. In the event that the Board votes but fails to reach a decision, any member of the Board may appeal within 7 days to the Special Committee. In either event the Special Committee shall review the matter, and its determination thereon shall be final. Appeals by the Director of NSA and/or the representatives of the Military Departments shall only be filed with the approval of the Secretary of Defense.

2. If any matter is voted on by the Board but —

   1. no decision is reached and any member files an appeal;

   2. a decision is reached in which the representative of the Secretary of Defense does not concur and files an appeal; no action shall be taken with respect to the

subject matter until the appeal is decided, provided that, if the Secretary of Defense determines, after consultation with the Secretary of State, that the subject matter presents a problem of an emergency nature and requires immediate action, his decision shall govern, pending the result of the appeal. In such emergency situation the appeal may be taken directly to the President.

3. Recommendations of the Board adopted in accordance with the foregoing procedures shall be binding on the Secretary of Defense. Except on matters which have been voted on by the Board, the Director of NSA shall discharge his responsibilities in accordance with his own judgment, subject to the direction of the Secretary of Defense.

4. The Director of NSA shall make such reports and furnish such information from time to time to the Board, either orally or in writing, as the Board may request, and shall bring to the attention of the Board either in such reports or otherwise any major policies or programs in advance of their adoption by him.

5. It shall also be the duty of the Board as to matters not falling within the jurisdiction of NSA;

1. To coordinate the communications intelligence activities among all departments and agencies authorized by the President to participate therein;

2. To initiate, to formulate policies concerning, and subject to the provision of NSCID No. 5, to supervise all arrangements with foreign governments in the field of communications intelligence; and

3. to consider and make recommendations concerning policies relating to communications intelligence of common interest to the departments and agencies, including security standards and practices, and, for this purpose, to investigate and study the standards and practices of such departments and agencies in utilizing and protecting COMINT information.

6. Any recommendation of the Board with respect to the matters described in paragraph e [5] above shall be binding on all departments or agencies of the Government if it is adopted by the unanimous vote of the members of the Board. Recommendations approved by the majority, but not all, of the members of the Board shall be transmitted by it to the Special Committee for such action as the Special Committee may see fit to take.

7. The Board will meet monthly, or oftener at the call of the Chairman or any member, and shall determine its own procedures.

2. A directive to the Secretary of Defense. This directive shall include the following provisions:

1. Subject to the specific provisions of this directive, the Secretary of Defense may delegate in whole or in part authority over the Director of NSA within his department as he sees fit.

2. The COMINT mission of the National Security Agency (NSA) shall be to provide an effective, unified organization and control of the communications intelligence activities of the United States conducted against foreign governments, to provide for integrated operational policies and procedures pertaining thereto. As used in this directive, the terms "communications intelligence" or "COMINT" shall be construed to mean all procedures and methods used in the interception of communications other than foreign press and propaganda broadcasts and the obtaining of information from such communications by other than intended recipients, but shall exclude censorship and the production and dissemination of finished intelligence.

3. NSA shall be administered by a Director, designated by the Secretary of Defense after consultation with the Joint Chiefs of Staff, who shall serve for a minimum term of 4 years and who shall be eligible for reappointment. The Director shall be a career commissioned officer of the armed services on active or reactivated status, and shall enjoy at least 3-star rank during the period of his incumbency.

4. Under the Secretary of Defense, and in accordance with approved policies of USCIB, the Director of NSA shall be

responsible for accomplishing the mission of NSA. For this purpose all COMINT collection and production resources of the United States are placed under his operational and technical control. When action by the Chiefs of the operating agencies of the Services or civilian departments or agencies is required, the Director shall normally issue instruction pertaining to COMINT operations through them. However, due to the unique technical character of COMINT operations, the Director is authorized to issue direct to any operating elements under his operational control task assignments and pertinent instructions which are within the capacity of such elements to accomplish. He shall also have direct access to, and direct communication with, any elements of the Service or civilian COMINT agencies on any other matters of operational and technical control as may be necessary, and he is authorized to obtain such information and intelligence material from them as he may require. All instructions issued by the Director under the authority provided in this paragraph shall be mandatory, subject only to appeal to the Secretary of Defense by the Chief of Service or head of civilian department of agency concerned.

5. Specific responsibilities of the Director of NSA include the following:

1. Formulating necessary operational plans and policies for the conduct of the U.S. COMINT activities.

2. Conducting COMINT activities, including research and development, as required to meet the needs of the departments and agencies which are authorized to receive the products of COMINT.

3. Determining, and submitting to appropriate authorities, requirements for logistic support for the conduct of COMINT activities, together with specific recommendations as to what each of the responsible departments and agencies of the Government should supply.

4. Within NSA's field of authorized operations prescribing requisite security regulations covering operating practices, including the transmission, handling and distribution of COMINT material within and among the COMINT elements

under his operations or technical control; and exercising the necessary monitoring and supervisory control, including inspections if necessary, to ensure compliance with the regulations.

5. Subject to the authority granted the Director of Central Intelligence under NSCID No. 5, conducting all liaison on COMINT matters with foreign governmental communications intelligence agencies.

6. To the extent he deems feasible and in consonance with the aims of maximum over-all efficiency, economy, and effectiveness, the Director shall centralize or consolidate the performance of COMINT functions for which he is responsible. It is recognized that in certain circumstances elements of the Armed Forces and other agencies being served will require close COMINT support. Where necessary for this close support, direct operational control of specified COMINT facilities and resources will be delegated by the Director, during such periods and for such tasks as are determined by him, to military commanders or to the Chiefs of other agencies supported.

7. The Director shall exercise such administrative control over COMINT activities as he deems necessary to the effective performance of his mission. Otherwise, administrative control of personnel and facilities will remain with the departments and agencies providing them.

8. The Director shall make provision for participation by repesentatives of each of the departments and agencies eligible to receive COMINT products in those offices of NSA where priorities of intercept and processing are finally planned.

9. The Director shall have a civilian deputy whose primary responsibility shall be to ensure the mobilization and effective employment of the best available human and scientific resources in the field of cryptographic research and development.

10. Nothing in this directive shall contravene the responsibilities of the individual departments and agencies for the final evaluation of COMINT information, its synthesis with information from other sources, and the dissemination of finished intelligence to users.

3. The special nature of COMINT activities requires that they be treated in all respects as being outside the framework of other or general intelligence activities. Orders, directives, policies, or recommendations of any authority of the Executive Branch relating to the collection, production, security, handling, dissemination, or utilization of intelligence, and/or classified material, shall not be applicable to COMINT activities, unless specifically so stated and issued by competent departmental or agency authority represented on the Board. Other National Security Council Intelligence Directives to the Director of Central Intelligence and related implementing directives issued by the Director of Central Intelligence shall be construed as non-applicable to COMINT activities, unless the National Security Council has made its directive specifically applicable to COMINT.

/s/   HARRY S. TRUMAN

The Biggest Secret in the World— The National Security Agency

They may be the biggest secret in the world, but they are no longer attempting to operate covertly; in fact, they are very public about their future plans (at least some of them!). They are rapidly becoming "Big Brother, Inc." Among their many activities, they have much information available on the Internet. . ."information," perhaps, may be interpreted better as "propaganda," but regardless what you call it, they are filling cyberspace singing their own praises and attempting to convince all who see their "pages" that they are providing a better, a safer, a more secure future for all of us. (Never mind that all it will cost us is our privacy, and eventually our freedom!)

Physical and Internet Addresses

This is probably the most underplayed of all the government agencies, yet their facilities and equipment are enough to boggle the mind, and they are adding to them, even now, to arrive at a staff of about 80,000. Throughout this chapter you will find that I have included many maps and photos of this location—even some aerial shots. Careful study of this documentation will give you an idea of the immensity of this organization.

Here is how you can reach them, if you wish:

National Security Agency, Public Affairs Office
Fort George G. Meade, Maryland 20755-6000
Phone: (301) 688-6524

Internet addresses: www.nsa.gov:8080
www.odci.gov/ic/usic/nsa.html
www.fas.org/irp/nsa/nsafacil.html

National Security Agency
Identification Division/Biometrics Consortium
R221, DIRNSA, Fort Meade, Maryland, 20755-6000
Phone: (301) 688-0278
Internet address: www.vitro.bloomington.in.us:8080/bc/

The Bible says that there is nothing new under the sun, and it surely applies to the goal of the NSA. Historically, men have recognized and spoken in protest of such activities.

> The first stage of the collapse of empires is **the consolidation of political and financial power under one government machine into which all problems are fed and from which all wisdom is to emerge**....Can politicians not sense the disasters toward which they are heading? Can they not perceive what the future holds for them and for us? [Emphasis added.]
>
> — C. Northcote Parkinson

Does this not sound exactly like the NSA? Again, they must be proud of the following, because they aren't trying to cover it up—it appears in one of their own brochures.

Internet Reports

Throughout this chapter, I will be inserting information about the NSA that appears on one or more of their "web sites." The following information concerns their "mission statement" and was found at http://www.hpcc.gov/reports/reports-nco/a.9.html (I won't be giving the location in the future...sufficient to say, it is extensive).

> *Information security is a primary mission of the National Security Agency.* In pursuing this mission NSA develops security technology and security products. [Author's

THE NSA INSIGNIA

Courtesy of NSA's Public Affairs Office, Ft. Meade, Maryland.

The National Security Agency's **insignia** of an **eagle inside a circle** symbolizes **"Supreme power and authority"** and **"perpetuity of its continuance, the symbol of eternity."** [Emphasis added.]

—NSA Brochure

note: As you read this further, keep in mind this security
may apply to others, **but not to them**—nothing will
keep them out of your business; in fact, specific features
are incorporated to let them in! (When we get to it, note
carefully the term "backdoor.")] Network security applications present significant challenges for the National
Information Infrastructure [translate that "Internet"].
NSA will initiate programs that address authentication,
wireless interoperability, and real-time operating aspects
of network security. NSA will develop authentication
techniques (e.g., biometric) *for network access control*
and will create a mechanism for establishing standards
of security and interoperability in emerging wireless
PC's and cellular networks. NSA and NIST will integrate
Smartcard and biometric technology to permit authentication of a person to a network. In collaboration with
NIST and hardware and software manufacturers, NSA
will develop technology to integrate real-time and data
communications in a secure multimedia, multi-terminal
network environment. [Emphasis added.]

Now, before we move on, let's examine in laymen's terms
what was covered in that previous paragraph. On the whole,
it adds up to the fact that they want positive (biometric) identification on all of us, and they're getting there as fast as they
can, at the expense of the taxpayer. . .*you're footing the bill
for your own surveillance and control!* But let's redefine some
of their specific terms (above).

In addition to the "Author's notes" I have inserted into the
copy furnished above, it is important that I comment on a
number of the other phrases in the revealing terminology
(double-speak). "Information security is **A** primary mission"
—they have many, and personally I'm more concerned about
what they are planning to do with the information than with
how they are "protecting" it and us.

The term "wireless interoperability" means they can
observe and/or access information from a number of desig-

nated sources via wireless operation, such as a cell phone, wireless PC, or other such devices. They readily tell us that the "authentication [identification] techniques" they plan to use are biometric in nature, and if you aren't approved "for network access," you won't be doing any business on the Super Information Highway. Note that they want "interoperability" again in the "emerging wireless PCs and cellular networks." This just means that they want all future wireless communications networks to develop their systems on the drawing boards with "interoperability", supposedly so they can "talk" with anyone, but basically they don't want some entrepreneur out there developing and encrypting a system that they don't have the capability of accessing (surveillance).

You notice they claim that *they will integrate Smartcard and biometric technology;* prior to this revelation, it was assumed that the international banking industry was the organization planning to biometrically identify us by tying biometrics with the Smartcard, specifically Citicorp, *et al* (and I'm convinced that they still are heavily involved)... now we find NSA claiming it is part of their mission to establish a standard for this positive identification.

"In collaboration with NIST and hardware and software manufacturers," means that they are using your tax dollars to underwrite private companies, to have them develop these "security" devices (more will be mentioned later in this chapter and further in the next chapter).

Finally, they want to "develop technology to integrate... in a secure multimedia multi-terminal network"—interpret "multimedia" as "anyone" and "multi-terminal" as "anywhere," and you will arrive at the fact that this is an oxymoron—because once anyone (interoperability) has access to anyone, anywhere, *there's nothing secure about it!* Below are several more statements about their mission which I must address.

> Over the past few years there has been a significant research program funded by ARPA, NSA, and other government agencies.... [Author's note: ARPA has

been very instrumental in this area; again NSA is footing
the bill, via the taxpayer].

. . . ARPA, NSA, and other agencies have conducted
and sponsored research programs to develop. . . speech
recognition [and it is their goal to teach their machines
to read foreign languages, in addition to those for which
we are footing the bill]. [Emphasis added.]

Another paragraph that they consider a "near-term goal"
is the development of a computer that will analyze the information and tell the "human" what is *relevant*. What?
You mean you're not ready to let your computer analyze your
information and determine what you ought to know? Then
you'd better not read the next paragraph!

A major effort needs to be initiated for development
of efficient and reliable *text summarization* technology.
. . . Prototype development *for text summarization and
relevance feedback* from users is a *near-term goal* of the
program. [Emphasis added.]

Now, speaking of secure, how secure do you feel letting
a computer analyze your data? What if it sees something that
it dismisses as unimportant (or not relevant), but might make
you alter your determination on a subject, if some small piece
had not been overlooked? No matter how sophisticated the
hardware, the best computer is no better than the operator
who feeds it the data. What if they had a fight with their
spouse before breakfast, and the kids were late for school,
and by Murphy's Law if their day could get any worse, it
probably would? It all boils down to that decades-old acronym:
GI - GO (garbage in, garbage out). Still think you want your
computer to summarize your data and tell you what it wants
you to know? The following paragraph doesn't require any
interpretation—it is very self-explanatory, and after sharing
it, I will move on to another topic. . . remember, all this

information has been gleaned from only **one** page from their Internet site.

> . . . access to multiple heterogeneous databases. . . is the major component of a large-knowledge base effort. NSA will develop a prototype. . . where the end-user of the data, the application builder, and the data administrator **all** see, not a collection of relatively unintelligible, difficult-to-access databases, but an **integrated information** space in terms **directly meaningful and accessible to them.** [Emphasis added.]

Foreseeing the Future with George Orwell and Aldous Huxley

In the 1940s, George Orwell wrote his famous (or infamous) futuristic book titled *1984*, the year in which his futuristic novel was set. Many of the technologies postulated are no longer science fiction—in fact, many are quite commonplace. But his introduction of "Big Brother is watching you" seemed too farfetched ever to occur; unfortunately, the technology for this kind of ruthless surveillance has passed the testing stage and is being inducted into use in any number of new electronic facilities that soon will be in our homes. There is the modem experience, E-mail and E-money, and better yet (just as in *1984)* two-way television sets. Keep in mind that anything that is "two-way" can be accessed by either party or parties, and if you are planning on that security that the NSA promises you, just remember that they are the ones holding the "key" to the "backdoor"—the ability to decode any encryption you may use and enable them to monitor any or all of your activities conducted on the system.

The television is probably the most prominent appliance of entertainment in our homes, and now with interactive capability (via the cable companies and fiber optics) any number of banks and a myriad of businesses and other groups are pushing for the day when your television screen also becomes your correspondence screen, your bookkeeping screen, your Internet screen, your check-writing screen, your direct-deposit/direct-transfer/direct-payment screen, *et al*, in addition to selecting your pay-per-view movie of the week. Here is what George Orwell said about the premise of his book:

> I do not believe that the kind of society I describe [in *1984*] necessarily will arrive, but I believe . . . that something resembling it could arrive. I believe also that totalitarian ideas have taken root in the minds of intellectuals everywhere.
>
> —George Orwell

His concept was right on the money—only the date was premature; the events were still in the covert drawing board/ testing stage in 1984. But by 1994—just ten more years— the situations he described not only were possible, they were impending!

Even before Orwell, in the 1930s, Aldous Huxley wrote a book titled *Brave New World*, about which Huxley had this to say in 1947:

> The theme of *Brave New World* is not the advancement of science as such; it is the advancement of **science as it affects human individuals** . . . .The sciences of matter can be **applied in such a way that they will destroy life** or make the living of it impossibly complex and uncomfortable . . . .A really **efficient totalitarian state** would be one in which the all-powerful executive of political bosses and their army of managers **control a population of SLAVES** who do not have to be coerced, because **they LOVE THEIR SERVITUDE**. To **make them love it** is the task assigned, in present-day totalitarian states, to the ministries of **PROPAGANDA**, newspaper editors, and school teachers . . . .**Unless** we choose to **decentralize** and to use applied science, not

as the end to which human beings are to be made the means, but as the means to producing a race of **free** individuals, **we have ONLY TWO ALTERNATIVES** to choose from; either **A NUMBER** of national, militarized **totalitarianisms**, having as their root the terror of the atomic bomb and as their consequence the destruction of civilization. . .**or else ONE SUPRANATIONAL TOTALITARIANISM**, called into existence by the **social chaos resulting from rapid technological progress** in general and atomic revolution in particular, and **developing, under the need for efficiency and stability**, into the **welfare-tyranny of Utopia**. . . . [Emphasis added.]   —Aldous Huxley, 1947

Mr. Huxley was incredibly prophetic and correct in his analysis of the two proposed alternatives to future government. It appears, however, that his *second* alternative vision for the future state-of-the-world was the more accurate alternative. It appears that the **Brave New-World-Order** of *supranational totalitarianism* is finally about to emerge and materialize through the supranational **United Nations** (or the U.N. will become the "middle-man" between freedom and a completely totalitarian state). This will result in a totalitarian system of global communism (probably via some interim system of welfare-state socialism). Note that he claims we will embrace this supranational totalitarian-type goverment because of the social chaos brought on by the rapid progress of technology and the need for "efficiency and stability" in our lives.

Consider that even though Huxley so accurately postulates these events, he viewed these events as a blessing to mankind, rather than detrimental. *There is none so blind as he who will not see!*

Origin, Location, and Definition of the NSA

The National Security Agency was founded in 1952 by President Harry Truman, not by legislation but by one of those infamous Executive Orders that permits a President to do an "end run" around both houses of Congress and enact into law something that he never could get passed by the legislature. At the moment, NSA consists of three major facilities: (1) the main facility at Fort Meade, Maryland; (2) the second facility, National Business Park, near Fort Meade; (3) the third facility, Friendship Annex, by the Baltimore-Washington International Airport.

A new reference book written by Thomas Parrish, and published as A Henry Holt Reference Book in 1996, is titled *The Cold War Encyclopedia*. This 500-page book is replete with interesting information. I am quoting here (from page 227) what they have to say about the NSA.

National Security Agency (NSA). With headquarters occupying a 1,000-acre tract at Fort George G. Meade, MD, and *personnel numbering at times more than 80,000*, the NSA during the Cold War was clearly *the largest intelligence body in the non-Communist world*. It was also by far the most secret U.S. intelligence agency. Established not by legislation (as was the Central Intelligence Agency—CIA) but under an order signed by President Truman on October 24, 1952, the NSA quietly came into being on November 4, 1952, a day when the attention of the news media was focused on the presidential election. The level of secrecy was so high that Truman's order not only carried the Top Secret classification but was labeled with a code name that was also secret.

Charged with the responsibility for all Department of Defense [DOD] activities relating to communications intelligence, the NSA operated an array of listening posts around the world, decrypted and analyzed the intercepted messages, and created U.S. signal intelligence [SIGINT] capacities—codes and ciphers, together with transmission methods and devices, with *heavy emphasis on the*

NSA Complex. Courtesy of NSA's Public Affairs Office, Ft. Meade, Maryland.

Aerial view of sprawling NSA Ft. Meade complex from a different angle. Digitized photo from NSA's database. Note the enormity of the parking area, able to accommodate thousands of vehicles. Courtesy of NSA's Public Affairs Office, Ft. Meade, Maryland.

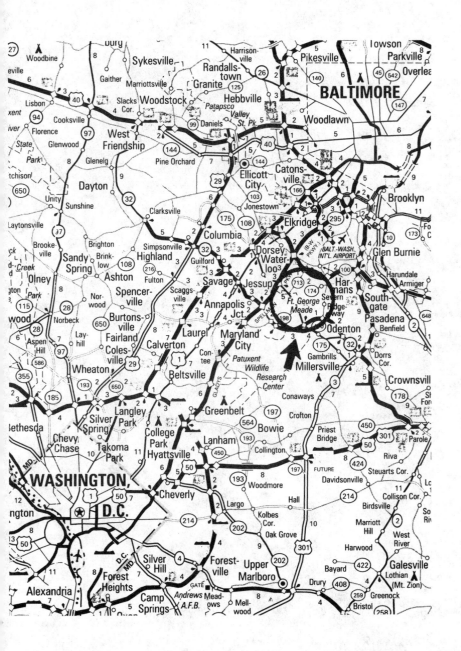

NSA's location between Washington, DC, and Baltimore, Maryland.

95-072 ANNE ARUNDEL CO. 3-24-95 1200 AM1 6- 18

1995 aerial photo of NSA Complex. Courtesy of Anne Arundel County, Maryland.

Note NSA's unguarded entrance on the road approaching the NSA facility at the Ft. Meade, Maryland, army base. Photos by Terry L. Cook, 1996.

development of computerization. In addition, the agency held the responsibility for preserving the security of its operations. [Emphasis added.]

The *1994 Grolier's* defines the National Security Agency and references James Bamford's excellent book, *The Puzzle Palace* (1982). I have quoted below the general definition, then subsequent excerpts pertinent to our subject matter.

National Security Agency

The largest and most secret of the intelligence agencies of the U.S. government, the National Security Agency (NSA), with headquarters at Fort Meade, Maryland, has two main functions: to protect U.S. government communications and to intercept foreign communications. It protects government communications by enciphering messages and taking other measures to ensure their secrecy. In its foreign intelligence function the NSA marshals a vast corps of intelligence analysts who use sensitive electronic equipment to monitor, decipher, and translate the communications of foreign governments. It could follow space rocket launchings in the former USSR and can overhear conversations between aircraft pilots and ground-control personnel in remote areas of the globe. The NSA was established in 1952 as a separately organized agency within the Department of Defense. It replaced the Armed Forces Security Agency. . . .The National Security Agency (NSA) is *responsible* for collecting signals intelligence *from all over the world* and for overseeing the integrity of American secret communications. [Author's note: Can you see what an easy step it is to move from exclusively military/government secret communications to personal, banking, buying, selling, trading, *et al*, communications, since they have been made "responsible. . . . for overseeing the integrity of American secret communications"?] Some sources suggest that there is a third highly secret

national intelligence agency responsible for satellite
surveillance. . . .
responsible for satellite surveillance. . . .

    A second form of clandestine collection is known as
signals intelligence—the interception of electronic communications and other emissions. Signals are intercepted
by a variety of methods, including the tapping of telephone lines and the monitoring of radio transmissions.
. . . [Emphasis added.]

Grolier's has this to say regarding the economic impact of
NSA on the surrounding urban areas:

>   Maryland's economy is dominated by activities in the
> Baltimore-Washington metropolitan areas, and these
> have changed markedly in the decades since World
> War II. Baltimore's traditional heavy manufacturing and
> port and rail activities have declined. At the same time,
> the growth of the federal government and government-
> related activities have spilled from the nearby District
> of Columbia to Maryland, including Baltimore. Today,
> government-related business is of major economic
> importance to the state. Federal-government installa-
> tions include Andrews Air Force Base, the Goddard
> Space Flight Center, the Agricultural Research Service,
> and Fort Meade, including the National Security Agency,
> Aberdeen Proving Ground, and Fort Detrick in the Balti-
> more metropolitan area.

It is easy to see how an organization with three facilities and
a payroll for 80,000± employees could have a tremendous
impact on the economics of the surrounding community.

    In 1995, HarperCollins of Great Britain published a book
by Christopher Andrew, titled *For the President's Eyes Only:
Secret Intelligence and the American President from Washington
to Bush.* Professor Warren Kimball, Rutgers University, has
this to say about the book:

NATIONAL SECURITY AGENCY WELCOMES PRESIDENT RONALD REAGAN

Above: In September 1986 Reagan became the first president to enter NSA headquarters at Fort Meade; NSA had tried without success to persuade previous presidents to visit. Reagan made unprecedented public use of SIGINT.

Right: Bush at NSA in May 1991. He was the first president to use the word SIGINT in public; it was, he claimed, a "prime factor" in his foreign policy. *(Both courtesy of the National Security Agency)*

Courtesy of NSA and For the President's Eyes Only, *by Christopher Andrew.*

Christopher Andrew has written far and away the best
study of how American presidents have used and mis-
used secret intelligence. The evidence is solid, the
argument persuasive. It should be required reading for
presidents, national security advisors, and Congressional
watchdogs.

David Kahn, author of *The Codebreakers* and *Hitler's Spies*,
provides even more accolades for this publication.

This is the most important book ever written about
American intelligence. Andrew has done what hardly any
other studies do—tell how the intelligence gathered by
so many people at such risk and cost is actually used
by the most powerful men in the world.

Next, I would like to quote some relevant passages from this
book, from the following pages (respectively): 197, 198, 250,
273, and 537.

. . . On October 24 Truman signed a top-secret eight-
page presidential memorandum entitled "Communications Inteiligence Activities," putting into effect the main
recommendations of the committee, with one significant
addition. In keeping with its enhanced authority, AFSA
was renamed the National Security Agency (NSA).
    Whereas CIA was brought into being by an act of Con-
gress, NSA was thus founded by a secret presidential
signature. The date of its foundation, November 4, 1952,
was deliberately chosen to keep it out of the news. . . .
Before long, both the new agency's budget and its
personnel outstripped those of the CIA. *NSA possessed
the largest bank of computers in the world.* For more than
two decades, however, even its existence was unknown
to the vast mass of American people. Those in the know
in Washington joked that **NSA** stood for **"No Such
Agency."**

. . . In 1947, Truman promoted the National Security Act, which founded the CIA. In 1948 he authorized the beginning, and during his second term the rapid expansion, of peacetime covert action by U.S. intelligence agencies. And in 1952, as one of his final acts as president, he founded NSA.

During his twenty-year retirement, Truman sometimes seemed amazed, even somewhat appalled, at the size and power of the intelligence community he had brought into being. . . . [Even as late as 1964 he wrote to Look magazine] that he had never intended CIA to do more than get "all the available information to the president. It was not intended to operate as an international agency engaged in strange activities." NSA was so secret that Truman did not mention it at all. He would probably have been pleased that his biographers have shown a similar disinclination to dwell on his responsibility for the creation of the biggest peacetime intelligence community in the history of Western Civilization. [Emphasis added.]

The pertinence of the following quote will be clear when you understand that the NRO manages satellite communication for the NSA. (See the next chapter, "NSA's Sister Intelligence Organizations.")

. . . Eisenhower approved the creation of a new agency, the National Reconnaissance Office (NRO), to manage satellite reconnaissance programs for the entire intelligence community. For the next generation, NRO was to be the most secret of all U.S. intelligence agencies. Its existence was not discovered by the media until 1973 and not officially acknowledged until September 1992.

Now, of course, the NRO is the second most secret organization. . . second to the NSA and its global activities. The following references are quoted because of the obvious implications, and the not-so-obvious. Therefore, allow me to give

you a head start to pick-up on key words. You will find William
Baker, president of Bell Labs mentioned significantly below
—Hint: the tie-in is via Bell/AT&T/Lucent Technologies.

. . . Its most influential members were two brilliant
scientists: William Baker, the president of Bell Labs, and
Edwin Land, the inventor of the Polaroid camera. "The
tutelage of Drs. Baker and Land," wrote Clifford, "turned
all of us into missionaries for intelligence collection by
'technical means': that is, electronic, photographic, and
satellite espionage." Baker and Land brought to a meeting . . . some of the first ultrahigh-resolution satellite
photographs. "We were awed and amazed," Clifford
recalls, "as we gazed for the first time upon photographs
taken of a tennis court from one hundred miles above
the ground, with resolution so clear that one could
clearly see a tennis ball lying on the court!". . . [the]
collection, however, seemed in danger of becoming a
victim of its own success. The intelligence explosion
generated by NRO and NSA threatened to swamp the
analysts who had to deal with it. . . . NSA's problems
were even greater. . . . collection by satellite, ground
stations, ships, and aircraft expanded so rapidly that,
even with the world's largest and most advanced banks
of computers and more personnel than any other Western
intelligence agency, NSA could barely cope with it. . . .
. . . the National Security Agency [is] the largest and
most expensive intelligence agency in the history of
Western civilization.

The Strange Chain of Command

Referring again to the documents available on the Internet,
furnished directly by NSA, I have learned that the Director
of Central Intelligence (DCI) serves both as head of the CIA
and the IC (Intelligence Community). The IC is a collection

of 13 intelligence agencies, including functions in the Department of Defense, Departments of Justice, Treasury, Energy, and State, as well as the CIA (see next chapter). Now, while not a military organization, *per se*, NSA is one of several "elements" of the IC administered by the Department of Defense.

John Deutch
*Former DCI and CIA Director
CFR and Trilateral Commission
Member. Courtesy of the CIA.*

Therefore, technically the DCI (formerly John Deutch, presently George Tenet) is head of the CIA and also head of NSA and other entities. Currently Lieutenant General Kenneth A. Minihan, USAF, is the Director of NSA (William P. Crowell is the Deputy Director). However, I have it on good authority that this is a case of "the tail wagging the dog," that is, the NSA Director really runs the show, even though technically he is under the headship of the DCI. Even the CIA has their own web page and offers a myriad of selections, mostly directed toward proving how "open" they are, one of which is a photo and full-page resume of John Deutch. Not to be outdone, the NSA proudly supplies a color photo and biography/resume for Lt. Gen. Kenneth A. Minihan, USAF, on the Internet. (Photo appears later in this chapter.) His credentials, training, and experience are impeccable. He is a native Texan who is married with three children. He has been in the Air Force since 1966. A complete list of his education and assignments are described in detail, including seven major awards or decorations. (All these other related agencies are discussed in the next chapter, "NSA's Sister Intelligence Organizations.")

Even though the current CIA Director/DCI is not listed as an official member of either the Council on Foreign Relations (CFR) or the Trilateral Commission, John Deutch has been affiliated with them for years.

Another of those Executive Orders that have been used so treacherously was signed into Law by Exec. Order 12333 of December 4, 1981, and describes in more detail (feel free to interpret that as "expands their area of control") the responsibilities of the NSA.

The Public Affairs Department of NSA has printed a brochure on itself, which they will be happy to send if you care to request it. Or if you just want additional information you may contact the NSA Public Affairs on (301) 688-6524, or you may "Visit the NSA Homepage on the Internet at http://www.nsa.gov:8080/". The brochure offers information on the following topics (and there is no question that the copy was prepared by a P.R. Department).

Establishment of NSA
NSA/CSS
NSA's Role in the Intelligence Community
The NSA Mission
Inside the NSA
NSA Facts and Figures
The Cipher Disk
The NSA Insignia [discussed in detail below]
The National Cryptologic Museum

The NSA's Occultic, Blasphemous, and Satanic INSIGNIA is Symbolic of Lucifer's Control Over the Entire Organization!

The above occultic insignia was designed by NSA in 1965, under the direction of then NSA Director Lt. Gen. Marshall S. Carter, US Army. Its design is blasphemous and satanic! For example, the information brochure to which I referred earlier that was supplied to me by the Public Affairs Office in Fort Meade, Maryland, conveys the nature of the occultic and freemasonic thought that was incorporated into the insignia's design at the time it was created. This is a very important spiritual issue. Therefore, I'm going to spend a considerable amount of time analyzing this evil symbol because it is vitally important that we fully comprehend its satanic origin. Accordingly, let's first consider what the NSA itself has to say about its insignia, then we'll analyze what occultic and freemasonic literature (including *The Secret Teachings of All Ages* by Manly P. Hall) reveal about this kind of symbolism. The NSA's brochure reads this way:

The created [symbol] is described as: an insignia which shall be **a circle** [meaning Lucifer is eternal] bordered white. In the Chief semicircle border, the words **National Security Agency**. In the base semicircle border, the words United States of America, separated on either side by a five pointed star, silver; in a field, blue, an American **eagle** [an occultic phoenix bird] displayed, wings inverted, all proper. The dexter and *sinister talons* clutching **a key,** silver. On the breast of the eagle, the escutcheon, chief blue, supported by paleways of **thirteen [the number 13** is a very powerful, satanic number in the occult and freemasonry] pieces red and white.

In heraldry, **the eagle** is a **symbol** of **courage, supreme power, and authority.** Use of **the eagle** in the **NSA insignia symbolizes the national scope of**

> the mission of the agency. . .The **key** in the **eagle's talons,** *representing the key* to security, evolves from the **emblem of St. Peter the Apostle** and **his power to loose and to bind.** The **shape** of the insignia, **a circle,** represents **perpetuity of its continuance, the SYMBOL OF ETERNITY** [emphasis added].

It should be extremely obvious to anyone who has had even a little Bible training that *the NSA is mocking and blaspheming God with this occultic claim to divine power.* For instance, let's turn to the appropriate Scripture in the Bible for a better understanding of this heresy. In Matthew 16:19 (KJV), Jesus told Peter the Apostle this:

> And I will **give unto thee the KEYS** of the kingdom of heaven: and whatsoever **thou** shalt bind on earth shall be bound in heaven: and whatsoever **thou** shalt loose on earth shall be loosed in heaven [emphasis added].

Jesus Christ gave to Peter (not to the NSA) the **keys** to heaven and the **power to "loose and bind."** Furthermore, only the kingdom of God is perpetual and eternal, **not the satanically inspired National Security Agency!** When we pray for our leaders, as God has ordained, let's remember to pray for all of the deceived souls at the NSA who war (usually unaware) against God's kingdom in these last days.

Now let's dissect the insignia and study the symbolism of each part (where available I have inserted illustrations).

Freemasonic/Occultic Definitions of What US Government and NSA Insignias Truly Represent

On page number "XC" (90) of a highly occultic and esteemed Freemasonic book called *The Secret Teachings of All Ages,* by the late Manly P. Hall, a 33rd degree Mason, the *occultic* secrets of the US government's origin and history and the NSA's occultic insignia are revealed.

The Occultic Insignia of
the National Security
Agency Signals That
Lucifer's Spirit Is Really
Running the Show from
Behind the Scenes!

*The late Manly P. Hall, highly esteemed freemasonic/occultic author.
Courtesy of his book* The Secret Teachings of All Ages.

National Security Agency Souvenir Coin.

European *mysticism* [occultism/freemasonry] was **not dead** at the time the United States of America was founded. The hand of *the Mysteries* [secret Masonic cults] *controlled the establishment of the new government,* for the **signature** of the Mysteries may still be seen on the *Great Seal of the United States of America* [see pyramid and eagle on back side of the U.S. dollar bill, enlarged below]. Careful analysis of the seal discloses a **mass of occult and Masonic symbols, CHIEF AMONG THEM is the so-called American EAGLE** . . . . Here again, only the student of symbolism [Masons] can see through the **subterfuge** and realize that the **American EAGLE** on the Great Seal **is but a conventionalized PHOENIX BIRD**, a fact plainly discernible from an examination of the original Seal design . . . .The Phoenix is the symbol of **spiritual victory** and achievement. . . . Both the single and double-headed eagles are, in reality, **Phoenixes**, a symbol of the accomplishment of **the Great Work** [meaning Satan's evil plan]. [Emphasis added.]

From Hunt's *History of the Seal of the United States.*

Obverse and Reverse of the Great Seal of the United States of America
The Great Seal of the United States of America, with its occultic Eagle/ Phoenix bird, pyramid, and Lucifer's "All-Seeing Eye," are evil occultic insignias symbolizing America's involvement in the New World Order.

Author Manly P. Hall warned us clearly *not to doubt* free-masonry's *occultic presence* and influence in the Great Seal's symbolism on page "XCI" (91) of his book as follows:

> If any one **doubts** the presence of **Masonic and occult influences** at the time the Great Seal was designed, he should give due consideration to the comments of **Professor Charles Eliot Norton of Harvard**, who wrote concerning the *unfinished Pyramid and the All-Seeing Eye* which adorned the reverse of the Seal, as follows: "The device adopted by Congress is practically

incapable of effective treatment; **it can hardly look otherwise than as a dull EMBLEM OF A MASONIC FRATERNITY.**" [Emphasis added.]

Furthermore, on the same page Hall had this to say about **who really created the United States in 1776:**

> Not only were many *founders* of the United States Government *Masons,* but they received aid from **a secret and august [majestic] body existing in Europe** which helped them **to establish this country for a PECULIAR AND PARTICULAR PURPOSE KNOWN ONLY TO THE INITIATED FEW [meaning to bring forth The New World Order].** The Great Seal [of the United States] **is the signature of this exalted body—unseen and for the most part unknown—** and the unfinished **pyramid** upon its [the Seal's] reverse side is a trestle board [supporting structure] setting forth *symbolically* **the task to the accomplishment of which the United States government was dedicated from the day of its inception.** [Emphasis added.]

Manly P. Hall's occultic explanation of America's national insignia should clarify what's presently going on spiritually in this country, because the **five Latin words inside the satanic circle of the Masonic pyramid**, with Satan's "All-Seeing Eye," translate to read: **"Announcing the birth of the New World Order" (ANNUIT COEPTIS NOVUS ORDO SECLOREM).**

Note in Hall's statement above how he freely admits that **freemasonry is "occultic"** in nature. But what does the word *occultic* mean? *Rodale's Synonym Finder* sums it up fairly succinctly as follows: "**Occultism**—cabalism, mysticism, esoterism, supernaturalism, theosophy, spiritualism, mediumism, magic, **black magic, sorcery, witchcraft,** and **diabolism** [of the devil]. *Roget's International Thesaurus* defines occultism similarly. Therefore, we may conclude clearly, without reservations whatsoever, that **freemasonry is deceptive and anti-Christian.** A few top-level Freemasons have admitted it openly in some of their Masonic publications. So why should Christians argue with them about whom they worship and serve?

But what does all this have to do with the NSA's insignia? We are getting to that, so let's continue. I realize that for some of you, I may be "telling you more than you want to know" about the NSA, but I feel it's necessary, since the NSA presently has the capacity to track, eavesdrop, and monitor/watch everybody, and they are enhancing their technical abilities of surveillance and control even more each year, funded by "black chambers projects" (undesignated funds used for top secret expenditures, hidden in the budgets of other legitimate intelligence organizations; referred to by Portland's major newspaper, *The Oregonian,* May 20, 1997, as " 'black budget'. . . hidden inside false accounts. . .within the Pentagon's budget"). NSA is becoming the "clearing house" or "watchdog" into which the other intelligence gathering organizations, both direct and indirect [defined in the next chapter] are funneling the information they collect. They currently have the second largest supercomputer in the world (allegedly) and are linked by satellite with World Wide Web's "CERN" database center in Europe, as well as NSA's own facilities scattered throughout the world. In order to improve the way they are perceived by the nation, in addition to an all-out "P.R." campaign, they are trying to "declassify" their secretive image by declassifying some of the older documents (30 to 40 years) whose data is no longer sensitive to national security. Don't fall for this illusion. . . the things that are really going on at present—and that will affect your lives in the immediate future—are still very much *classified / Top Secret.* They are collecting information from all over the world, which politically speaking would be a very dangerous thing to do, concentrating that much power in the hands of one organization, even if it had no connection with fulfillment of biblical prophecy (which it obviously could: read Revelation 13).

Exposing the NSA's occultic background and covert activities is one of the major thrusts of this book. Please take advantage of my extensive research to enlighten yourself, and subsequently share with others as an evangelizing tool. I'm believing God that the information in this book will be instrumental in leading a multitude of people to a saving relationship with Jesus Christ.

Breakdown of the NSA Insignia

The National Security Agency conveys to Luciferians many occultic messages with its esoteric insignia. This insignia uses two five-pointed stars inside a satanic "eternal circle." Again, Manly P. Hall explains the occultic significance of these symbols in his book, *The Secret Teachings of All Ages.* And in spite of the fact that the stars are not inverted, Hall still refers to them as *pentagrams* (p. CIII—103). This book of pre-Masonic occultists is a rare and prized possession of the Masonic Order. It displays and defines/explains many occultic, freemasonic drawings that define the true satanic origin of this kind of thought. Please take a moment to peruse the following illustrations from this publication, in addition to those appearing above.

Freemasonic writer Manly P. Hall defines *the circle* occultically in this manner:

> The **circle** is the Plan of Divine Activity [esoteric language meaning Lucifer's unholy plan]. According to Qabbalists, the life of the SUPREME CREATOR [he means Lucifer here because Satan is the god of freemasonry] permeates all substance, all space, and all time, but for diagrammatic purposes, the Supreme, All-Inclusive Life is limited by **circle 3**, which may be called " the boundary line of Divine existence." The Divine Life permeating the area bounded by **circle 3** is focused at **Point 1**, which thus becomes the personification of the impersonal life and is termed **"the First Crown."** The creative forces pouring through **Point 1** come into

Note the "nine" five-pointed (pentagram) stars inside the satanic circle, along with "nine" drops, symbolizing the Ninth Degree of freemasonic initiation rites, during which Masons become "born again." Also note the satanic "skull & bones" in the center of the serpent-circle, symbolizing death. Occultists celebrate death frequently with the use of this symbol. It also mocks Christ's death at Golgotha, the place of the "skull."

Phoenix or Eagle—Which? Courtesy of The Secret Teachings of All Ages.

Egyptian Phoenix

From Wilkinson's *Manners and Customs of the Ancient Egyptians.*

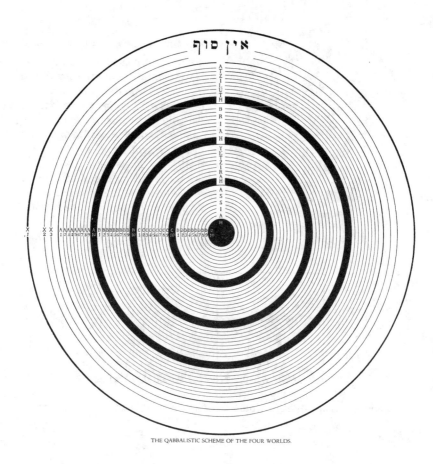

THE QABBALISTIC SCHEME OF THE FOUR WORLDS.

Masonic/Occultic "eternal" circle of Lucifer. Courtesy of The Secret Teachings of All Ages.

The double-headed eagle—the supreme symbol. (The resurrected phoenix bird.) Courtesy of The Secret Teachings of all Ages.

From Khunrath's *Amphitheatrum Sapientiae, etc.*

THE ENTRANCE TO THE HOUSE OF THE MYSTERIES.

This symbolic figure, representing the way to everlasting life, is described by Khunrath in substance as follows: "This is the portal of the amphitheatre of the only true and eternal Wisdom—a narrow one, indeed, but sufficiently august, and consecrated to Jehovah. To this portal ascent is made by a mystic, indisputably prolaptic, flight of steps, set before it as shown in the picture. It consists of seven theosophic, or, rather, philosophic steps of the Doctrine of the Faithful Sons of the Doctrine of the Faithful. Seven is along the way of God to the Father, either directly by inspiration or by various means, contemplating and investigating in a Christiano-Kabalistic, divino-magical, physico-chemical manner, the nature of the Wisdom, work with the sweat of the brow. The bodies of sense, contemplating and investigating in a Christiano-Kabalistic, divino-magical, physico-chemical manner, the nature of the Wisdom, Goodness, and Power of the Creator; to the end that they die not sophistically but live theosophically, and that the orthodox philosophers so created may with sincere philosophy expound the works of the Lord, and worthily praise God who has thus blessed these friends of God." The above figure and description constitute one of the most remarkable expositions ever made of the appearance of the Wise Man's House, and the way by which it must be entered.

GRAND ARCHITECT OF THE UNIVERSE

"If one takes into consideration the immense development which these secret societies have attained; the length of time they are perservering in their vigour; their furious aggressiveness; the tenacity with which their members cling to the association and to the false principles it professes; the persevering mutual cooperation of so many different types of men in the promotion of evil; one can hardly deny that the **SUPREME ARCHITECT** of these associations (seeing that the cause must be proportional to the effect) can be none other than he who in the sacred writings is styled the **PRINCE OF THE WORLD**; and that Satan himself even by his physical cooperation, directs and inspires at least the leaders of these bodies physically cooperating with them." Acta Sancta Sedis, vol, i, p. 293, July 13th, 1865.

ANTICHRIST

COUNCIL OF 13

COUNCIL OF 33

THE "300"

B'NAI B'RITH

GRAND ORIENT

ILLUMINATI

COMMUNISM

SCOTTISH RITE

YORK RITE

WHITE MASONARY: ROTARY, ELKS, YMCA, ETC.

BLUE LODGE

PRO-MASONS — "MASONS WITHOUT THE APRON"

BRITISH ISRAELISM

CATHOLIC and PROTESTANT-LIBERALISM

MATERIALISM   DEIFICATION OF MAN   OCCULTISM

THE MASONIC PYRAMID
ILLUMINISM AND FREE MASONRY — FATHER OF LIES

Reprinted from The Mark of the New World Order.

Time capsule monument to be opened in 100 years (2094). Note caption below date: "New World [Order] Airport Commission."

Note the occultic/Masonic floor tile a short distance from the dedication plaque.

New Denver airport Masonic dedication plaque, March 19, 1994. Photos by Terry L. Cook, 1997, Denver International Airport, Colorado.

Photo of the State of Colorado's Masonic Seal on the wall of the Colorado Capitol Building in Denver, Colorado. Note the Masonic "All-Seeing-Eye" of Lucifer inside the occultic triangle (similar to the dollar bill).

—Photo: Courtesy of Rodney Frank

manifestation as the objective universe in **the inter-
mediate space, circle 2**. [Emphasis added.]

What Hall is really saying here is that "the circle" is nothing
more than a secret, hidden, or esoteric symbol of worship. This
Luciferic circle symbol is typical of various witchcraft circles
used internationally by devil worshipers. In fact, the initiation
rites of freemasonry and witchcraft are virtually identical.
This is why Masons call their meeting lodges "Masonic Temples."
A temple is a place of worship and Masons secretly worship
Satan in their "Blue," "Scottish Rite," and "York" lodges or
temples.

Below I am going to quote a number of excerpts from Hall's
comprehensive book on occultism/mysticism and its history,
filtering down to modern times. **Please receive this warning:** you will note that there is much reference to the Bible
and the scriptures therein; to Paul and other apostles; to God;
even to the great "I Am." This is a perfect case of distorting
the truth and making it a lie. Without exception, when they
interpret biblical truths, they twist them out of shape or use
them out of context, so that they no longer constitute sound
doctrine. Anytime an author *readily admits* that the historical
evidence *documents an occultic history, you can rest assured
that it does, and any use of scripture will be twisted, out of
context, and manipulated to support some occultic mystical
principle, including their use of symbolism, both graphic and
verbal.*

> *Every pagan nation had (and has) not only its state
> religion, but another into which the philosophic elect alone
> have gained entrance.* Many of these ancient cults van-
> ished from the earth without revealing their secrets, but
> *a few have survived the test of ages and their mysterious
> symbols are still preserved.* Much of the ritualism of free-
> masonry is *based on the trials to which candidates were
> subjected* by the ancient hierophants before **the keys
> of wisdom** were entrusted to them. [Author's note:

these are also the keys to loose and bind, mentioned earlier, that Jesus gave expressly to Peter and the Church.]

Few realize the extent to which the ancient secret schools influenced contemporary intellects and, through those minds, posterity. Robert Macoy, 33°, in his *General History of Freemasonry,* pays a magnificent tribute to the part played by the ancient Mysteries in the rearing of the edifice of human culture. He says, in part: "It appears that all the perfection of civilization, and all the advancement made in philosophy, science, and art among the ancients are due to those institutions which, **under the veil of mystery,** sought to illustrate the sublimest truths of religion, morality, and virtue, and impress them on the hearts of their disciples. . . [p. 21 (XXI)].

"There is a certain bird which is called a Phoenix. This is the only one of its kind and lives five hundred years. . . . "

. . .the general resemblance in shape between the phoenix and the eagle [is] a point which the reader should carefully consider, for **it is reasonably certain that the modern Masonic eagle was originally a phoenix. . . .**The phoenix was regarded as *sacred to the sun. . . .*Modern Masons should realize the *special Masonic significance of the phoenix. . . .*The phoenix was a most appropriate symbol of the immortality of the human soul, for just as the phoenix was reborn out of its own dead self seven times seven, so again and again the spiritual nature of man rises triumphant from his dead physical body [reincarnation?].

. . .In the Mysteries it was customary to refer to initiates as *phoenixes* or *men who had been born again,* for just as physical birth gives man consciousness in the physical world, so the neophyte, after **nine degrees in the womb of the Mysteries, was born into a consciousness of the spiritual world. This is the mystery of initiation to which Christ referred when**

he said, "Except a man be born again, he cannot see the kingdom of God" (John iii:3) . . . [p. 90 (XC), emphasis added].

DON'T YOU BELIEVE IT! They are misusing this scripture to support their theory of reincarnation. . .the phoenix bird goes down in flames, then is resurrected, or "rises from the ashes." Hall says, "The phoenix is a fitting symbol of this spiritual birth." Not even close! They carefully manage to ignore the Bible's words about "it is appointed unto man **once** to die, and after that the judgment." We will not rise from the ashes "seven times seven," as Hall claims. For the human race, it will be "ashes to ashes, and dust to dust" until the day the Lord returns to resurrect the "dead in Christ," which in one place the Bible tells us will rise first, and in another place "those who are alive will not precede those who are asleep [dead]." But the ones (in Christ) who are alive and remain will be changed in the twinkling of an eye. . .and so shall they ever be with the Lord. Quite a different scenario than Hall postulates.

However, he wants us to know that this occultic/Masonic mysticism had (and still has) great influence on the affairs of the United States. He continues on page 90 (XC):

> European mysticism was not dead at the time the United States of America was founded. **The hand of the Mysteries controlled in the establishment of the new government, for the signature of the Mysteries may still be seen on the Great Seal of the United States of America.** Careful analysis of the seal discloses a **mass of occult and Masonic symbols**, chief among them the **so-called American eagle**—a bird which Benjamin Franklin declared unworthy to be chosen as the emblem of a great, powerful, and progressive people. Here again **only the student of symbolism can see through the subterfuge** and realize that the American eagle upon the Great Seal is but a conven-

tionalized phoenix, **a fact plainly discernible from an examination of the original seal**.... In a colored sketch submitted as a design for the Great Seal by William Barton in 1782, an actual phoenix appears sitting upon a nest of flames. This itself demonstrates a tendency towards the use of this emblematic bird. [Emphasis added.]

On page 91 (XCI), Hall has this to say:

If any one doubts the presence of Masonic and occult influences at the time the Great Seal was designed, he should give due consideration to the comments of Professor Charles Eliot Norton of Harvard, who wrote concerning the unfinished pyramid and the All-Seeing Eye which adorned the reverse of the seal, as follows: "The device adopted by Congress is practically incapable of effective treatment; it can hardly (however artistically treated by the designer) look otherwise than as a dull emblem of a Masonic fraternity" (the *History of the Seal of the United States).*

. . . *Not only were many of the founders of the United States Government Masons, but they received aid from a secret and august body existing in Europe,* which helped them to *establish this country for a peculiar and particular purpose known only to the INITIATED FEW.* The Great Seal is the signature of this exalted body—**unseen and for the most part unknown**—and the unfinished pyramid upon its reverse side is a trestleboard *setting forth symbolically the task to the accomplishment of which the United States Government was dedicated from the day of its inception.* [Emphasis added—you will recognize part of the above from earlier use, but I wanted you to see it context.]

On page 99 (XCIX) Hall goes into the mythological search for the Holy Grail and the Spear of Longinus (alleged to be the weapon used to spear the side of Christ at the crucifixion to assure that He was dead). He concludes his examination of the evidence with this bit of heresy: "Moreover, to the Christian, the search for the Holy Grail is the search for the real Self. . . ." (The capital "S" on self is Hall's.)

As Hall continues to lay his foundation for the fact that freemasonry is built upon occultism and mysticism, he feels that we should have a basic knowledge about the "black arts—black magic."

The Theory and Practice of Black Magic

Some understanding of the intricate theory and practice of ceremonial magic may be derived from a brief consideration of its underlying premises.

First. The visible universe has an invisible counterpart, the higher planes of which are peopled by good and beautiful spirits; the lower planes, dark and foreboding, are the habitation of evil spirits and demons under the leadership of the Fallen Angel and his ten Princes.

Second. By means of the secret processes of ceremonial magic it is possible to contact these invisible creatures and gain their help in some human undertaking. Good spirits willingly lend their assistance to any worthy enterprise, but the evil spirits serve only those who live to pervert and destroy.

Third. It is possible to make contracts with spirits whereby the magician becomes for a stipulated time the master of an elemental being [demon].

Fourth. True black magic is performed with the aid of a demoniacal spirit, who serves the sorcerer for the length of his earthly life, with the understanding that after death the magician shall become the servant of his own demon. For this reason a black magician will go to inconceivable ends to prolong his physical life, since there is nothing for him beyond the grave.

The *most dangerous form of black magic is the scientific perversion of occult power* for the gratification of personal desire. Its less complex and more universal form is human selfishness, for *selfishness is the fundamental cause of all worldly evil.* **A man will barter his eternal soul for temporal power,** and down through the ages a mysterious process has been evolved which **actually enables him to make this exchange.** In its various branches the black art includes nearly all forms of ceremonial magic, necromancy, witchcraft, sorcery, and vampirism. Under the same general heading are also included **mesmerism and hypnotism,** except when used solely for **medical purposes,** and **even then there is an element of risk for all concerned.** [Author's note: This is a position by Hall on this subject that even most "intellectual" Christians refuse to acknowledge.]

Though the demonism of the Middle Ages seems to have disappeared, there is abundant evidence that in many forms of modern thought...black magic has merely passed through a metamorphosis, and although its name be changed its nature remains the same [p. 101 (CI), emphasis added].

As Christ was leaving, one of the last commissions He gave to His disciples and the Church included "casting out demons" until His return. Knowing that this function is no longer a very frequent part of the ministry of the local church, one preacher I knew impertinently asked in a sermon, "If there are no more demons to cast out, where'd they all go?" Of course, this is a rhetorical question...since, like the angels, they don't die—there are still plenty to go around (possibly by different names, as Hall suggests). When He left, Christ seemed to think there would be plenty, since He was so specific in His instructions to continue casting them out till His return. Therefore, we cannot agree with Hall's previous paragraph that demonism disappeared in the Middle Ages, although we do agree with him that the black arts just keep changing their names and reappearing...*maybe they're the phoenix bird!*

On page 117 (CXVII), Hall gets into the fundamentals of Qabbalistic teachings, including what I call the "occultic/Masonic circle" with its mystical, complex mathematical interpretations (it is pictured above). This is the section where he describes "I AM" as a point in the middle.

In the chapter titled "The Mystery of the Apocalypse" (page 185, CLXXXV), he addresses, from a **mythological position**, the prophecies we find in the biblical Book of Revelation. Naturally, everything means something other than the Christian sound doctrine, which we espouse, but what else would you expect? (That, too, is a rhetorical question!)

Did you think I forgot The New World Order? Not so! Hall discusses "the new order" of things, people, and the world to come many times, especially on page 203 (CCIII), following his statement that ". . .eventually civilization will destroy itself in one great cataclysmic struggle. . ." and of course the "new order" will be built upon the foundation of the former world order (by then allegedly defunct),·to which he furthers refers as: ". . .this spherical ant-hill in Chaos." The final paragraph in his book (p. 204, CCIV) sums up the lie and encourages you to "jump right in"—in much the same way as we would present salvation to a non-Christian, then invite him to accept Christ. Remember how we all have been taught that in the Church there could not be a counterfeit if there were not an original truth to copy and distort. Well, I think this is one of Satan's biggest counterfeits.

> . . .Only transcendental philosophy knows the path. Only the illumined reason can carry the understanding part of man upward to the light. Only philosophy can teach man to be born well [Author: Now, who can determine how or where he is born, or to whom?], live well, to die well, and in perfect measure *be born again*. Into this band of the *elect*—those who have chosen the life of knowledge, of virtue, and of utility [hardly a biblical definition of the elect]—the philosophers of the ages invite YOU [emphasis added].

The Leadership of the NSA

Lieutenant General Kenneth A. Minihan, USAF Current Director of the National Security Agency and Central Security Service Fort Meade, Maryland

Courtesy of NSA's Public Affairs Office.

Lieutenant General Kenneth A. Minihan is the combined Director of both the NSA and the Central Security Service (NSA/CSS). Remember this connection as we delve further into the workings of the NSA and its sister intelligence organizations (see next chapter). He is stationed at the Fort George G. Meade Army Base, Maryland (the location of the NSA headquarters). As the Director of both of these organizations, he is responsible for the NSA, as well as a combat support agency of the Department of Defense with military and civilian personnel stationed around the globe. *General Minihan is THE* senior uniformed intelligence officer in the entire Department of Defense.

The General first entered the Air Force in 1966 as a distinguished graduate of the Florida State University Reserve Officer Training Corps program. He has served in many prestigious positions throughout his career, including senior intelligence officer for the Air Force and in other senior staff officer positions in the Pentagon, Electronic Security Command, Kelly Air Force Base, Texas, and the Defense Intelligence Agency, Washington, DC, among others. He has commanded squadrons, groups, and a major air command both in the United States and abroad. He has been the assistant chief of staff, intelligence, Headquarters US Air Force, Washington, DC, and most recently the Director of Defense Intelligence.

His experience and education appear to make him imminently qualified to run this agency, or at least as well as anyone can be expected to. I suspect at the moment that it may be a case of "the tail wagging the dog" around the NSA/CSS.

His education is also very impressive. He holds a B.A. degree in Political Science from Florida State University, an M.A. degree in National Security Affairs from the Naval Postgraduate School, Monterey, California, and is a graduate of the Harvard University Program for Senior Executives in National and International Security in Massachusetts, as well as the US Air Force's Air War College, Alabama.

General Minihan has worked in the intelligence field for most of his very impressive military career. It started at Langley Air Force Base and concluded with his present assignment as Director of both the NSA/CSS at Fort Meade, with one stint along the way as Chief of the Office of Support to Military Operations and Plans at the NSA.

The general is a native Texan and a family man, married to Barbara Gleason of Elkhorn, Wisconsin, with three children, Mike, Tom, and Katie. This has been a condensed "digest" version of General Minihan's resume, but the unabridged version is available on NSA's website, if you care to pursue it.

General Minihan is obviously a very bright, talented, and respected intelligence leader. The fact that he has been chosen to run Big Brother's NSA, the most sophisticated intelligence organization in the entire world (as well as the other positions that fall within his job description), leads me to believe that the New-World-Order leaders must trust him implicitly and unequivocally.

Who is the Real Leader of the NSA? Could it be Minihan's Civilian Deputy Director, William P. Crowell?

Very little is known or available regarding this man. It is possible, however, that Mr. Crowell may be the real leader of the NSA behind the scenes, with Minihan simply serving as the covering front man. It is further possible that he has strong ties to the New World Order globalists and that he may take orders directly from them.

How I Was Able to Obtain This and Other Unclassified Information about the Illustrious National Security Agency

Ooops! I almost wrote *notorious* instead of *illustrious*. I wonder if that's what is referred to as a "Freudian slip"? According to *Miriam Webster's Collegiate Dictionary,* Tenth Edition, it is "a slip of the tongue that is motivated by and reveals some unconscious aspect of the mind." In that case, I'd better confess. . . it was probably a Freudian slip!

Although the *internal* operations of the National Security Agency are kept *highly secret,* there is quite a bit of *superficial,* publicly obtainable information available if one merely knows where to look. Obtaining this information requires doing a little basic research and investigation and making a few phone calls. But with a little investigation, some common sense, and a small amount of cash, one readily can acquire a substantial amount of information about the NSA. For example, I spent about a month gathering the above and below information and documentation.

As a former police investigator and a commercially licensed pilot with a strong background in aeronautics, I used this knowledge, background, and training to contact the Federal Aviation Administration in order to obtain aeronautical airspace charts of the NSA's facility in Maryland. After a few phone calls, I was sent the Fort Meade aeronautical charts that pilots use for navigating over that area. Surprisingly, I discovered that there were **no restrictions** against civilian

pilots flying near or over that area. Frankly, I expected to see depictions of "restricted airspace" on these charts near the NSA headquarters area, but I was shocked to observe none whatsoever! I have reproduced portions of these "Sectional" and "World Aeronautical Charts" below for your enlightenment and perusal.

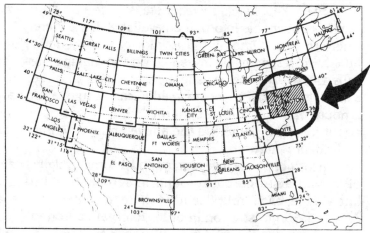

WASHINGTON
SECTIONAL AERONAUTICAL CHART
SCALE 1:500,000

Lambert Conformal Conic Projection Standard Parallels 33°20′ and 38°40′
Horizontal Datum: North American Datum of 1983 (World Geodetic System 1984)

60 *TH EDITION August 15, 1996*
Includes airspace amendments effective *August 15, 1996*
and all other aeronautical data received by June 20, 1996

Information on this chart will change; consolidated updates of chart changes are available every 56 days in the AIRPORT / FACILITY DIRECTORY (A/FD). Also consult appropriate NOTICES TO AIRMEN (NOTAMs) and other FLIGHT INFORMATION PUBLICATIONS (FLIPs) for the latest changes.

This chart will become *OBSOLETE FOR USE IN NAVIGATION* upon publication of the next edition scheduled for *FEBRUARY 27, 1997*

PUBLISHED IN ACCORDANCE WITH INTERAGENCY AIR CARTOGRAPHIC COMMITTEE SPECIFICATIONS AND AGREEMENTS, APPROVED BY:
DEPARTMENT OF DEFENSE • FEDERAL AVIATION ADMINISTRATION • DEPARTMENT OF COMMERCE

The Washington Sectional Chart. Note on this aeronautical chart that there is no restricted fly zone over the NSA facility.

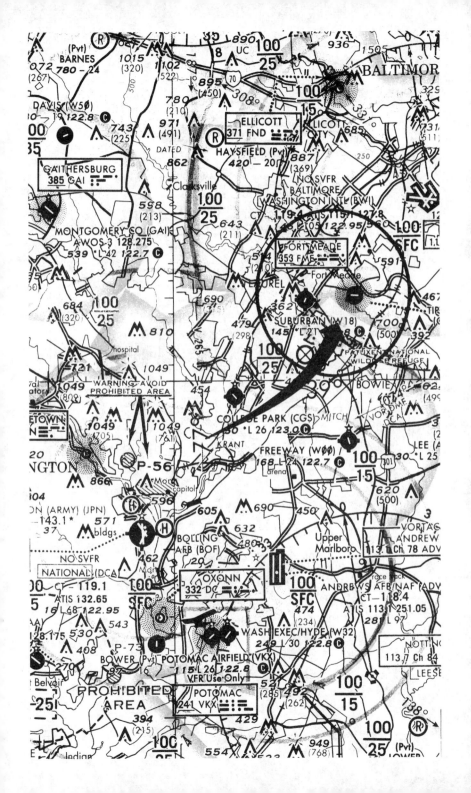

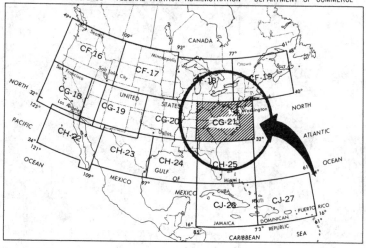

WORLD AERONAUTICAL CHART
SCALE 1:1,000,000
Lambert Conformal Conic Projection Standard Parallels 33°20' and 38°40'
Horizontal Datum: North American Datum of 1983 (World Geodetic System 1984)
Topographic data corrected to January 1996
27 TH EDITION *September 12, 1996*
Includes airspace amendments effective *August 15, 1996*
and all other aeronautical data received by July 18, 1996
Consult appropriate NOTAMs and Flight Information
Publications for supplemental data and current information.
This chart will become *OBSOLETE FOR USE IN NAVIGATION* upon publication of
the next edition scheduled for *OCTOBER 9, 1997*
PUBLISHED IN ACCORDANCE WITH INTERAGENCY AIR CARTOGRAPHIC COMMITTEE
SPECIFICATIONS AND AGREEMENTS, APPROVED BY:
DEPARTMENT OF DEFENSE • FEDERAL AVIATION ADMINISTRATION • DEPARTMENT OF COMMERCE

World Aeronautical Chart No. CG-21

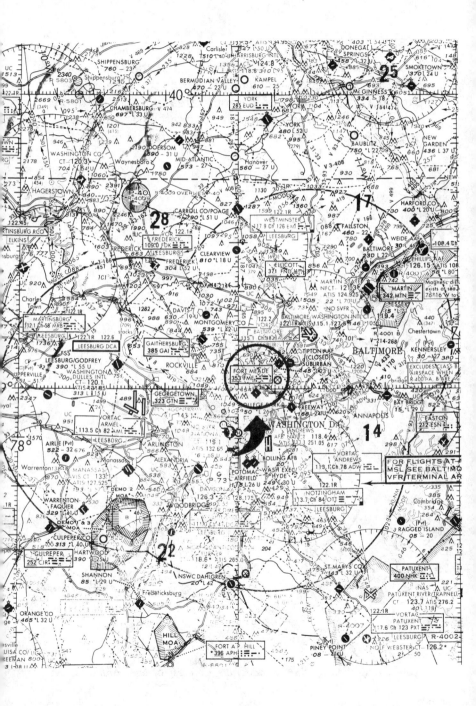

Then I called the local Chamber of Commerce in NSA's area and requested a good street map of the area near the NSA in Fort Meade. They were delighted to send me an excellent highway map of the entire area that actually depicts where the NSA is located relative to nearby freeways, streets, and airports. A portion of this map also is shown below.

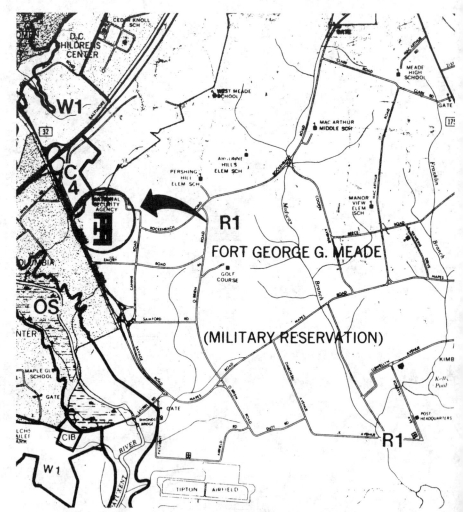

Zoning map showing NSA headquarters. Courtesy of Anne Arundel County.

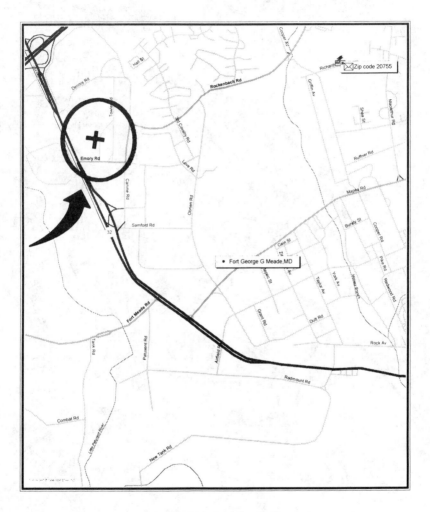

Current Map. NSA, Ft. George Meade, Maryland.

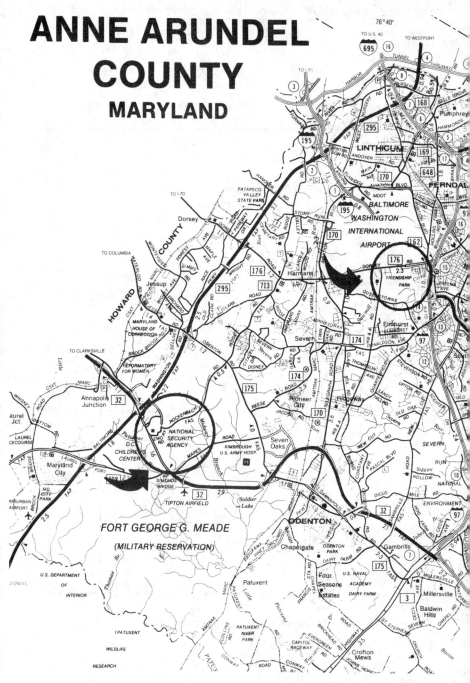

ANNE ARUNDEL COUNTY
MARYLAND

NSA's huge Friendship Annex facility, located near the Baltimore / Washington, DC, airport (top circle.) NSA's headquarters facility at Ft. George Meade, Maryland (bottom circle).

Since I'm also a licensed real estate broker with a strong background in real estate, I called the Anne Arundel County Planning and Code Enforcement Division in Annapolis, Maryland, to ascertain the availabilty of any publicly available tax assessment maps of the NSA complex at Fort Meade. They sent me a copy of Tax Assessment District Zoning Map #4, which covers that area. They also told me how to reach a company that sells aerial maps of the area.

On calling that company, I learned that they produce several publicly available high-definition aerial and infrared maps of Fort Meade (and many other areas) for various government and private organizations. After paying substantial fees (believe me, they were not cheap!), I was able to obtain several excellent aerial and infrared photographs of the National Security Agency complex located near the Fort Meade Army Base.

Furthermore, **the NSA itself** will send you a wealth of basic information on its history, background, and present leadership, if you simply call its Public Affairs Office at the number indicated at the beginning of this chapter, or access its **Internet** website address at **www.nsa.gov:8080**—this is what I did to acquire all the information in this chapter. But again, *don't allow this apparent availability and openness to deceive you! The NSA is still the most secretive organization on earth.* They simply are attempting to convince us otherwise by launching this very impressive, effective, and deceptive public-relations "marketing" maneuver. . . so don't forget the term "doublespeak" from Orwell's book *1984*—they are masters of its use! Keep in mind that all intelligence agencies are experts at playing mind games via deceptive tactics and the spread of "disinformation." That's what the intelligence business is all about in the first place! With this slick P.R. smokescreen, the NSA is hoping that most of us will buy the illusion that they **are not as secret as they truly are**, when in fact, there is no other organization in the entire world that's more clandestine than they!

Throughout this book I will be referencing excerpts from

a myriad of publications, and in a few cases I will recommend highly that you obtain a copy for your own use and read it in its entirety. Such a book is James Bamford's *The Puzzle Palace: A Report on America's Most Secret Agency.* There were many attempts to prevent its publication, and a comprehensive dossier was compiled on Bamford, under the code name *Esquire.*

Another item I believe you should purchase and study in its entirely is a six-part special feature of *The Baltimore Sun,* which ran from December 3-15, 1995 (it is still available for purchase from *The Sun* in a combined format for $6.95).

The large (all caps, 1-3/8" tall), bold headline reads: "AMERICA'S FORTRESS OF SPIES," but above the photo (which appears *above* that gigantic headline), appear the words: NO SUCH AGENCY. After you have read enough to be "in the know," you will recognize this as a pun, based on a joke that was going around early in the existence of the secret group ultimately emerging as the NSA. It was alleged in humor that the acronym NSA stood for "No Such Agency." Here are a few comments from that special edition pertaining to Bamford.

Author unearthed dossier spies had collected on him

In 1982, AFTER author James Bamford published his landmark book on NSA, *The Puzzle Palace,* he filed a Freedom of Information Act request for any files the agency might have compiled on him. He was told there was nothing.

Then, on a hunch, he repeated the request, this time asking for files that used the code name Esquire, a mysterious notation he'd spotted on another document.

He hit the jackpot. NSA officials nervous about his research had assigned the code name to Mr. Bamford, a lawyer. Over many months, he received hundreds of **sanitized** Esquire-related documents showing that dozens of employees, up to the NSA director, attorney

Order
Now!

an information service of the Baltimore Sun

NSA: America's Fortress of Spies

Here's what's in *The Sun's* NSA series. Full-color reprints of the entire NSA series are available for $6.95 through SunSource, The Baltimore Sun Information Store. Call 410-332-6800 to reserve your copy now. Outside the Baltimore area call (800) 829-8000, Ext. 6800.

Part 1

NSA eavesdrops on allied presidents, military strongmen, drug dealers and trade negotiators. Click here to read it on-line.

Part 2

Maryland's largest employer is one of America's strangest workplaces.

Part 3

NSA has a secret within a secret: eavesdroppers undercover abroad.

Part 4

Scores of countries thought their coded messages were secure. Was NSA reading over their shoulders?

Part 5

Trolling for foreign secrets, NSA routinely picks up Americans' overseas calls. And it's legal.

Part 6

The next war may be fought with computers. NSA is getting ready.

- The Fortress of Spies page
- Read an excerpt from Part 1
- Intelligence Sources on the Web

SUNSOURCE HOME

SUNSPOT | CLASSIFIED | NEWS | SPORTS | CRABHOUSE | SEARCH | OUR TOWN | THE SUN | HELP

general, and national security adviser, had been involved
in discussions of what to do about *The Puzzle Palace* and
its author.

The Esquire files showed that NSA officials had tried
to acquire early proofs of the book from the publishers,
Houghton Mifflin Co., without revealing their identity.
Memos detailed NSA's attempts to keep track of Mr.
Bamford's research at other government agencies, noting
which documents he inspected and copied.

And the files revealed that serious consideration was
given to prosecuting the writer for revealing secrets
about NSA . . . . [Ultimately] no charges were filed. *The
Puzzle Palace* became a best seller. And an updated
edition is planned for publication next year.

References to NSA are rare in government documents

Compared with the tightlipped NSA, the CIA is about
as secret as an Elks lodge.

The Library of Congress catalog lists 522 books on
the CIA and just 12 on NSA—and four of those are
different editions of *The Puzzle Palace,* still the only book
devoted exclusively to NSA.

The Puzzle Palace has become the definitive publication
on the dealings of the NSA—secret and otherwise. Bamford
is now considered and quoted as the top authority on the
NSA, and invariably whenever a newspaper, magazine, or
government agency, *et al,* do an article, speech, etc. on NSA,
without fail they will quote from *The Puzzle Palace* as the
undisputed authority. I wholeheartedly concur with this
evaluation, therefore, I, myself, will be quoting from Bamford
throughout this book, beginning below with excerpts from
pages 133 to 141.

Office of Telecommunications and Computer Services:
Whereas most government offices or large corporations

measure in square feet the space taken up by their computers, **NSA measures it in acres.** "I had five and a half acres of computers when I was there," said General Carter. "We didn't count them by numbers; it was five and a half acres." Even though the emphasis today is on increased capacity and decreased size, one NSA employee, when recently told the statistic, commented, "It's double that today."

Resting today in the cavernous subterranean expanses below the National Security Agency's Headquarters-Operations Building is probably **the greatest concentration of computers the world has ever known.** It is a land where computers literally talk back and forth to each other and where, using what is known as "brute force," they are able to spit out solutions to complex statistical problems in nanoseconds rather than the decades it once might have taken.

NSA, like its predecessors, has been a silent partner in America's computer growth from the very beginning, yet because of what one NSA computer expert called its "policy of anonymity," NSA's role has been almost totally hidden. When the Association for Computing Machinery sponsored an observance in honor of the twenty-fifth anniversary of its founding, NSA simply observed in silence. Likewise, when the "pioneers" gathered at COMPCON-76, the quarter-century anniversary meeting of the Institute of Electrical and Electronic Engineers' Computer Society, NSA again exhibited an advanced case of shyness. Apparently, the fact that America uses computers in its SIGINT and COMSEC activities is still a national secret.

. . .Today the **NSA's enormous basement**, which stretches for city blocks below the Headquarters-Operations Building, undoubtedly **holds the largest and most advanced computer operation in the world**.

. . .On top of this [the capacity and speed of their computers], NSA in 1983 plans to put into operation

secretly an enormous worldwide computer network codenamed Platform which will tie together fifty-two separate
computer systems used throughout the world. Focal
point, or "host environment," for the massive network
will be NSA headquarters at Fort Meade. Among those
included in Platform will be the British SIGINT organization, GCHQ.

. . . About 1976 . . . all Agency computer functions
were transferred to the newly reorganized Office of Telecommunications and Computer Services, known generally as the T Organization.

. . . Several floors above and to the rear of Gatehouse
3, behind a solid steel-gray door pasted with warning
signs and controlled by cipher lock, is the center of NSA's
worldwide eavesdropping net. If NSA is America's ear,
the T Organization's massive Communications Center
is the ear's drum. Inside, row after row of rat-a-tat-tatting
crypto machines bare the world's secrets on multicolored,
six-ply carbon paper, each sheet repeating the word
CLASSIFIED on one side while the other side repeatedly
warns against disclosure under penalties specified by the
espionage laws.

The chatter of Soviet transport pilots, the latest home
communique from the Kuwaiti ambassador to Algeria,
the singsong of a Chinese merchant telephoning an
order for spare parts to a supplier in Kuala Lumpur—
whatever the net snares crackles back to the Puzzle
Palace over the Agency's own supersecret communications network, SPINTCOM, which is short for Special
Intelligence Communications. The intercepts make their
way via SPINTCOM to a synchronous satellite 22,300
miles over the equator and are then beamed down to
a pair of giant dish antennas hidden in a wooded area
behind NSA. From there the intelligence flows via a
$500,000, three-quarter-mile-long underground cable
past a $2.2 million antenna control facility and into the
COMM Center to be distributed to analysts, linguists, and

codebreakers.

Also zapping in to the Puzzle Palace via the twin earth terminals is another worldwide circuit, this one reserved for the most important and immediate of intelligence messages. The Critical Intelligence Communications network, or CRITICOM, is designed to flash to the President and a handful of other senior officials intelligence alerts and warnings of the highest priority—an imminent coup in a Middle East sheikdom, for example, or the assassination of a world leader, or the sinking of a Soviet sub. It is the goal of NSA to have such a CRITIC message on the President's desk within ten minutes of the event. [Emphasis added.]

Budget and Personnel of the NSA

Usually one can determine the magnitude or scope of an organization by examining its annual budget and the number of personnel involved in supporting the functions of the organization.

Recently, the CIA was sued to force it to reveal the size of the budget for US espionage. The article below appeared in the May 20, 1997, edition of Portland's largest newspaper, *The Oregonian*, in Section A-5, National.

Scientists sue to reveal CIA's spy budget

The Federation of American Scientists sued the Central Intelligence Agency **(CIA)** on Monday to force it to reveal one of Washington's worst-kept secrets: the size of the budget for U.S. espionage.

The amount of the "black budget," is hidden inside false accounts and classified compartments within the Pentagon's budget. It has been reported to be about $29 billion a year, give or take a billion.

The CIA spends about $3 billion a year. The agency's director and the secretary of defense allocate most of the rest to military intelligence services such as the

National Security Agency **(NSA)**, which conducts electronic eavesdropping, and the National Reconnaissance
Office **(NRO)**, which builds spy satellites. [Read details
about the NRO and CIA in the next chapter on "Sister"
Organizations of the NSA.)

Intelligence spending is officially a state secret, and
it has been since the CIA was created 50 years ago. But
the veil of secrecy has slipped somewhat.

The Federation of American Scientists, founded in
1945 as a research group concerned with national
security policy, has decoded some of the secret sections
of the Defense Department's budget where intelligence
spending is hidden. But the number remains officially
classified. [Some of the findings of the FAS on specific
topics are examined later in this chapter.]

Although I seriously question the validity of the information
contained therein, the FAS website reveals the following
details of the NSA budget and staff (which I suspect probably
are grossly underestimated because they really don't want
the "enemy" to obtain this info and use it against them in
some way).

Budget and Personnel

While the CIA budget is regularly the subject of public
reports which are generally rather consistent, **the NSA
budget is less frequently subject to press speculation**, and published reports vary widely, **with some
estimates running as high as $10 billion.** A principal
source of confusion is the distinction between NSA
proper and the associated military elements of the
Central Security Service (CSS). These service elements
have historically been quite expensive, encompassing
many thousands of personnel at overseas ground stations.
In fact, the NSA turns out to be not much larger than
that of CIA, and surprisingly, much more readily discern-
able from official public sources.

The annual R-1 and P-1 military budget documents provide total figures for RDT&E and procurement for all Defense Agencies, as well as funding for each individual agency, except for NSA and the Defense Intelligence Agency (DIA). Simple arithmetic reveals the total for these two agencies, and since NSA is much larger than DIA, the bulk of this remainder must be NSA. *Contracts with NSA are routinely announced by the Defense Department, which shyly refers to NSA as the "Maryland Procurement Office."*

Unfortunately, there was until recently no "O-1" for the operations and maintenance account, but each year testimony is given to Congress which displays the operations and maintenance budget for Defense Agencies. As with the R-1 and P-1, this display provides a total figure for all Defense Agencies, as well as funding for each individual agency, with a few exceptions. One of the amusing examples of the foolish inconsistency with which the "secret" budget is publicly discussed is the presentation of the operations and maintenance budget, which coyly provides an **aggregate figure for intelligence and communications (about $2.8 billion)**. This includes **NSA** and **DIA**, as well as the Defense Information Systems Agency (**DISA**), which is included in the aggregate to avoid revealing the intelligence portion of this account (a reticence which does not extend to the RDT&E and procurement accounts). However, DIS has no reticence in revealing its annual operations and maintenance budget (nearly $400 million) in its annual report. Again simple arithmetic reveals the total for DIA and NSA, and the bulk of this remainder **(about $2 billion) must be NSA** [emphasis added].

Remember what I told you about "disinformation"? The previous paragraph is a perfect example of a convoluted explanation of their funding. Perhaps they didn't lie (which I never would rule out!), but they have made it so confusing

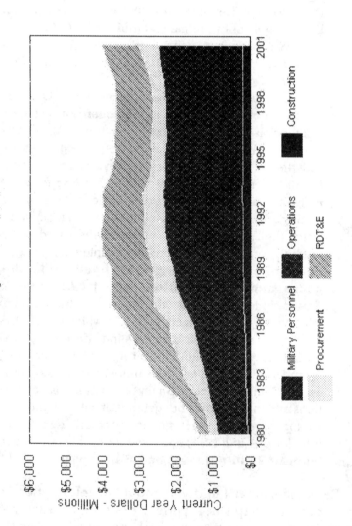

National Security Agency
Estimated Budget - Current Dollars

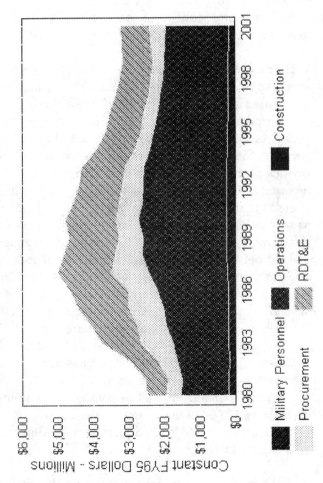

National Security Agency
Estimated Budget - Constant Dollars

that even if it's the truth and you use the "simple arithmetic" which the FAS recommends, you'll be lucky to arrive at a conclusion anywhere near the actual spending of the NSA.

By the way, if you are having trouble with all these "alphabet soup" abbreviations, there is an exhaustive appendix in *The Puzzle Palace* (seven pages) entitled "Acronyms and Abbreviations," in which Bamford identifies the organizations pertinent to his study on the NSA, and many have detailed descriptions, making it a very handy tool.

The FAS website continues on budget and personnel information:

> The operations and maintenance account consists of spending for contractor services and civilian employees (uniformed service members are funded through the military personnel account). NSA reportedly has about 20,000 employees in Maryland, with a $831.7 million payroll in 1990. Based on the precedent of other Defense Agencies, most (over 90%) of these are civilians. The reported 20,000 civilian employees is consistent with an operations and maintenance budget of about $2 billion, as seen by dividing the typical cost of a civilian government employee (about $100,000, which is about equally divided between direct pay and purchases of supplies and contract services). These estimates are also consistent with the approximately 5 million square feet of NSA office space at Ft. Meade, somewhat less than the Pentagon, which houses somewhat more than 20,000 personnel. Other published estimates that NSA has between 38,000 and 52,000 employees clearly also include the personnel of the Central Security Service military components, as well as contractor personnel. As many as 12,000 of these personnel are housed at the Friendship Annex at Airport Square near the Baltimore Washington International Airport.

I'm glad there is an organization, such as the FAS, who is willing to fearlessly call these entities to account for their spending and actions—if our Congress won't do it. However, all this fancy dancing footwork—such as "all these speculations seem like they would be about right," etc., etc.—could be avoided if they would just come right out and issue a true budget in black and white, at least to Congress, if not publicly through the media.

That very thorough article I mentioned in *The Baltimore Sun,* arrived at a decidedly larger amount . . . $8 billion, and they had this to say in reference to the budget of the NSA:

An $8 billion effort

Keeping the world wired isn't easy, and it isn't cheap.

NSA listens from a fleet of billion-dollar satellites and through an ordinary electrical socket on the wall of a foreign mission. The eavesdroppers are in the van along Embassy Row in Washington and in the bunker at Misawa Air Base on the northern tip of Japan. They're aboard that U.S. Navy cruiser steaming through the Mediterranean and in the cockpit of the U-2 spy plane above the Bosnian landscape.

The price tag for the entire budget network is secret, but it only begins with NSA's annual budget of about $3.6 billion [probably inflation since the NSA's report of about $2 billion in 1990 (above)]. Those eavesdropping satellites may cost another $3 billion, from the budget of the National Reconnaissance Office. The Army, Navy and Air Force provide NSA with 30,000 or so servicemen and women who staff listening posts, adding about $2 billion.

The total: at least $8 billion a year for U.S. signals intelligence, by the calculation of John Pike, an intelligence watcher at the Federation of American Scientists [FAS] and ardent student of the Pentagon's "black" budget that conceals NSA's spending.

The Sun's special feature also addresses the size and how it affects the Maryland economy.

National Security Agency headquarters

From this 650-acre campus, NSA operates its global eaves
network and designs secure communications systems. In
buildings is the largest concentration of computing pc
mathematicians and linguists in the world.

A **National Business Park tower:**
Private office tower leased by NSA
since 1992 for its Technology and
Systems Organization, which buys
and maintains the agency's
computers and other hardware.

B **Supercomputing facility** (under
construction): A $47 million
building to house supercomputers
used to break foreign codes and
sort the intelligence that streams
into the agency.

C **Museum and conference
center:** Former Colony 7 Motel —
purchased by NSA to prevent
foreign spies from using the motel
to eavesdrop — houses the
National Cryptologic Museum.

D **Operations complex:** The hub

of NSA's eavesdropping or signals
intelligence (SIGINT) operations.
The 3-million-square-foot
compound includes four buildings:
the U-shaped original 1957
headquarters; the nine-story 1966
building, dubbed the "SIGINT
Hilton"; and the pair of glass towers
— encased in copper mesh to
prevent leaking electronic signals
from reaching enemy
eavesdroppers — completed in 1984
and 1986.

E **Support Activities Building 1:**
Administrative offices and storage.

F **Military housing:** Dormitories
for military intelligence battalions
that provide support for NSA.

G **Child Development Center:** The

largest day-care center i:
opened in 1992 with spa
children.

H **Microwave tower:** L:
capacity microwave rel:
used for government
communications. Likely
used to intercept micro
between foreign officials
York and Washington.

I **Support Activities B**
Includes the recently re
NSA archives, holding 1
pages of records.

J **Information Security**
Headquarters for NSA's
writing the codes and d
the equipment to make
government communica

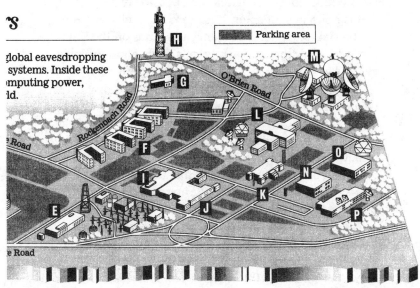

's

global eavesdropping
systems. Inside these
mputing power,
ld.

-care center in the state
1992 with space for 305

ave tower: Large-
icrowave relay tower
vernment
ations. Likely has been
ercept microwave links
reign officials in New
Vashington.

t Activities Building 2:
ie recently renovated
res, holding 11 million
cords.

ition Security complex:
ers for NSA's other role:
codes and designing
ient to make sure U.S.
t communications are

not picked up by foreign spies.

K Microchip plant: Wearing white
spacesuits to prevent dust
contamination, agency employees
craft the microchips that are the
brains of NSA computers. The air
is changed 360 times per hour
inside the "clean room."

L Research and Engineering:
This scientific research center
opened in 1988 and includes a
15,000-book library. A site for NSA's
Secure Distance Learning Network,
a two-way round-the-world video
hookup for technical courses.

M Satellite communication field:
The four huge microwave dishes
serve as the principal downlink site
for information beamed by satellite

from NSA's worldwide field sites.

N Support Activities Building 3:
Includes 1.6 million data tapes in
tape library. Also includes lockers,
classrooms and armory for NSA's
police force.

O Support Activities Building 4:
Includes office space and a
warehouse.

P Systems Processing Center:
Includes the NSA model shop as
well as workshops for plating,
woodworking, welding, metal
working and painting; research
labs; echo-free chambers for
acoustic testing.

JEROLD COUNCIL : SUN STAFF

Sprawling complex fuels Md. economy

It is not a nest of spies. It is more like a city of them.

The National Security Agency's campus off the Balti-more-Washington Parkway swells with enough spies every day to populate College Park or Salisbury.

The 7 million square feet of office space at NSA's headquarters and the outlying locations could fill 10 U.S. Capitol buildings. The electricity consumed there could keep the lights glowing in a city of 50,000 people. [However, when the city loses its lights, for any of a myriad of reasons, you can be guaranteed that the NSA won't lose theirs!—they have adequate alternate power sources in place to protect their operation.]

The agency's day-care center is the largest in the state, with room for 300 children. And the shuttlebus and car-pool service is the largest on the East Coast.

NSA has its own 400-member police force, television network, and power plant....

NSA's $930 million Maryland payroll is the largest in the state....

Though some Marylanders confuse NSA with NASA and few know more than its name, the agency may be the state's most powerful economic engine.

In 1993, NSA gave Maryland companies 14,000 contracts totaling more than $700 million...[not including all the secret projects NSA is subsidizing in other states and around the globe].

"It's a tremendous economic impact," said James D. Fielder, deputy secretary of DEED. "Those businesses that work off the contracts have employees and facilities. It multiplies."

And what do its neighbors in the community have to say about NSA? I would describe their attitude as one of "can't live with them—can't live without them!" *The Sun* included the following information.

Officials use subterfuge to get data they need

Anne Arundel County planners sometimes become so frustrated with NSA's secrecy that they turn the tables and spy on the spies: They shoot aerial photos of agency parking lots in an attempt to estimate the number of employees. [Remember, I told you about aerial photos which will appear throughout this chapter.]

"NSA is Anne Arundel County's largest employer," say Alexander D. Speer, the county demographer.

Obviously, they are having difficulty with fiscal planning for the county when any reliable statistics are top secret and you have to depend upon the accuracy of the information supplied to you by NSA. That's kind of like asking the fox to guard the hen house. Mr. Speer continues, "It makes us nervous not to know how many people are employed there. We could get a new business here with 100 employees and think it's a great thing, but even [as small as] a 2% drop at NSA could blow it out of the water." I wouldn't want to be responsible for maintaining a sound fiscal policy in the county with a situation this volatile on my hands. Although, I truly am amused at their solution . . . turning the tables on them and spying on the spies. More power to you!

Before I conclude my references to *The Baltimore Sun* article, I want to call one more thing to your attention. In their website page describing the contents of this special feature and how to obtain it, they state: "And you'll learn how NSA operatives may practice by eavesdropping on you." I don't think that requires any more comment—it's self-explanatory!

Employment Opportunities at NSA

The NSA has to have an elaborate hiring system to employ such a large number of people, although I would expect them to have a relatively small turnover—it doesn't sound like leaving would be very good for one's health! The website calls them Employment Opportunities and, of course, declares that the NSA is an equal opportunity employer and US citizenship is required for all applicants.

The National Security Agency expects to fill a limited number of full-time positions and student positions in the following fields:

MATHEMATICS
COMPUTER AND
ELECTRICAL/ELECTRONICS ENGINEERING

COMPUTER SCIENCE
ASIAN, MIDDLE EASTERN, OR SLAVIC LANGUAGE
(EXCEPT RUSSIAN)

I guess they have all the Russians they can use...or maybe they assume that Russia is "over the hill," so to speak, and their needs are not likely to increase. (This would be a premature assumption, indeed!)

Have you ever given consideration to how the CIA and FBI recruit bright young people into an area of employment that will require them to learn how to "lie, cheat, steal, and kill"? Well, NSA has given its brain-power to that problem and arrived at an ingenious solution...just like anything else you want to indoctrinate into adolescents, *you start them young!* I'll bet they would sure know how to put all those sneaky little juvenile hackers to good use. Let's face it—if they are smart, they'd rather have the hackers on their side than on the outside hacking in to everything they are working so hard to keep secret. The Employment Opportunities bulletin also states: "In addition CLERICAL, COMPUTER, ANALYTIC, AND ACCOUNTING positions are available to local *high school students* through the **High School Work Study Program.**"

Following are copies of the website pages, which I have highlighted.

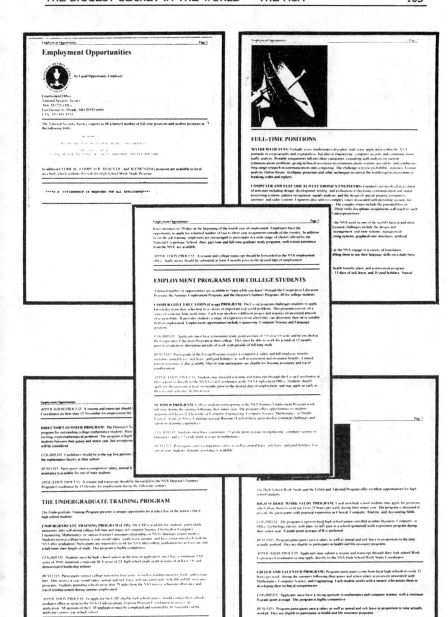

Employment Opportunities

An Equal Opportunity Employer

Employment Office
National Security Agency
Attn: M322 (ADE)
Fort George G. Meade, MD 20755-6000
FAX: 410-859-4591

The National Security Agency expects to fill a limited number of full-time positions and student positions in the following fields:

In addition CLERICAL, COMPUTER, ANALYTIC, and ACCOUNTING positions are available to local area high school students through the High School Work Study Program.

*****U.S. CITIZENSHIP IS REQUIRED FOR ALL APPLICANTS*****

FULL-TIME POSITIONS

MATHEMATICIANS: Virtually every mathematics discipline finds some application within the NSA.

COMPUTER AND ELECTRICAL/ELECTRONICS ENGINEERS:

EMPLOYMENT PROGRAMS FOR COLLEGE STUDENTS

COOPERATIVE EDUCATION (Co-op) PROGRAM:

SUMMER PROGRAM:

DIRECTOR'S SUMMER PROGRAM:

THE UNDERGRADUATE TRAINING PROGRAM

UNDERGRADUATE TRAINING PROGRAM (UTP):

EMPLOYMENT PROGRAMS FOR HIGH SCHOOL STUDENTS

HIGH SCHOOL WORK STUDY PROGRAM:

GIFTED AND TALENTED PROGRAM:

Mathematical **$**ciences **P**rogram

Mathematics and NSA: A Long Term Partnership . . .

Grants Information

Sabbatical Information

Back to the NSA Home Page

MATHEMATICAL SCIENCES PROGRAM

Grants for Research in Mathematics and Cryptology

INTRODUCTION

The NSA Mathematical Sciences Program continues its efforts at funding high quality mathematical research in the areas of Algebra, Number Theory, Discrete Mathematics, Probability, Statistics, and Cryptology. The program began in 1987 when the then director of the National Security Agency, Lieutenant General William E. Odom, announced the expansion and enrichment of Programs for research in cryptology and related areas. This effort is currently being vigorously supported by the Agency.

Grant proposals submitted to the program are reviewed by the NSA Mathematics Review Panel which is appointed and administered by the American Mathematical Society.

AREAS OF INTEREST

The NSA Mathematical Sciences Program is interested in supporting self-directed research in the following areas of mathematics (including possible computational aspects): Algebra, Number Theory, Discrete Mathematics, Probability, and Statistics.

---

4. the investigator's demonstrated awareness of previous approaches to the problem

The NSA Mathematical Sciences Program attempts to have a wide geographic and institutional distribution of support, and NSA encourages proposals from traditionally underrepresented groups

TECHNICAL EVALUATION

The research proposals submitted to the NSA Mathematical Sciences Program will be reviewed each year by the NSA Mathematics Review Panel. The membership of this panel will be determined independently of NSA, currently by the American Mathematical Society. Each proposal will be evaluated by peer reviewers chosen by the Panel members. Once each year, the Panel will meet to evaluate the reviews and provide the Program Director with a rank ordering of the proposals based on scientific merit. Funding decisions will be based on this ranking.

DISCLOSURE OF INFORMATION

Although it is the intent of the NSA Mathematical Sciences Program that the research it supports will produce only unclassified results, it should be recognized that research in cryptologic areas may produce information whose disclosure could harm U.S. national security. Thus, the following disclosure policy is incorporated in each NSA grant

"It is expected that the recipient may make formal public disclosure of the scientific and technical information resulting from this agreement (e.g., release articles for appropriate professional publications, or present papers at scientific meetings or symposia). Such disclosure is authorized as long as a copy of the article or paper, report, etc. shall be provided to the Government, preferably in advance but at least concurrent with public disclosure. It is also understood and agreed that the recipient may utilize the scientific and technical information resulting from this work in consulting or disbursing this and related information with other qualified individuals or groups of individuals, where appropriate. For furthering research. In the event that the researcher believes information generated during the research may require classification, the researcher shall notify NSA and request that the information be reviewed for classification prior to further dissemination.

WHO MAY SUBMIT

Awards will be made only to nonprofit institutions. Such awards will be based on a formal proposal submitted by an organization on behalf of the principal investigator(s). It is NSA's intent to maintain America's high capabilities in mathematics. Therefore, for mathematics grants the principal investigators supported by the grant must be U.S. citizens or permanent residents.

WHEN TO SUBMIT

The deadline for submission of all grant proposals is **15 OCTOBER** of each academic year. For proposals to be eligible for review by the NSA Mathematical Sciences Review Panel, proposal must be received no later than that date. Awards will generally be made in **November** of the next year.

[lower left document — largely illegible]

WHO TO SUBMIT

The proposal must be in the office of the Mathematical Sciences reviewed in that cycle. Please allow at least 10 days for mail

THE FOUR FUNDING CATEGORIES

The NSA Mathematical Sciences Program now supports research in each of four distinct funding categories. In order to decide which category applies to one's specific research objectives, please consider the following program descriptions.

I. The Young Investigators Grant

This award is available to promising investigators within ten years after beginning an academic career. The basic award is a bottom line figure of $40,000 per year for each of two years to cover the direct costs of up to two summer months salary per year plus fringes, a small amount for travel and expenses, and a university payment in lieu of indirect cost of 15% of the direct costs. Young Investigator proposals will be graded more generously than Standard Grant proposals. Subject to the same 15% in lieu of indirect costs, a young investigator proposal may also ask for support of a graduate student (other than tuition) not to exceed $5,000 per student per year, as well as limited funds for computer equipment

II. The Standard Grant

This is a continuation of the grants program which has been in operation by the Mathematical Sciences Program since 1987. Support will be given for no more than one month of summer salary each year for the principal investigators. Financial support for a named graduate student(s) who is working toward a degree for the investigators and miscellaneous expenses for supplies, travel, etc. The Standard Grant can also include support for workshops, postgraduate assistants, and certain equipment purchases. The section entitled "FINANCIAL SUPPORT" provides additional information concerning budgets.

An applicant for a Standard Grant may not also submit a proposal for a Young Investigators Grant or a Senior Investigators Grant. However, the review panel may recommend that a Standard Grant proposal be switched to one of the other categories. A proposal for a Standard Grant may ask for support of a graduate student. In this case, in addition to describing the proposed research, the proposer should list the names of any graduate students who have received degrees under her or his direction in the last 10 years. Each

---

[lower right document — largely illegible]

the proposals will be reviewed by the NSA Sciences panel based on the principal investigators' present status and condition of the proposal's description in **Section I** of present proposal.

of scientists who have demonstrated their effectiveness in pursuing research in cryptology, those who wish to begin research in the cryptologic area, and those wishing to support particular graduate students. Support for travel, week-long, and

supported should be identified. The proposals will be ranked by the NSA reviewers panel according to the scientific merit of the research and the principal investigation's present status at the time of the award, and as above on above students.

IV. Conferences, Workshops and Special Situations

These are single year proposals to fund a specific, well-publicized conference. A special year or an otherwise innovative program at a university in one of the areas supported by research areas. The budget may include travel expenses for principal speakers and participants, honoraria for speakers and honoree expenses for participants. It is expected that conference proposals will be submitted to other agencies as well as NSA, and the stipend awarded by NSA will normally not exceed $20,000. These proposals will be reviewed by members of the NSA review panel commensurate throughout the year. Efforts to promote attendance by minorities and women are encouraged. Registration fees should be set at a level to minimize fiscal activities but no additional fund or lodging requirements (and perhaps not each requiring an individual conference proceedings).

The budget for this category should not include any salary reimbursement. Therefore, it is inappropriate that any university indirect costs be incurred. The budget should include expected income from registration fees.

Upon request the Program Director can provide the investigator with a letter from the National Security Agency explaining this policy to the institutional research office.

WHAT TO SUBMIT

The format required for a proposal to the Mathematical Sciences Program has changed considerably from previous years. It is important for a principal investigator to read the section very carefully and follow all instructions. An before an original and eleven (11) copies of the entire package should be furnished. One copy should contain original signatures of all parties to the proposal. The proposal must contain the following.

Title Page — The principal investigator should remove or replicate the appropriate SAMPLE TITLE PAGE found on a link at the bottom of this page and fill in all the required information, especially indicating all copies whether a list of Reviewers/Nonreviewers is or is not enclosed. The Mathematical Sciences Program

NSA's Mathematical Sabbatical

Questions you may have

Just what is the NSA?

What is the NSA math environment like?

Will I still be able to publish my work?

How long do NSA sabbaticals last?

What kind of compensation can I expect?

GRANT ADMINISTRATION

FURTHER INFORMATION

Full-time positions are listed as *Mathematicians* (virtually every mathematics discipline finds some application with the NSA, primarily in cryptography and cryptanalysis), Computer and Electrical/Electronics Engineers, Computer Scientists, and Language Specialists. They offer a better than average benefits package, and they tell you about the application process.

Employment Programs for College Students—They offer a "limited number" of opportunities to "earn while you learn" through the *Cooperative Education (Co-op) Program*. They tell you the eligibility requirements, the benefits package, and the application process.

Summer Employment Work Program—Students work full time during the summer following their junior year, in some form of electronics, computers, mathematics, or specified foreign languages. They tell you the eligibility requirements, the benefits package, and the application process.

Director's Summer Program—A 12-week summer workshop program for outstanding college mathematics students. They tell you the eligibility requirements, the benefits package, and the application process.

The Undergraduate Training Program (UTP)—A unique opportunity for a select few of the nation's finest high school students. They tell you the eligibility requirements, the benefits package, and the application process.

Employment Programs for High School Students—*The High School Work Study Program* and the *Gifted and Talented Program* offer excellent opportunities for high school students. They tell you about eligibility requirements, benefits packages, and application processes.

Next, they get into their opportunities for the "Mathematical $ciences Program—Mathematics and NSA: A Long-Term Partnership. . ." (That is an exact quote! I guess since they are spending our $$$ they can afford to get creative.)

In addition to the research and development companies the NSA is surreptitiously supporting, they offer a Grant program for research in mathematics and cryptology. The website pages introduce you to the program, tell you NSA's areas of interest, selection criteria, technical evaluation, disclosure of information, who may submit, when to submit, where to submit. The Four Funding Categories are: (1) The Young Investigator's Grant; (2) The Standard Grant; (3) The Senior Investigator's Grant; and (4) Conferences, Workshops, and Special Situations. Then they tell you what to submit, information on joint submissions, and grant administration.

The next program is the **NSA Mathematical Sabbatical Program**. It gives a general introduction, then answers these questions: "Just what is the NSA? What is the NSA math environment like? Will I still be able to publish my work? [Answer: Publishing is important to all serious mathematicians. NSA provides ample opportunity to inform your contemporaries of your work. The in-house publication, *Cryptologic Quarterly,* is one such forum. Because of the nature of the work, however, *publications outside the NSA community must be cleared through our public information office. This is also true after you leave our employ,* but only for work directly related to your research at NSA. And of course, any classified techniques you are involved with cannot be reported.] How long do NSA sabbaticals last? What kind of compensation can I expect? How are sabbatical applicants screened? How do I apply?"

NSA Employee Handbook

Of course, what good is a good employee without a good employee handbook? The NSA apparently has a quite extensive manual, but the following is first and foremost in it.

Security Guidelines

This handbook is designed to introduce you to some of the basic security principles and procedures with which all NSA employees must comply. It highlights some of your security responsibilities, and provides guidelines for answering questions you may be asked concerning your association with this Agency. Although you will be busy during the forthcoming weeks learning your job, meeting co-workers, and becoming accustomed to a new work environment, you are urged to become familiar with the security information contained in his handbook. Please note that a listing of telephone numbers is provided at the end of this handbook should you have any questons or concerns.

Introduction

In joining NSA you have been given an opportunity to participate in the activities of *one of the most important intelligence organizations* of the United States Government. At the same time, you have also assumed a trust which carries with it a most important individual responsibility—the safeguarding of sensitive information vital to the security of our nation.

While it is impossible to estimate in actual dollars and cents the value of the work being conducted by this Agency, the information to which you will have access at NSA is without question critically important to the defense of the United States. Since this information may be useful only if it is kept secret, it requires a very special measure of protection. The specific nature of this protection is set forth in various Agency security regulations and directives. The total NSA Security Program, however, *extends beyond these regulations.* It is based upon the concept that security begins as a state of mind. The program is designed to develop an appreciation of the need to protect information vital to the national defense, and to foster the development of a level of awareness which will make security more than routine compliance with regulations.

At times, security practices and procedures cause personal inconvenience. They take time and effort and on occasion may make it necessary for you to *voluntarily forego some of your usual personal perogatives.* But your compensation for the inconvenience is the knowledge that the work you are accomplishing at NSA, within a framework of sound security practices, contributes significantly to the defense and continued security of the United States of America. [He might just as well stand up and wave the flag!]

I extend to you my very best wishes as you enter upon your chosen career or assignment with NSA.

Philip T. Pease
Director of Security

INITIAL SECURITY RESPONSIBILITIES
Anonymity

Perhaps one of the first security practices with which new NSA personnel should become acquainted is the *practice of anonymity*. In an open society such as ours, this practice is necessary because information which is generally available to the public is available also to hostile intelligence. *Therefore, the Agency mission is best accomplished apart from public attention. Basically, anonymity means that NSA personnel are encouraged not to draw attention to themselves nor to their association with this Agency. NSA Personnel are also cautioned neither to confirm nor deny any specific questions about NSA activities directed to them by individuals not affiliated with the Agency.*

The ramifications of the practice of anonymity are rather far reaching, and its success depends on the cooperation of all Agency personnel. Described below you will find some examples of situations that you may encounter concerning your employment and how you should cope with them. Beyond the situations cited, your judgment and discretion will become the deciding factors in how you respond to questions about your employment.

Answering Questions About Your Employment

Certainly, you may tell your family and friends that you are employed at or assigned to the National Security Agency. There is no valid reason to deny them this information. However, you may not disclose to them any information concerning specific aspects of the Agency's mission, activities, and organization. You should also ask them not to publicize your association with NSA. [The secrecy begins!]

Should strangers or casual acquaintances question you about your place of employment, an appropriate reply would be that you work for the Department of Defense. If questioned further as to where you are employed within the Department of Defense, you may reply, "NSA." When you inform someone that you work for NSA (or the Department of Defense) you may expect that the next question will be "What do you do?" It is a good idea to anticipate this question and **to formulate an appropriate answer** [in other words, plan your lie in advance!]. Do not act mysteriously about your employment, as that would only succeed in drawing more attention to yourself. [Emphasis added.]

Naturally, this is only one part of the Employee Handbook and is not an exhaustive description of the covert operations and training required. In fact, they are told to study it carefully, as the security is explained in greater detail further on in the Handbook.

NSA Operations Division

The "Federation of American Scientists (FAS)," introduced earlier in this chapter, seems to have appointed itself the watchdog over NSA and its affiliates. This is the same group that is trying to get the intelligence budgets publicly revealed. On their website location, they have some very good information on a wide array of subjects pertaining to the NSA. I will be referring to pertinent items, but will furnish reduced copies of the entire sheets for your perusal, beginning with this title, "Operations."

The SIGINT or foreign intelligence mission of NSA/CSS involves the interception, processing, analysis, and dissemination of information derived from foreign electrical communications and other signals. SIGINT itself is composed of three elements: Communications Intelligence (COMINT), derived from the interception and analysis of foreign communications; Electronics Intelligence (ELINT), technical and intelligence information derived from electromagnetic radiations, such as radars; Telemetry Intelligence (TELINT), technical and intelligence information derived from the interception, processing, and analysis of foreign telemetry.

I find it almost amusing that these scientists state that: "All requirements levied on NSA must be for foreign intelligence. *Yet, the precise definition of foreign intelligence is unclear*" [emphasis added]. In the same paragraph they state: "NSA limits its collection of intelligence to foreign communications and confines its activities to communications links *having at least one foreign terminal.* Nevertheless, this is based upon an *internal regulation* and *is not supported by law or executive branch directive.* Although NSA limits itself to collecting communications with at least one foreign terminal, it may still *pick up communications between two Americans* when international communications are involved. . . .Whenever NSA chooses particular circuits or 'links' known to carry foreign communications. . . it collects **all** transmissions that go over those circuits. Given current technology, **the only way for NSA to prevent the processing of communications of US citizens would be to control the selection, analysis, or dissemination phases of the process**" [emphasis added].

In case you had any remaining doubts, they should be dispelled by now. . .they readily admit above that the way the current technology operates, **NSA would have to set up special parameters in its software programs** in order to prevent **eavesdropping on US Citizens**. However, neither

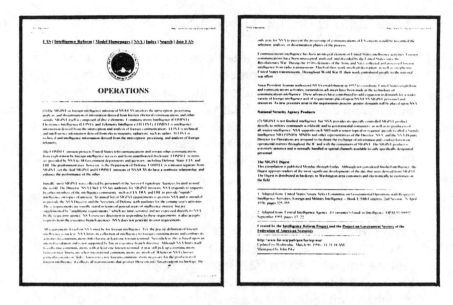

should this information surprise you, since we discussed earlier in this chapter how they practice and hone their skills by spying on individuals, via the phone lines (and whatever other devices they are using these days which are still ultra top secret).

The FAS prepared these many papers on the NSA for the *Intelligence Reform Project* and the *Project on Government Secrecy*.

Organization and Functions of the NSA

The FAS has addressed the subject of "Organization and Functions" of the NAS on their website. Remember, if you want to pull this stuff off at full size, it's all readily available on the Internet.

This eight-page paper delves deeper in the relationship between the intelligence communities and divisions of NSA.

I'll just touch on the highlights.

"COMINT [one of the three SIGINT divisions] is technical and intelligence information derived from foreign communication by *other than the intended recipients*. . . . Intercept and processing of press, propaganda and other public broadcasts, except for processing encrypted or *"hidden meaning"* passages in such broadcasts; oral and wire interceptions conducted under DoD Directive 5200.24; or censorship."

Next, a lengthy analysis is given on the Central Security Service, which we have proven previously in this chapter to be operating under the auspices of the NSA, whether directly or indirectly. This FAS paper describes the CSS Components, as well as NSA's Directorates and Groups.

> Unlike other intelligence organizations such as CIA or DIA, NSA is particularly reticent concerning its internal organizational structure. The following description is based on the best available current information. The best comprehensive treatments of NSA's organization are found in Jeffrey Richelson's *The U.S. Intelligence Community* (Ballinger, Cambridge, 1989) and James Bamford's *The Puzzle Palace* (Houghton Mifflin Company, New York, 1982). [Author's note: I wholeheartedly concur with their conclusion on these two books—I have already used and praised and recommended *The Puzzle Palace,* and now I would like to encourage you to get a copy of *The U.S. Intelligence Community,* as well. This publication contains many excellent "organizational charts" which really simplify getting a mental image of how these intelligence-gathering groups are connected in the "web." I am including the one on the NSA in this chapter, and a number of them in the next chapter on Sister Organizations.] It was reported (Bill Gertz, "Electronic Spying Reoriented at NSA," *The Washington Times,* 27 January 1992) that the A Group had been expanded to include all of Europe, in addition to Eastern Europe and the USSR, and that the B Group, focused on Communist

Figure 2-4. Organization of the National Security Agency.

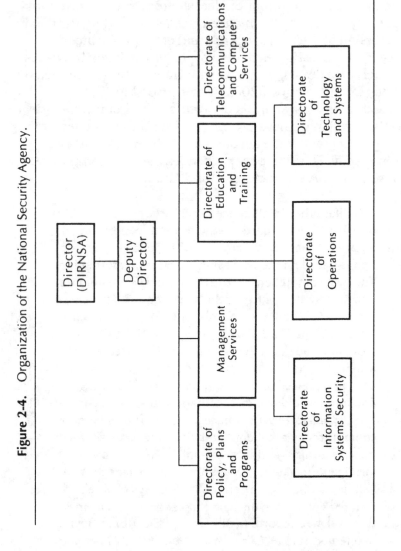

Courtesy of The U.S. Intelligence Community, by Jeff Richelson.

Asia, had been combined with the G Group, collecting against the rest of the world. The most detailed insight into NSA organization is found in the **NSA Employee's Security Manual**, posted on the Internet on 6 April 1994 (grady@netcom.com in igc:alt.pol.org.ns), which provided building locations for the security offices of each of the groups, among other interesting tidbits. Additional information, primarily related to information security developments, is reported in the computer trade press, such as "More Changes at NSA," *Federal Computer Week,* 22 August 1994, p. 4.

We are informed further that NSA is organized into five Directorates [although there are six shown in the organizational chart included above]: Operations Directorate, Technology and Systems Directorate, Information Systems Security Directorate, Plans, Policy, and Programs Directorate, and Support Services Directorate. A brief description of what they do and to whom they report is included. Then the FAS gives definitions of all those "Groups" mentioned above, along with a paragraph on the function of each. I will just list them for you below.

A Group — Former Soviet Bloc

B Group — Asia

C Group — Policy & Resources (??) [Note: question marks are the FAS', not the author's.]

D Group — Director

E Group — Contract Support (?)

F Group — (no group with this designation has been identified)

G Group — Operations (?) / All Others (?)

H Group — (no group with this designation has been identified)

I Group — Information Security Programs

J Group — Legislative Affairs

K Group — Operations Research (?)

ORGANIZATION AND FUNCTIONS

CENTRAL SECURITY SERVICE

CENTRAL SECURITY SERVICE COMPONENTS

L Group — Logistics
M Group — Administration
N Group — Programs
O Group — no group with this designation has been
    identified)
P Group — Production
Q Group — Plans & Policy
R Group — Research & Engineering
S Group — Standards & Evaluation
T Group — Telecommunications
U Group — General Counsel
V Group — Network Security (?)
W Group — Space
X Group — Special Access Systems (???) (The function and
    designation of this Group is undetermined.)
Y Group — ??? (The function and designation of this Group
    is undetermined.)
Z Group — (no group with this designation has been
    identified)

Of course, there's just an off chance that my overly suspicious nature makes me say this, but I'll just bet the ones
they fail to identify (F, H, O, Y, and Z) are the ones that would
interest us most...and very well may affect us most! And
would you care to speculate on what goes on in the X Group,
titled "Special Access Systems," for which the FAS could not
obtain information?

NSA Facilities and the Trojan Spirit

The FAS has given a good oversight of the many facilities
and locations of the NSA...both the headquarters at Ft.
Meade, as well as the other divisions. In this area I have
included many photos/maps/illustrations to aid you in getting
a mental picture of the layout.

In addition to the general details, they have included an
enlightening description of businesses sponsored by NSA,
such as Laboratory for Physical Sciences, College Park, MD,

Supercomputer Research Center, Bowie, MD, and E-Systems (which was an NSA company) and a chart revealing the nature and number of E-Systems' supercomputers (see my book on supercomputers). E-Systems was founded by NSA but is now owned by Raytheon Corp. In the same report they provide another chart with this caption: "Gunter Ahrendt's *List of the World's Most Powerful Computing Sites* shows the NSA at Fort Meade as the world's second most powerful supercomputer." I suspect that if you included the supercomputers of all their affiliates around the globe, they likely are no longer in second place.

"The National Security Agency operates a **global network** of ground stations for the **interception** of **civil** and military satellite communications traffic" [emphasis added]. They are located at: Bad Aibling, Kasserne, Germany; Menwith Hill, Harrogate, UK; Misawa Air Base, Misawa, Japan; Rosman Communications Research Station, Rosman, NC; Sugar Grove Naval Communications Facility, Sugar Grove, WV; Yakima Research Station, Yakima, WA. "Additional COMSAT intercept activities are conducted at Geraldton, Australia, and Bude, Cornwall, UK, . . . [as well as] facilities at Pine Gap, Australia and Buckley Air National Guard Base, Colorado." (I have included some maps and photos of the Pine Gap operation.)

There is one last point that I want to call to your attention. "The CBOF incorporates tactical and strategic units through TROJAN and other satellite networks. . . .TROJAN SPIRIT supports split-based connectivity between CONUS-based processing and production centers and forward-deployed forces." As in so many other examples of their nomenclature, they have selected occultic, mystical, mythological, *et al*, names for their activities.

"Trojan" may prove to be an apt name for projects of the NSA. Here is a definition (first), followed by some information from *Grolier's Encyclopedia.*

Trojan Horse A huge wooden horse left behind on the beach by the Greeks, who had *pretended to give up the*

FAS | Intelligence | Model Homepages | NSA | Index | Search | Join FAS

FACILITIES

Most NSA employees, both civilian and military, are headquartered at Fort George G. Meade, MD. The rest of the workforce is scattered at CONUS and overseas field locations. NSA is one of the largest employers in the state of Maryland. Its workforce represents an unusual combination of occupational specialties including engineers, physicists, mathematicians, linguists, computer scientists.

NSA reportedly has about 20,000 employees in Maryland, with a $831.7 million payroll in 1990 (1). This estimate is consistent with the approximately 5 million square feet of NSA office space at Ft. Meade, somewhat less than the Pentagon, which houses somewhat more than 20,000 personnel. Other published estimates that NSA has between 38,000 and 52,000 employees clearly also include the personnel of the Central Security Service military components, as well as contractor personnel (2).

NSA FACILITIES FOCUS PLAN -- 1989 (3)

NSA conducted the most significant upgrade of NSA's facilities in its history, based on a blueprint, the Facilities Focus Plan, prepared and approved in 1989. The 1989 Facilities Focus Plan provided for the upgrading of over 2.5 million square feet of space and will involved the movement of over one-half of the NSA work force. When completed, NSA will have achieved a long-sought goal of a minimum of 70 square feet of office space per person across NSA.

In 1991 alone, NSA added over one million square feet of new space to the NSA inventory by opening the new REE Building, the SPL state-of-the-art microelectronics Production Facility, the System Processing Center, and the Columbia Annex. These facilities were occupied by thousands of NSA employees. In addition, the total renovation of the Headquarters Building was 60 percent complete and the offices were partially re-occupied, providing work space for another 1,000-plus employees. As NSA moved people into these new spaces, the areas they leave were fully renovated and other employees moved into expanded spaces. (a process NSA called "decompression"). In 1992 NSA completed the renovation of SAB 1 for parts of ISL and begin the renovations of FANX 2 for the National Cryptologic School and FANX 3 for another key component.

In addition to executing the Facilities Focus Plan, many other major facilities projects are under way or have been completed. The Twin Towers Utility Upgrade on the Headquarters Building provided improved air conditioning for people and equipment. The 3,000-ton Chiller Plant constructed in front of the Headquarters Building provided much-needed cooling for OPS I occupants. The Chiller Plant's Main Distribution Loop delivers over 430,000 gallons of chilled water per hour to OPS I. This project required over 200 helicopter airlifts to put equipment in place on the OPS 1 Building. The Road Improvements

Project provided a much-needed upgrade to the road network throughout the NSA Headquarters complex. The replacement of the 16-year-old Uninterrupted Power Systems protected NSA's most critical mission operations. The OPS I Sprinkler Project met the latest fire/safety codes. Extensive asbestos removal was conducted in OPS I and the Headquarters Building to provide an asbestos-free environment for NSA employees.

Upgrades in 1991 and 1992 included the installation of additional landscaping and efforts to repaint and clean up the corridors prior to President Bush's visit in 1991, along with the addition of a marble signpost at the intersection of Route 32 and Canine Road, and the redecorating of the OPS 2B lobby --- all of which were intended to "create a dignified and professional look," at NSA. But some work spaces remained overcrowded and unattractive (with some offices working under such crowded conditions that everyone in each row must interrupt their work to move each time a teammate enters or exits the aisle). Work space requirements and safety regulations were not complied with.

NSA DRAWDOWN PLAN -- 1992 (4)

In 1991 NSA planners anticipated possible personnel and Operations and Maintenance budget cuts, and began planning for reduced lease, utility, and facility support costs commensurate with projected budget reductions. The NSA Drawdown Plan was approved by the Critical Issues Group (the current Board of Directors) in January 1992, briefed to and approved by DIRNSA in February 1992, and presented to and approved by several Congressional staffs in March 1992.

The Plan's strategy focused on the reduction of nine leased buildings. This would not only decrease rent and utility costs, but also such facility support costs as security, grounds, maintenance, bus service, mail runs, and local travel time.

Another major goal of the plan is to accommodate the 1992 NSA agency restructure by consolidating several key components into fewer buildings, bringing many of the elements in closer proximity to NSA Headquarters at Ft. Meade and enhancing the efficiency of SIGINT resources and support services. The Technology and Systems Organization will be housed in NBP 1, R&E, and CANX; Operations elements are to be consolidated at the Ft. Meade complex. Several Support Services elements will be relocated to the OPS 3 and APS 20 buildings, and the Information Systems Security Organization will be consolidated in FANX 3 and OPS 3.

Over the course of the four year implementation, the Drawdown Plan will affect 21 NSA-owned or leased buildings -- over 1.2 million square feet will be involved -- and 506 organizations, ranging from 10 to 200 people will be moved. The plan compromises more than 1,700 activities, ranging from building designs and construction to furniture and communications installation to the actual organizational moves. The plan is further complicated by over 3,000 constraints, or dependent activities. Constraints are activities that must precede or succeed one another. Therefore, if one activity is delayed, it can delay another activity, which in turn delays two more activities, which in turn delay several more activities, and so on and so on... These constraints, combined with the large volume of work to be accomplished, are what make this plan so complex.

From the beginning, the Drawdown Plan assumed an aggressive schedule. However, since the original plan was devised, two major changes occurred.

The first involved a key aspect of the plan, the leasing of NBP 1. Prior to the 1992 NSA reorganization, the building had been completely designed for its new occupants, the majority of whom were coming directly from the OPS 1, OPS 2B, and APS 20 buildings However, as a result of the Agency reorganization, the slated occupants of the building completely changed; elements from throughout NSA were scheduled to move to NBP I, home of the new Technology and Systems Organization This meant that the floor plans, seating arrangements, communications systems, etc, had to be readjusted. The Drawdown team was able to rectify the situation with no delay to the already tight schedule.

The second major alteration involved the relocation of the Naval Security Group (NSG) from its Nebraska Avenue headquarters to OPS 3, a direct result of the Federal Base Closure Act. Prior to the decision to relocate NSG, FANX 3 was scheduled to be rehabbed, floor by floor, over the course of 3 years. However, because DDI personnel must vacate their OPS 3 spaces to make room for the 1995 arrival of NSG, the rehab of FANX 3, DDI's new home, must be completed in 18 months. This aggressive schedule requires that the entire FANX 3 building be empty during the rehab. The Drawdown Plan had to be altered to allow for temporary retention of ITB and indefinite retention of APS 20 to accommodate the FANX 3 personnel. This major revision did not lengthen the original 4-year Drawdown schedule

The NSA Drawdown Plan includes the termination of leases for FANX 1, APS 8, and APS 9; the complete renovation and occupancy of FANX 2; the consolidation of the National Cryptologic School in FANX 2; the consolidation of the Operations Organization in the Headquarters complex; and the transfer of all personnel from FANX 3 in preparation of the building rehab, with scheduled completion by mid-1995.

Equally significant is the complete interior construction and occupancy of NBP 1 When leased in 1992, NBP 1 was essentially a "hollow building." Crews had to construct everything from floors and ceilings to heating and air conditioning systems to communication lines and sprinkler systems to walls and furniture.

By late 1996, the plan's scheduled completion date, NSA will fully reoccupy the newly renovated FANX 3 and termination of leases for Parkway Center, APS 5, APS 10, APS 11, APS 13, and the International Tower Building.

The implementation of the NSA Space Drawdown Plan required the combined efforts of many organizations -- the Support Services Organization for design, construction, maintenance, custodial, transportation, furnishings, and security operations; the Army Corps of Engineers for project lease management; the Technology and Systems Organization for communications fit-up and support; the Plans, Policy, and Programs Organization for financial programming and budgeting.

Focusing on quality customer support, the Space Drawdown Plan tries to minimize the inconvenience to NSA personnel as much as possible. Other than the time required to pack and unpack, moves are completed overnight, with minimal office downtime Whenever possible, customers may retain their telephone numbers at their new location And, although double (and sometimes triple) moves are occasionally necessary, the team takes great pains not to "hopscotch" their customers all over the Agency The NSA Space Drawdown Plan is a team effort, requiring the coordination of many different Agency elements, which continued until the final move was completed in late 1996.

FORT GEORGE G. MEADE
Ft. Meade, Maryland

Fort Meade's mission is to provide a wide range of support to 56 tenant organizations from all four services and to several federal agencies. Major tenant units include the National Security Agency (NSA), the US Army Intelligence and Security Command, the Naval Security Group Activity, and the 694th Intelligence Wing (US Air Force).

Fort George G. Meade, Maryland, is an Army installation dedicated to providing support to servicemen, women, DoD civilians and their families. Located midway between the cities of Baltimore, Washington, DC, and Annapolis, near the communities of Odenton, Laurel and Columbia, The installation lies four miles east of Interstate 95 and one-half mile east of the Baltimore-Washington Parkway between Maryland State Routes 175 and 198. Fort Meade is home to approximately 9,200 military personnel as well as 29,000 civilian employees. Approximately 7,500 family members reside on post. The economic impact of Fort Meade to local civilian communities is approximately $2 billion annually. This reaches the community in the form of $300 million in military payroll, $1.2 billion in civilian payroll, and nearly $500 million in contracts. Virtually a city in itself, Fort Meade has 65 miles of paved roads, and 28 miles of secondary roads and 1,670 buildings. There is also a bank, modern exchange mall, credit union, post office, hospital, chapels and many other facilities.

Fort George G. Meade became an Army installation in 1917. Authorized by an Act of Congress in May 1917, it was one of 16 cantonments built for troops drafted for the war with the Central Powers in Europe. The present Maryland site was selected on June 23, 1917. Actual construction began in July. The first contingent of troops arrived here that September. The post was originally named Camp Meade for Major General George Gordon Meade, whose defensive strategy at the Battle of Gettysburg proved a major factor in turning the tide of the Civil War in favor of the North. During World War I, more than 100,000 men passed through Fort Meade, a training site for three infantry divisions, three training battalions and one depot brigade.

In 1928, when the post was renamed Fort Leonard Wood, Pennsylvanians registered such a large protest that the installation was permanently named Fort George G. Meade on 5 March 1929. This action was largely the result of a rider attached to the Regular Army Appropriation Act by a member of the House of Representatives from the Keystone State. Fort Meade became a training center during World War II. Its ranges and other facilities were used by more than 200 units and approximately 3,500,000 men between 1942 and 1946. The wartime peak-military personnel figure at Fort Meade was reached in March, 1945-70,000. With the conclusion of World War II, Fort Meade reverted to routine peacetime activities, but later returned to build-up status. Many crises, including Korea, West Berlin and Cuba, along with Vietnam-related problems, were to come.

One key post-World War II event at Fort Meade was the transfer of the Second US Army Headquarters from Baltimore, on 15 June 1947. This transfer brought an acceleration of post activity because Second Army Headquarters exercised command over Army units throughout a then seven state area. A second important development occurred on 1 January 1966, when the Second US Army merged with the First US Army. The consolidated headquarters moved from Fort Jay, NY, to Fort Meade to administer activities of Army installations in a 15-state area.

In August 1990, Fort Meade began processing Army Reserve and National Guard units from several states for the presidential call-up in support of Operation Desert Shield. In addition to processing Reserve and National Guard units, Fort Meade sent two active duty units-the 85th Medical Battalion and the 519th Military Police Battalion-to Saudi Arabia. In all, approximately 2,700 personnel from 42 units deployed from Fort Meade during Operation Desert Shield/Desert Storm.

The National Security Agency was established by presidential directive on 4 November 1952. In 1957 NSA consolidated its headquarters operations at Fort George G. Meade, Maryland. Its headquarters complex at Fort Meade is dominated by two high-rise buildings completed in 1986 and dedicated by then President Ronald Reagan in a special ceremony. The complex includes an operations building, a technical library and other facilities which house logistics and support activities. NSA is supported by elements of the Army, Navy, Marines and Air Force, whose officers and enlisted personnel constitute approximately 20 percent of the agency work force. The remainder are civilians who are permanently assigned and who reside in the Baltimore/Washington area.

A large number of the agency's semi-skilled and clerical employees have been drawn from the local area. NSA has developed special educational programs, in conjunction with local high schools, to help prepare students for employment with the agency. NSA works with US employment offices and civic groups in the area to promote employment of the handicapped. Graduates coming from high schools and college campuses may move into one of three broadly defined professional occupational areas. Some specialize in cryptology (making and testing US codes and ciphers), others become specialists in the data-processing fields, and the remainder (especially mathematicians, scientists and engineers) will work in research and development.

NSA has always placed great emphasis on the training and development of its people. The establishment of the National Cryptologic School as a separate professional structure is a true symbol of this concern and represents further enhancement of the agency's already extensive training activities. Additionally, the agency has a number of educational programs-both undergraduate and graduate-established with the Johns Hopkins University, American University, George Washington University, University of Maryland and Catholic University, as well as its own special courses. Also a number of NSA professional personnel teach part time at these local universities.

Gunter Ahrendt's List of the World's Most Powerful Computing Sites shows the NSA at Fort Meade as the world's second most powerful supercomputer. This listing ranks sites according to ratings which "are ratios to a Cray Y-MP1 based on NASA NPB BT Size A benchmark reports. Figures prefixed '~' denote approximations usually based on comparable programs, figures suffixed '?' denote relative guesses based on Intel Paragon peak Gflops ratios."

Number Installed	Computer Type	Total Y-MP1 equivalents	Each Y-MP1 equivalent
1	Cray T3D MC1024-8	220.16	3.44 @ 16 cpus
4	Cray C916/161024	183.04	2.86 @ 1 cpu
5	Cray J916/161024	52.8	0.66 @ 1 cpu
1	TMC CM-5/256-128	22.4	2.80 @ 32 cpus
6	Cray Y-MP8E/81024	48	1.00 @ 1 cpu
1	Cray T94/4128	16.4	4.10 @ 1 cpu
1	SRC Terasys	~ 9	
1	Cray 3/SSS [+3Q95]	179.73	?

FRIENDSHIP ANNEX
Airport Squares
Linthicum, Maryland

(5) As part of the effort to provide improved facilities, reduce fragmented operations, and "decompress" the work force, the FANX 2 and FANX 3 Buildings underwent complete renovations, with FANX 2 housing the National Cryptologic Training Facility (NCS), and FANX 3 serving as the second campus for the Information Systems Security Organization. All INFOSEC resources in the Parkway Center and Airport Square Buildings 10, 11, and 20, as well as select elements from OPS 3, were consolidated with

existing INFOSEC elements at FANX 3, and all non-INFOSEC elements were relocated either within the Airport Square Complex or back to Fort Meade.

Renovations on the two-story FANX 2 Building were completed in the second quarter of FY94. As well as meeting all Federal accessibility standards, it provided the NCS with 100 classrooms of different sizes; space for nonsecure training; space for a satellite training/video center; and a 300-seat auditorium. A state of the art thermal ice storage system to supply air conditioning, raised floor throughout, a sprinkler system, a central fire alarm system, a public address system, and 20 transport rooms to enhance communications distribution were also provided.

The FANX 3 design was completed in October 1993. Construction began in January 1994 with planned completion in July 1996. Final move-in of INFOSEC personnel will take place in January 1997. FANX 3 renovations include an ice storage HVAC system, primary power, and energy efficient modular lighting. In addition, FANX 3 will be equipped with a highrise fire detection and prevention system, new elevators, select TEMPEST protection, and an emergency generator.

INFOSEC will occupy all operational space in FANX 3 with the exception of the utility infrastructure and support services on the first floor. While all support services will remain, several will be moved to accommodate utility expansion and installation of the Confirm System in the inner lobby. A joint Facilities Engineering/Corps of Engineers/INFOSEC FANX 3 design and construction center has been opened in Room B1119E of FANX 3.

As many as 12,000 NSA personnel are housed in 1 million square feet of leased space at the Friendship Annex at Airport Square Technology Park and Industrial Park near the Baltimore Washington International airport (6). The Friendship Annex is connected to Ft. Meade and other Washington area facilities through the Washington Area Wideband System (WAWS), a coaxial cable network established in the mid-1970s.

NATIONAL BUSINESS PARK
Ft. Meade, Maryland

An additional 240,000 square feet of office space are leased at the National Business Park, across the BW Parkway from the main facility at Ft. Meade (7).

LABORATORY FOR PHYSICAL SCIENCES
University of Maryland
College Park, MD

NSA work in the design and development of specialized chips for national security uses is supported by a recently opened Laboratory for Physical Sciences building at the University of Maryland at College Park. This laboratory conducts research on a range of projects of interest to NSA, including optical communications and computer networks (8).

SUPERCOMPUTER RESEARCH CENTER
Bowie, MD

NSA sponsors the Supercomputer Research Center in Bowie, Maryland, which includes government, academics and industry in an effort to benefit all sectors from its research activities (8).

E-Systems

Dallas, TX

Gunter Ahrendt's <u>List of the World's Most Powerful Computing Sites</u> shows E-Systems in Dallas TX (formerly listed as "NSA") as the third most powerful site. This listing ranks sites according to ratings which "are ratios to a Cray Y-MP1 based on NASA NPB BT Size A benchmark reports. Figures prefixed '~' denote approximations usually based on comparable programs, figures suffixed '?' denote relative guesses based on Intel Paragon peak Gflops ratios."

As of 10 July 1995 the third ranked facility was listed as E-Systems,Dallas,Texas, with

Number Installed	Computer Type	Total Y-MP1 equivalents	Each Y-MP1 equivalent
8	Cray C916/16512	366.08	2.86 @ 1 cpu
9	Cray J916/16512	95.04	0.66 @ 1 cpu

This listing is compiled based in part on information provided in confidence or anonymously. The Dallas entry was based on information supplied by an individual who indicated that during the summer of 1994 the NSA advertised employment opportunities a Dallas newspaper, with the advertisement noting that a certain number of Cray C916's were being installed at a Dallas site, with a planned increase in 1995 to the current number. As this listing is widely publicized on the internet, reader feedback usually corrects erroneous entries, and thus far this listing has not been disputed. In addition, the total number of Cray C916's in the world (all of which are included in this listing) is consistent with published production of this computer by inclusion of the computers at the Dallas facility.

E-Systems has two facilities in the Dallas vicinity (E-Systems, Inc. Form 10-K, For the Fiscal Year Ended December 31, 1994, Securities and Exchange Commission File Number 1-5237). Buildings at the Greenville TX facility cover 2,936,000 square feet, with activities including offices, engineering, research and development, production: airborne electronic systems installation, and aircraft overhaul and maintenance. The Garland TX facility has 1,407,000 square feet of building, including offices, engineering, research and development, production facilities: radiation laboratory, electronic components, high powered transmitters, and radar antennas and other products.

It would seem that the NSA Crays are at one or the other site, most likely the Greenville site, which would seem to be the SIGINT side of the company (Garland appears to be the defense electronics (ie non SIGINT) side of the company, and thus the Crays are out at Greenville.) However, the 10-K form also lists: "Other Properties" with a total of 1,243,000 square feet, including offices, production and depot maintenance of electronic, equipment and systems. This includes approximately 899,000 square feet at various locations owned by the United States Government and operated by the Company. These would appear to be depot maintenance for RIVET JOINT and other airborne SIGINT systems, but it cannot be excluded that this also includes some unacknowledged NSA facility where all the Crays have been stashed (such as perhaps the overly large Federal Building in downtown Dallas??).

REGIONAL SIGINT OPERATIONS CENTERS / SATELLITE INTERCEPT OPERATIONS

Army national SIGINT responsibilities include management of the creation and operation of the Regional SIGINT Operations Centers (RSOC) at Fort Gordon, GA, Bad Aibling Station, Germany, and Menwith

Hill Station, England, as well as continued Army support to the National Security Agency (NSA) and its worldwide mission stations (10). Other RSOC locations include the Lackland Air Force Base Training Annex, in San Antonio, Texas, which supports Southern Command, and Pacific Command support from Kunia on Oahu, Hawaii.

The National Security Agency operates a global network of ground stations for the interception of civil and military satellite communications traffic (11).

Bad Aibling Kasserne, Germany, conducts satellite communications interception activities, and is also a downlink station for geostationary SIGINT satellites.

Menwith Hill, located 13 kilometers west of Harrogate, UK, collects against Russian satellite communications under Project MOONPENNY, and is also a downlink station for geostationary SIGINT satellites.

Misawa Air Base, Misawa, Japan, satellite communications intercept activities include collecting against Russian Molniya, Raduga and Gorizont systems under project LADYLOVE at a facility 6 kilometers northwest of the main airfield, known as the "Hill."

Rosman Communications Research Station, near Rosman, NC, has a total of twelve antennas for satellite communications interception, for communications connectivity with other intelligence facilities, and possibly also for downlinks from geostationary SIGINT satellites.

Sugar Grove Naval Communications Facility, near Sugar Grove, WV, intercepts Pacific INTELSAT/COMSAT satellite communications traffic routed through the COMSAT ground station at Etam, WV. This facility has four antenna, with diameters of 9.2, 18.5, 32.3 and 46 meters.

Yakima Research Station, near Yakima, WA, intercepts Pacific INTELSAT/COMSAT satellite communications traffic.

Additional COMSAT intercept activities are conducted at Geraldton, Australia, and Bude, in Corwall, UK. The Bad Aibling and Menwith Hill facilities are also used for downlink of high altitude SIGINT satellite product, as are facilities at Pine Gap, Australia, and Buckley Air National Guard Base, Colorado.

Other NSA facilities, including: Clark AFB, Phillipines; Sinope, Turkey; Heraulion, Greece; Berlin, Germany; and Eielson AFB, AK, have closed, with others, such as San Vito dei Normani, Italy, have transfered to other agencies (in this case, to Air Force Space Command) (12).

National SIGINT Operations Center (NSOC)
Ft. Meade, MD

The NSA National SIGINT Operations Center (NSOC) provides round-the-clock continuous service and support to customers through a worldwide communications network. NSOC is provided with the most modern integrated data and telecommunication infrastructure possible to meet the real time requirements of military and other intelligence consumers at every echelon (13).

Medina Regional SIGINT Operations Center (RSOC)
Lackland (Medina) Training Annex
San Antonio, TX (14)

The 19 August 1993 activation of the Medina Regional SIGINT Operations Center (RSOC) at the Lackland Training Annex (also known as the Medina Training Annex) in San Antonio, was a direct result of the end of the Cold War, which confronted the intelligence community with a downsizing force structure and withdrawal of forces deployed overseas. The Medina RSOC consolidates SIGINT assets, analytical databases, and experience personnel from various locations. It also provided tactical analysts an environment to keep their cryptologic skills sharp, supporting a pool of capable people which can deploy wherever they are needed. By 1996, over 1,000 Army, Navy, Marine Corps, Air Force, and National Security Agency civilian personnel will work at Medina. This consolidated SIGINT joint environment improved the ability to deliver timely, tailored intelligence to customers.

CONUS-based Regional Operations Facility (CROF)/
Regional SIGINT Operations Center (RSOC)
513th Military Intelligence Brigade
Fort Cordon, (15)

In early 1993 the relocation of the 513th Military Intelligence Brigade's from Fort Monmouth New Jersey to Fort Cordon, Georgia was initiated. Under the terms of the AR 5-10 Study, the 513th will be developed into a power projection support element. As part of this process, the NSA established a CONUS-based Regional Operations Facility (CROF) at Fort Gordon. The Regional SIGINT Operations Center uses current operations and troop facilities as well as a new 38,000 square-fool building to support 300 Army, Air Force, Navy and Marine Corps SIGINT personnel. The CBOF incorporates tactical and strategic units through TROJAN and other satellite networks to support requirements from theater commanders and Joint Task Force (JTF) components, as well as intelligence preparation of the battlefield. TROJAN SPIRIT supports split-based connectivity between CONUS-based processing and production centers and forward-deployed forces.

Menwith Hill
Harrowgate, UK

Menwith Hill in the UK is the principal NATO theater ground segment node for high altitude signals intelligence satellites (16) . Although this facility is jointly operated with the UK's General Communications Headquarters (GCHQ), GCHQ is not privy to the intelligence down-linked to Menwith Hill, since tapes containing the data are returned via air to the United States for analysis.

Menwith Hill Station was established in 1956 by the US Army Security Agency (ASA). Inside the closely-guarded 560 acre base are two large operations blocks and many satellite tracking dishes and domes. Initial operations focused on monitoring international cable and microwave communications passing through Britain. In the early 1960s Menwith Hill was one of the first sites in the world to receive sophisticated early IBM computers, with which NSA automated the labor-intensive watch-list scrutiny of intercepted but unenciphered telex messages. Since then, Menwith Hill has sifted the international messages, telegrams, and telephone calls of citizens, corporations or governments to select information of political, military or economic value to the United States.

Every detail of Menwith Hill's operations has been kept an absolute secret. The official cover story is that the all-civilian base is a Department of Defense communications station. The British Ministry of Defence describe Menwith Hill as a "communications relay centre." Like all good cover stories, this has a strong element of truth to it. Until 1974, Menwith Hill's Sigint specialty was evidently the interception of International Leased Carrier signals, the communications links run by civil agencies -- the Post, Telegraph and Telephone ministries of eastern and western European countries. The National Security Agency took over Menwith Hill in 1966. Interception of satellite communications began at Menwith Hill as early as

1974, when the first of more than eight large satellite communications dishes were installed.

In 1984, British Telecom and MoD staff completed a $25 million extension to Menwith Hill Station known as STEEPLEBUSH. The British government constructed new communications facilities and buildings for STEEPLEBUSH, worth L7.4 million. The expansion plan includes a 50,000 square foot extension to the Operations Building and new generators to provide 5 Megawatts of electrical power. The purpose of the new construction was to boost an cater for an 'expanded mission' of satellite surveillance. It also provides a new (satellite) earth terminal system to support the classified systems at the site. With another $17.2 million being spent on special monitoring equipment, this section of the Menwith Hill base alone cost almost $160 million dollars.

Rosman Research Station
Rosman, NC

The Rosman Research Station is located in the Pisgah National Forest of North Carolina's Smoky Mountains, near Balsam Grove, NC, off Route 215 approximately 11 kilometers north of Route 64. The station, which closed in 1994, was operated by approximately 250 NSA, Bendix Field Engineering and TRW employees.

The National Aeronautics and Space Administration began operations at the Rosman Spaceflight Tracking Station in 1963, and ceased activities there in January 1981. During NASA's tenure the station supported a number of space projects, including the Apollo and Apollo-Soyuz missions. The station at Rosman was turned over to the General Services Administration by NASA on 1 February 1981. The facility was converted by the Department of Defense for use as a Communications Research Station, a process which was completed in early July 1981. Initially there were approximately 35 contract personnel living in the area, but when the project became operational in July, this number increased to approximately 75 employees. The NSA role at Rosman apparently began almost immediately thereafter. By 1985 this number was reported to have grown to 250 employees, with annual payroll at $5 million, an average of $20,000 a year [*The Asheville Citizen 20 June 1985*]. For FY85 NSA requested $500,000 for construction of an electric substation to provide additional electric transformer capacity that is required to support station operations. It is difficult to ascertain the total number of satellite receiving antenna at the facility. These at least include two very large dishes, approximately 27.5 feet in diameter (the size of the biggest dish left by NASA), and a smaller 6.2 meter radome.

The Rosman Station was used to intercept telephone and other communications traffic carried by commercial and other communications satellites in geostationary orbit over the Western hemisphere. Potential targets of interest could include Latin American military, diplomatic and commercial traffic as well as domestic US traffic and drug traffickers in the Caribbean.

1. Shelsby, Ted, "NSA Employment Cuts will Hurt Maryland Economy, But Exactly How Much?" *Baltimore Sun*, 6 December 1991, page 9-C.

2. Spy Agency Staff Lacks Diversity, Director Says," *The Washington Times*, 1 November 1993, page A6

3. Adapted from: "Not Just a Pretty Face," *NSA Newsletter*, July 1992, page 11.

4. Adapted from: "Drawing Down for the Future -- NSA consolidates its resources ," NSA Newsletter, August 1994, pages 8-9]

5. Adapted from "Facilities Update -- Facelifts for FANX II and FANX III," *NSA Newsletter*, February 1993, page 6.]

6. "Supersecret Security Agency of Inestimable Aid to County," *The Washington Times*, 2 January 1993, page A9.]

7. "Supersecret Security Agency of Inestimable Aid to County," *The Washington Times*, 2 January 1993, page A9.

8. Adapted from: VADM James McConnell, "New World, New Challenges -- NSA Into the 21st Century," *American Intelligence Journal*, Spring/Summer 1994, page 10.

9. Adapted from: VADM James McConnell, "New World, New Challenges -- NSA Into the 21st Century," *American Intelligence Journal*, Spring/Summer 1994, page 10.

10. LTG Ira C. Owens (Deputy Chief of Staff for Intelligence, United States Army), "Army Intelligence In Transition 'Changing Horizons,'" *American Intelligence Journal*, Autumn/Winter 1993-1994, pages 17-20.

11. Richelson, Jeffery, *The US Intelligence Community*, (Ballinger Publishing, New York, 1989) second edition, pages 183-187.

12. Munro, Neil, "The Puzzle Palace in Post-Cold War Pieces," *Washington Technology*, 11 August 1994, page 1, 14.

13. Adapted from: VADM James McConnell, "New World, New Challenges -- NSA Into the 21st Century," *American Intelligence Journal*, Spring/Summer 1994, page 10.

14. Adapted from: Colonel Michael S. Cassidy, "SIGINT: An Important Part of Air Force Intelligence," American Intelligence Journal, Spring/Summer 1994, page 20.

15. Adapted from: "Intelligence Community Notes," *Defense Intelligence Journal*, 1993, number 2, pages 97-98.]

16. Ball, Desmond, Pine Gap, (*Allen & Unwin, Sydney, 1988*), page 61

Created by the Intelligence Reform Project and the Project on Government Secrecy of the Federation of American Scientists

http://www.fas.org/irp/nsa/
Updated on Monday, December 23, 1996 - 7:06:21 AM
Maintained by John Pike

FAS | Intelligence | Model Homepages | NSA | Index | Search | Join FAS

siege of Troy. Told by Sinon that it was an offering to Athena, *the Trojans broke down their city wall to bring it inside. At night, warriors emerged and captured the city.*

Trojan In Greek mythology the Trojan War pitted a coalition of Greek principalities against TROY, a city located on the coast of what is now Anatolia, just south of the entrance to the Dardanelles. The war was the subject of HOMER's *Iliad and Odyssey.*
. . . Using a **stratagem** devised by ODYSSEUS, the Greeks **feigned retreat**. . . leaving behind as a "gift" the Trojan Horse. Inside the large wooden horse was concealed a squad of Greek soldiers. . . . the soldiers entered Troy and great slaughter followed. [Emphasis added.]

I am convinced that the NSA's *"strategem"* is "feigning" openness and accessibility, and that what they really are doing is using the "Trojan Horse" technique to undermine not only our current privacy, but our future activities, as well, including those mentioned in Revelation about buying and selling.

Fort George G. Meade

Fort Meade, like all the others, has its own personal Home Page on the Internet. After welcoming us, they tell us about other information available "on-line," including a couple of E-mail addresses, then state: "The Meade Home Page is part of the Department of Defense computer system, and all information from this resource is unclassified, non-sensitive, and in compliance with Privacy Act requirements."

On their second page they state: "Fort Meade provides a base of operations for numerous strategic, tactical, and support organizations. Below is a listing of the major tenant organizations on the base:" The intelligence or security units are: **National Security Agency**, 694th Intelligence Group, 902nd Military Intelligence Group, 704th Military Intelligence Brigade, Naval Security Group Activity, Defense Information

School, 55th Signal Company (Combat Camera), and the US Army Central Personnel Security Clearance Facility. Other groups operating from Fort Meade include: 1st Recruiting Brigade, Defense Courier Service (this probably should have been listed with intelligence gathering organizations), US Army Field Band, First Army-East, and the US Army Claims Service.

This is one busy little beehive . . . or *not so little!* There are reported to be in the neighborhood of 80,000 employees just at the NSA. Rather like their *not* establishing a "no fly" zone over their location, at their website they proudly present two maps—regional and local—showing their exact location and how to get there. Aren't you overwhelmed with their openness, willing cooperation, and concern for the Privacy Act? Is that a Trojan Horse I see?

FAS Maps of the NSA

The scientific "watchdog" of the intelligence community, with heavy emphasis on the NSA, has provided on its website a number of maps of NSA facilities—Friendship Annex, Close-up view of Fort Meade grounds near the NSA Headquarters Building, a floor plan of the headquarters building, and the National Business Park.

The photos that follow were picked up from the FAS website, which accounts for the "third generation" quality. You can see them clearer and full size (8½ " × 11") by inquiring at the FAS Internet address:

(http://www.fas.org/irp/facility/nsaftmed.htm)

The photos are preceded by a couple of pages telling about the dates of construction, naming of roads, and other historic data about the facilities of Fort Meade.

Following the photographic evidence, the FAS provided yet more maps and illustrations defining the facility layout. Their title page reads: "National Security Agency, Fort Meade— (Ground-Truth photos and description of this site are also available)—Floorspace Analysis."

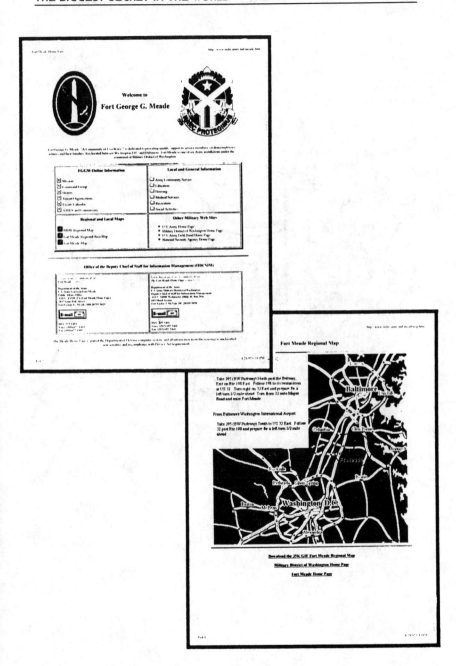

:e 795x562 pixels http: www.fas.org irp nsa nsamead.gif

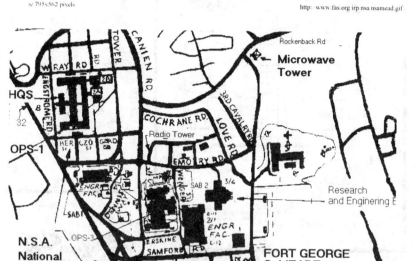

**NSA HQ "OPS"
FACILITY**

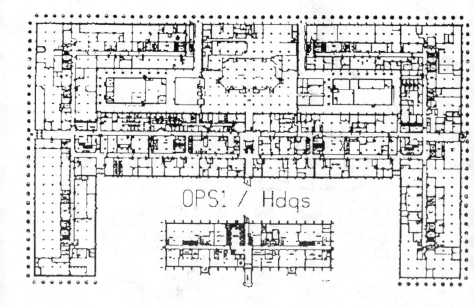

Internal layout diagram of NSA's headquarters "ops" facility.

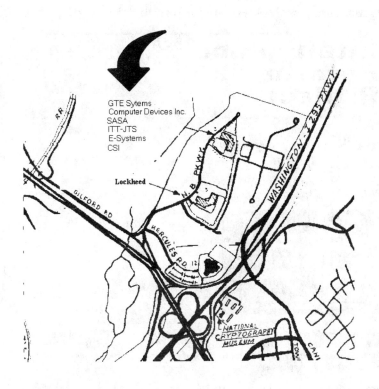

Note that E-Systems was originally an NSA operation. E-Systems Corp. since has been sold to Raytheon Corp. (Raytheon Corp. also controls the HAARP Program in Alaska. (See Chapter 12 on HAARP.)

FAS Homepage | **Intelligence** | **Facilities** | **Index** | **Search** | **Join FAS**

F Intelligence
A Reform
S Project

National Security Agency
Fort Meade, MD

When NSA moved to Fort Meade in 1957, the roads around the original complex (OPS 1) were simply named East, West, North, and South. It wasn't until the construction of the Headquarters Building (then known as Annex-1) neared completion in 1965 that NSA looked at renaming those four roads and a new loop road east of the building complex.

NSA requested that the Fort Meade Post Memorialization Board approve new names. Since Fort Meade is an Army post, memorialization projects such as roads, parks, memorials, and buildings have to be approved by the Base Commander.

Army regulations allow memorializations for deceased service personnel and civilians from other Services or the Department of Defense. The overriding requirement in all cases is that the individual had made outstanding contributions or performed heroic actions which contributed materially to the Agency's mission. Following approval in 1965, NSA began to memorialize deceased American cryptologists by naming roads around the NSA buildings in their honor.

As NSA expanded and buildings were added to its complex, new roads were constructed connecting the buildings through a huge web of parking lots and access roads. Eventually nine roads were named for deceased American cryptologists. A varied group of both civilians and military, these men and their accomplishments reflect the diversity that makes up the history of American cryptology.

The following individuals were honored:

The following individuals were honored:

- LTGEN Ralph Canine, USA, was the first Director-of NSA from 1952 to 1956. Before that he was Director of NSA's predecessor, the Armed Forces Security Agency. He served in various Army commands and received numerous decorations including the Distinguished Service Medal, the Silver Star, the Bronze Star, and the Legion of Merit. General Canine died in March 1969 at age 73.
- RADM Jefferson R. Dennis, USN, was Deputy Director of Operations at NSA when he died in February 1958 at age 49. Admiral Dennis had a long and distinguished career in Navy cryptology, including Commander, Naval Security Group.
- Dr. Howard T. Engstrom was Deputy Director of NSA from October 1957 to August 1958. Dr. Engstrom died in November 1964 at age 65. He served in the Navy, attaining the rank of Captain, and was awarded the Distinguished Service Medal. Dr. Engstrom also served as Deputy Director of Research and Development for NSA.
- LTGEN Graves B. Erskine, USMC, died in 1973 at the age of 76. Though General Erskine never served at NSA, he was Assistant to the Secretary of Defense for Special Operations, who oversaw NSA in its early days. He later was the DOD representative to the United States Communications Security Board. General Erskine had a long and distinguished career in the Marine Corps. During World War 11 he was awarded the Distinguished Service Medal, the Silver Star, and the Legion of Merit.
- Henry I. Herczog, who had served NSA and its predecessor agencies for 17 years, died in September 1960 at age 40. Mr. Herczog was head of the NSA Office of General Studies and had been president of GEBA since its inception.
- LTGEN John A. Samford, USAF, was Director of NSA from 1956 to 1960. Prior to his term at NSA, he had been the Director of Intelligence for the United States Air Force and served under General Canine. General Samford died in 1968 at age 63.
- COL Harry H. Towler, Jr., USAF, an office chief, died in October 1959 at age 45. Col Towler played a major role in the formation of the Air Force Security Service in 1948-49.
- RADM Joseph N. Wenger, USN, one of the pioneers of American cryptology, died in 1970 at age 69. He was a major architect of the process that unified American cryptologic efforts leading towards the establishment of NSA. Admiral Wenger was NSA's first Vice Director (Deputy Director).
- Dr. William D. Wray, a group chief, died in November 1962 at age 52. Dr. Wray had served with NSA and its predecessor agencies since 1942 and was awarded the Exceptional Civilian Service Award posthumously.

Robert Hanyok, " Wray Road, Dennis Way -- How the NSA roads were named," NSA Newsletter, January 1996, pages 6-7

Operations

Ground Truth: National Security Agency, Fort Meade   http://www.fas.org/irp/facility/nsaftmed.htm

Operations

Research & Engineering

New Supercomputer Center

Army INSCOM at Ft Meade

Overhead: NSA -- Ft Meade   http://www.fas.org/irp/overhead/nsameade.htm

Key	Address	Building	Occupant	Floors	Area m2	Staff
		National Business Park		12		
	9800 Savage	Headquarters				
	9800 Savage	OPS 1				
	9800 Savage	OPS 2A				
	9800 Savage	OPS 2B				
		OPS 3				
	9808 Savage	SAB 1				
	9814 Savage	SAB 2				
		Research & Engineering				
		Engineering Facility				
		Engineering Facility				
		Special Processes Lab				
		Supercomputer Center				

NSA Ft Meade

N 400 meters

Overhead: NSA -- Ft Meade

http: www.fas.org irp overhead nsameade htm

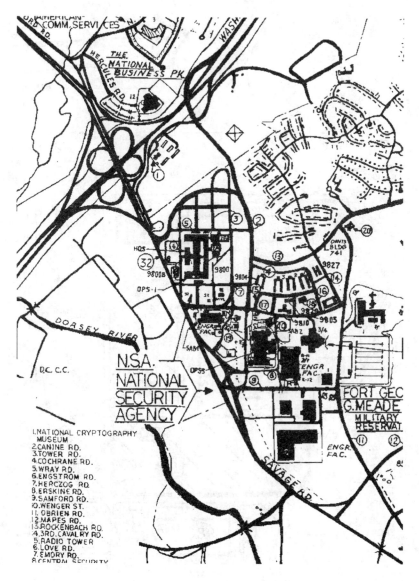

Overhead: NSA -- Ft Meade   http://www.fas.org/irp/overhead/nsameade.htm

NSA Ft Meade

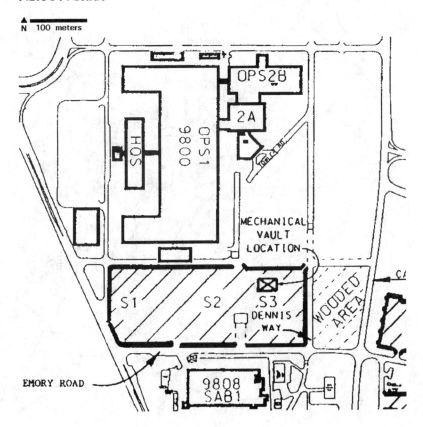

Overhead: NSA -- Ft Meade   http: www.fas.org irp overhead nsameade.htm

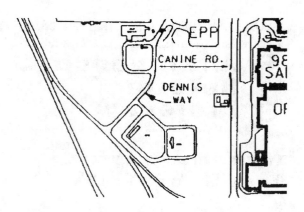

FAS Homepage | **Intelligence** | **NSA** | **Overhead** | **Index** | **Search** | **Join FAS**

http://www.fas.org/irp/overhead/nsameade.htm
Maintained by **John Pike**
Updated Sunday, May 05, 1996 - 9:12:58 AM

FAS Homepage | Intelligence | Overhead | Index | Search | Join FAS

F Intelligence
A Reform
S Project

National Security Agency
Friendship Annex - FANX

NSA FANX

▲
N 400 meters

NATIONAL SECURITY AGENCY

Overhead: NSA -- Friendship Annex

http://www.fas.org/irp/overhead/nsafanx.htm

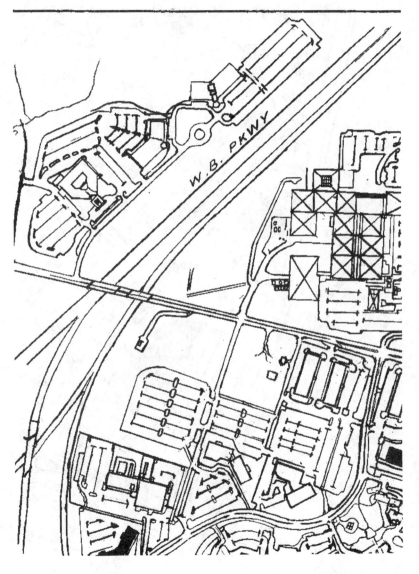

Overhead: NSA -- Friendship Annex   http://www.fas.org/irp/overhead/nsafanx.htm

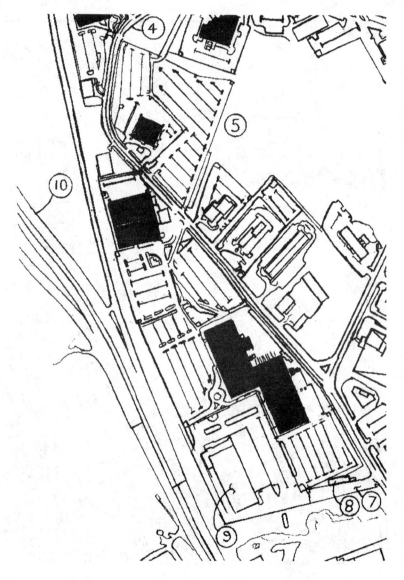

FAS | Intelligence Reform | Overhead | Index | Search | Join FAS

F Intelligence
A Reform
S Project

Menwith Hill, UK

"Overseas Collection Site
With Covered Antennae"

The 1996 Strategic Assessment by the National Defense University includes a chapter on Intelligence which includes the following aerial photograph, captioned "Overseas collection site with covered antennae."

Next FAS provides us with detailed maps of the Friendship Annex (FANX).

The FAS, as was mentioned earlier in this chapter, does not concern itself exclusively with activities within our borders, but reveals many foreign operations of the NSA. They have included a photo of the Menwith Hill, UK, project, with the following caption: "Overseas collection site with covered antennae."

One of the other foreign NSA observation/listening posts is located in Alice Springs, Australia. This linked facility (owned by the NSA) is also known as "Pine Gap." Just to bring you up to speed on Pine Gap operations, I am extracting several quotations from the excellent 554-page reference book, *The U.S. Intelligence Community, Third Edition* (1995), by Jeffrey T. Richelson, published by Westview Press, Inc. I will be quoting Richelson through a number of chapters in this book, but the following comes from the chapter titled "Signals Intelligence," beginning at p. 180.

> RHYOLITE/AQUACADE and MAGNUM satellites have been controlled since the beginning of their respective programs from a facility in Alice Springs, Australia, commonly known as Pine Gap. Officially, the facility is the Joint Defence Space Research Facility and is code-named MERINO. The facility consists of seven large radomes, a huge computer room, and about twenty other support buildings. The radomes (which resemble gigantic golf balls with one of the ends sliced off) are made of Perspex and mounted on a concrete structure. They were intended to protect the enclosed antennas against dust, wind, and rain and to hide some of the operational elements of the antennas from Soviet imaging satellites.
>
> The first two radomes at Pine Gap were installed in 1968 and remain the facility's largest. . . . The seventh radome, which was built in 1980, houses a second communications terminal.

Originally, the main computer room was about 210 square feet, but it was expanded twice in the 1970s to its present size—about 60,000 square feet. Its immense size requires that operators at each end of the room communicate with each other using headphones.

. . .The Signals Analysis Section is staffed solely by CIA personnel—no Australian citizens or contractor personnel are included. Many of the individuals in the section are linguists who monitor the voice intercepts.

As of January 1986 there were 557 people employed at Pine Gap—273 Australians and 284 Americans. Although in theory Pine Gap is a joint facility, the fifty-fifty relationship holds only with respect to the gross number of personnel and is achieved by counting Australian housemaids, cooks, and gardeners who work at the base as "equal" to the CIA personnel who conduct the actual operation.

. . .Two other major control stations are located in the United Kingdom and Germany. In 1972-1974 NSA began augmenting its listening posts at Menwith Hill (which it took over from the Army in 1966) and Bad Aibling, West Germany, to permit the planned CHALET system to downlink its intercepted communications to those sites. **Information received at either location can be transmitted directly via DSCS satellite to Fort Meade** [emphasis added].

Outside Input

In case you may be considering the possibility that only right-wing radicals and/or Christians are concerned about the way things are headed with the tracking, spying, listening, surveillence techniques of the NSA and its sister organizations (see the next chapter), I will share a few comments/articles from the "loyal opposition," neither Christian nor right wing.

An article by Charles Dupree appeared in the publication, *Claustrophobia*, August 1993, Vol. 2, No. 7. Here is what is said about Dupree:

Joint Defense Space Research Facility at Alice Springs, Australia (Pine Gap), the ground control station for RHYOLITE and ORION satellites. Huge surface and underground secret NSA communications facility located in central Australia. Photo Credit: Desmond Ball. Courtesy of The U.S. Intelligence Community by Jeffrey T. Richelson.

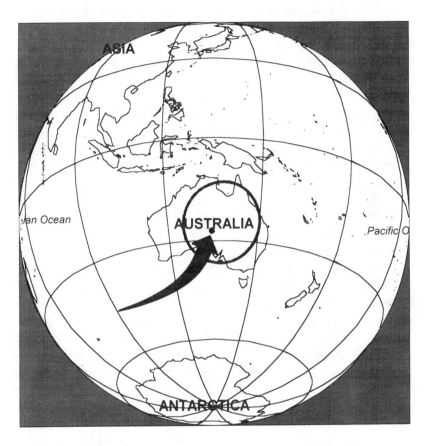

Approximate location of NSA's Alice Springs / Pine Gap facility.

Charles Dupree writes user documentation for a Silicon Valley software company. In recent years he has become concerned at **the intrusive power of the National Security Agency,** but this is probably just the effect of his antisocial habit of reading [emphasis added].

The Internet address for this article, titled "NSA: The Eyes of Big Brother," is:
(http://www.austinlinks.com/Crypto/claustrophobia.html)
After referencing his resources (primarily the books we have already mentioned), he makes some pertinent observations connecting what is occurring in this arena to the Big Brother's activities in the Orwell book, *1984.* Then the following topics are discussed: The Creation of the NSA; Watching and Listening; Project Shamrock; The Huston Plan; Project Minaret; and concluding with Uncontrolled Activities. The NSA doesn't appear to be *controlled by* or *answer to* anybody, even Congressional committees inquiring about their concern with the legality of their operations. . .according to Dupree's article, such a concern never crossed their minds (and probably was the least of their concerns). The NSA has taken care to be sure that they are **exempted** from the same legal restrictions concerning US citizens and eavesdropping without the wiretap authorization that regulates other agencies, corporations, and individuals.

In an inquiry by one of these committees, Dupree reports: ". . .CIA director William Colby had testified that the NSA was **not always able to separate the calls of US citizens from the traffic it monitors.** The general counsel of the NSA, Roy Banner, joined Allen as witness. He was asked if, in his opinion, the NSA could **legally intercept overseas telephone calls from U.S. citizens** despite the legal prohibition on wiretapping. He replied, '**That is correct.**'. . .When the committee's chief counsel said to Allen, 'You believe you are consistent with the statutes, but **there is not any statute that prohibits your interception of domestic communi-**

cations.' When deputy director Buffham was asked about
the legality of domestic aspects of the Huston Plan, he said,
'Legality? That particular aspect didn't enter into the discussions.' " [Emphasis added.]

Dupree begins his conclusion with the following astute
observation:

> The unchecked ability to intercept and read communi-
> cations, including those of U.S. citizens within the country,
> would be dangerous even if carefully regulated by elected
> officials held to a public accounting.

And finally, Dupree concludes with a statement by Senator
Schweiker of one of the committees investigating the NSA.

> Senator Schweiker of the Church committee asked
> NSA director Allen if it were possible to use NSA's
> capabilities "to monitor domestic conversations within
> the United States if some person with malintent desired
> to do it," and was probably not surprised by Allen's "I
> suppose that such a thing is technically possible." Cer-
> tainly Senator Church feared the possibility:
> **"That capability at any time could be turned
> around on the American people and no American
> would have any privacy left, such is the capability
> to monitor everything: telephone conversations,
> telegrams, it doesn't matter. There would be no
> place to hide.** If this government ever became a tyranny,
> if a dictator ever took charge in this country, the tech-
> nological capacity that the intelligence community has
> given the government could enable it to impose total
> tyranny, and there would be no way to fight back, because
> the most careful effort to combine together in resistance
> to the government, no matter how privately it was done,
> is within the reach of the government to know. Such is
> the capability of this technology.
> "I don't want to see this country ever go across the

bridge. I know the capability that is there to make tyranny total in America, and we must see to it that this agency and all agencies that possess this technology operate within the law and under proper supervision, so that we never cross over that abyss. That is the abyss from which there is no return. . . ." [Emphasis added.]

And that was written some time ago, before the NSA's latest increase in supercomputers! Imagine what the Senator might say if this were written today, knowing that the NSA now measures its computer power by the "acre." Senator Schweiker was inferring with absolute accuracy the information implied by the hearings with the NSA's leaders and counsel, and he also accurately extrapolated that information to its ultimate conclusion, if left to continue uncontrolled and unsupervised, with no accountability to the citizens and/or Congress.

Again, I urge you to visit the website cited above and obtain copies of this article.

In June, 1992, the *Houston Chronicle* requested an interview with the NSA to discuss NSA's activities regarding cryptography. Apparently NSA wasn't willing to have a face-to-face interview with the *Chronicle's* reporter, but to further their "we-have-nothing-to-hide" image, agreed to answer in writing questions presented to them. (See the next two pages.)

The October 12, 1996, edition of *The Oregonian,* Portland, Oregon's, major newspaper, contained an article by John Hendren (Associated Press) titled "A career of secrecy." It deals with companies trying to safeguard financial transactions. The sidebar reads: "A company founded by an ex-researcher of the National Security Agency develops high-tech keys to keep transactions private." Doug Kozlay was the founder of Information Resource Engineering, and he seems to have pushed ALL the right buttons on every front, although he obviously views each as "progress" and a boon to mankind in the future. . .which if you have read my previous book, *The Mark of the New World Order,* you will recognize as NOW!

Houston Chronicle Interview with the NSA

The following is the written response to my request for an interview with the NSA. To the best of my knowledge and according to their claims, it is the government's first complete answers to the many questions and allegations that have been made in regard to the matter of cryptography.

I would like to remind my readers that any qualified readers who care to address any of the issues raised herein. Please read to offical or host your (713) 236-6825

NATIONAL SECURITY AGENCY
CENTRAL SECURITY SERVICE
Serial: Q41 11-92-9

15 June 1992
Mr. Jim Abernathy
Houston Chronicle
P.O. Box 4265
Houston, TX 77210

Dear Mr. Abernathy

Thank you for your inquiry of 3 June 1992 on the subject of cryptography. Attached please find answers to the questions that you provided our Agency. If any further assistance is needed, please feel free to contact me or Mr. Jerry Volker on my staff on (xxx)

xxx-xxxx

Sincerely,

MICHAEL S CONN
Chief
Information Policy

1. Has the NSA ever imposed or attempted to impose a weakness on any cryptographic code to see if it can thus be broken?

2. Has the NSA ever imposed or attempted to impose a weakness on the DES or DSS?

3. Is the NSA aware of any weaknesses in the DES or the DSS? The RSA?

4. Has the NSA ever taken advantage of any weaknesses in the DES or the DSS?

5. Did the NSA play a role in designing the DSS? Why, in the NSA's analysis, was it seen as desirable to create the DSS when the apparently more robust RSA already stood as a de facto standard?

6. What national interests are served by limiting the power of cryptographic schemes used by the public?

7. What national interests are served by limiting the export of cryptographic technology?

8. What national interests are at risk, if any, if secure cryptography is widely available?

9. What does the NSA see as its legitimate interests in the area of cryptography? Public cryptography?

10. How did NSA enter into negotiations with the Software Publishers Association regarding the export of products utilizing cryptographic techniques? How was this group chosen, and to what purpose? What statute or elected representative authorized the NSA to engage in the discussions?

The Software Publishers Association (SPA) went to the National Security Advisor to the President to seek help from the Administration to bring profits tabulate clients and speed to the process for exporting mass market software with encryption. The National Security Advisor directed NSA to work with the mass market software representative on their request.

ii. What is the status of these negotiations?

These negotiations are ongoing.

12. What is the status of export controls on products using cryptographic techniques? How would you respond to those who point to the fact that the export of RSA from the U.S. is controlled, but that its import into the U.S. is not?

To the best of our knowledge, most countries who manufacture cryptographic products regulate the export of such products from their countries by providers similar to those existing within the U.S. Some even control the import into their countries. The U.S. complies with the guidelines established by I. Of ant for these products.

Regarding the export of RSA from the U.S., we are unaware of any restrictions that have been placed on the export of RSA for authentication purposes.

13. What issues would you like to discuss that I have not addressed?

None.

14. What question or questions would you like to pose of your critics?

None.

NOTE: In clarify misunderstandings regarding this Memorandum of Understanding (MOU) that MOU does not provide NSA any veto power over NIST proposals. As was discussed publicly in 1989, the MOU provides that if there is an issue that cannot be resolved between the two agencies, then such an issue may be referred to the President for resolution. I indeed please find a copy of subject MOU which has been made freely available in the past by both NSA and NIST to all requesters. At the House Judiciary Committee hearings on 7 May, 1992, the Director of NIST responded that he had never referred an issue to the White House since his assumption of Directorship in 1990.

MEMORANDUM OF UNDERSTANDING

BETWEEN

THE DIRECTOR OF THE NATIONAL INSTITUTE OF STANDARDS AND TECHNOLOGY

AND

THE DIRECTOR OF THE NATIONAL SECURITY AGENCY

CONCERNING

THE IMPLEMENTATION OF PUBLIC LAW 100-235. Recognizing that:

A. Under Section 2 of the Computer Security Act of 1987 (Public Law 100-235), (the Act), the National Institute of

Here is a quote from the article. (The "dateline" is BALTIMORE
. . .a neighborhood of the NSA.)

> You could say Doug Kozlay holds the key to the U.S.
> Treasury.
> Four million times a year, Uncle Sam makes computer-
> ized payments totaling $2 trillion to private companies.
> Not a dollar goes through unless the electronic key
> Kozlay invented turns in an electronic lock, verifying that
> the transaction is authentic and hacker-free. [Author's
> note: That sounds as if you are putting all your eggs in
> one basket and trusting Mr. Kozlay with the *supposedly*
> only key. Then he tells us how safe it is. Seems awfully
> naive to me, especially since the worst offenders are
> equipped with a key to the back door, the NSA, IRS, *et
> al.* There is much information available about the "clip-
> per-chip" and other devices to gain access to so-called
> "private" information.]
>
> A former researcher for the cloak-and-dagger
> **National Security Agency,** Kozlay turned espionage
> into entrepreneurship and founded Information Resource
> Engineering in 1983. He makes the codes and scram-
> bling devices that let seven of the nation's top 10 banks
> and 1,400 European financial institutions s ;nd financial
> transactions safely across computer networks.
>
> . . .Kozlay ponders issues such as what money will
> look like in the future. He carries one likely form: a proto-
> type electronic checkbook.
>
> People are counterfeiting checks using a lot of new
> technology that everybody has access to today, such as
> personal computers and laser printers, he said.
>
> **He envisions future consumers using electronic
> cash cards with all the anonymity and easy spending
> of paper money. He sees us wearing tiny personal
> computers as we now wear wristwatches** [emphasis
> added].

Biometrics—A Rapidly Growing Industry

Biometrics — it no longer sounds like a term from the latest sci-fi movie. In fact, the concept has been developed and implemented in many different areas of business, banking, government, etc. Why? Because as technology progresses toward the end times, absolute positive identification will be mandatory. A machine is unable to tell if a piece of paper or plastic is really presented to it by you, rather than just another stolen document. Therefore, it must have some kind of link to a part of your physical anatomy. . . something that is unique only to you. Presently, equipment is tied in to your fingerprints, palm prints, eyes (retinal scanning), thermal scanning of the blood vessels in your face (a face scan), voice recognition, DNA genotyping, and some others which the high-tech industries have implemented in the cause of security and limited access.

As with any new technology, lots of people want to get in on the ground floor and advance to the cutting edge, where the monetary proceeds loom large. (If you are considering an investment in such an enterprise, please be warned: these newer companies may be obsolete before time to pay their first dividends, especially if they are not adequately able to fund research and development to stay ahead of the curve. At present, technology is doubling about every 18 months. These high-tech corporations see the handwriting on the wall, and they are doing all the research and development they can to try to advance with the rapidly moving progress; otherwise, they will be producing things that are no longer needed, or can no longer be used.)

This is not an issue pertaining only to the United States, in fact, as usual with new technology, Europe may be somewhat ahead of us. An organization has been established in London called Association for Biometrics (AFB). Its stated purpose is to get together a group of interested organizations and (1) provide a single point of contact for potential customers, the media, government, and legislators; and (2) to

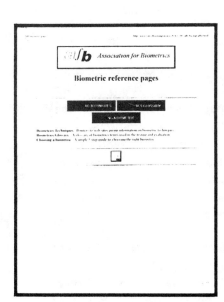

establish international standards and testing methodologies for biometrics. They claim that membership is inexpensive and urge anyone to join who could benefit from information about this technology.

The media has not overlooked the importance of biometrics and its possible future implications. The *E. E. Times Online,* February 2, 1997, Issue: 939, contained an article by Larry Lange titled: "Biometry: Human-Tracking System goes global," with a dateline of Stanford, California.

> **Biometric identification using such technologies as fingerprint and retinal scanning is well under way worldwide.** After debuting in Australia in 1987, national computerized fingerprint systems exist in several countries. The Japanese telco giant NTT is developing a fingerprint-recognition method, and the U.S. Department of Energy's Sandia National Laboratories is assessing equipment from several vendors in the retinal scanning industry, including EyeDentify (Baton Rouge, LA) and Recognition Systems, Inc. (Campbell, CA).
>
> **Transponder technology is routinely implanted in animals**; the pet market most predominantly, at 3 million ID chips and counting. LifeChip, produced by the Destron Fearing Corp. (St. Paul, MN) and the Trovan electronic identification tag, from Electronic Identification Devices, Ltd. (Santa Barbara, CA), offer a chip etched with a 10-or 64-bit ID code. Available for $10 at local animal shelters, the chips are small enough to inject with a syringe, and the ID number is read by a handheld scanner.
>
> These implantable transponders are finding their way into the livestock industry, as well, with tags implanted in pigs, sheep, cows, and horses. **Texas Instruments, Inc. is also manufacturing an alternative called TIRIS, a radio-frequency identification technology for vehicle identification and livestock monitoring.**

Though the Trovan dealer's agreement prohibits placing a chip under human skin, there's nothing to say one can't be worn on a bracelet, and such devices are being utilized by nursing-home and prison administrators to track people [not to mention the 50,000+ used by the military on the civilian refugees at Guantanamo Bay, Cuba, to track them and keep track of services being provided]. Even ski resorts are putting the chips inside lift tickets.

Widespread tracking of human beings is not far away. The Department of Defense's Advanced Research Projects Agency (ARPA) [funded by the NSA] **recently awarded Eagle Eye Technologies** (Oak Hill, VA) **a contract to build a bracelet-sized mobile terminal designed for compatibility with existing satellite communication systems.** The contract is overseen by the U.S. Army Space and Strategic Defense Command at Huntsville, AL. **Suggested uses**, according to Eagle Eye, include "tracking Alzheimer's patients, children, executives, probationers and parolees, and military personnel"—**a market that could conceivably ENCOMPASS THE WORLD's entire populace in just a few decades.**

So-called smart cards are widely catching on, too. The DoD's Multi Technology Automated Reader Card (MARC) looks to "record, revise, and transfer medical-treatment data" and store soldiers' "readiness information," such as personal, legal, and medical information. **The MARC card was developed for President Clinton's aborted plan for universal health care.**

France and Germany have incorporated **all** their social-services data into national ID systems: **Is the United States, with its rich store of digital data, poised to follow suit?**

Copyright ®   1997 CMP Media, Inc. [Emphasis added.]

The Human Identification System, An Identification and Forensics Tool, has a website expanding on the use and newly acquired speed for verifying fingerprints (see following text on the Biometrics Consortium).

NSA Enters the Picture

Now, you might be asking just how the NSA ties in with all this, especially on a global scale, supported by US taxpayers' funds. Below is another article obtained from the Internet titled "Spying," originating in Great Britain. The US citizens definitely are not the only ones concerned with the activities of the NSA, particularly in Europe and other global sites. Read these concerns, expressed from England.

> **Who runs Britain?** It's not really a trick question; I'm not after "The 100 biggest multi-nationals who control 85% of world trade and most of the governments," not "The Illuminati" nor "Thatcher! Still," even though any of them could conceivably be true. Nope, who officially runs Britain? The Government, right? Which really comprises not just the Conservative Party but also the civil service, the other parliamentary parties, the House of Lords, the courts, the whole establishment, in other words. Well, there are parts of Britain, mainland Britain, where there appears to be no control whatsoever exercised by any UK authorities. Or indeed anyone else, according to the Government.
>
> The areas in question are **electronic listening posts** operated by the American **National Security Agency (NSA),** the most famous of which is that at Menwith Hill near Harrogate in North Yorkshire, although the NSA does operate other posts, including one in the West Country and a brand new ultra high-tech operation at Edzell in Scotland. Menwith Hill has been the scene of repeated protest trespasses by a local woman, a Ms. Percy; the Ministry of Defence has been trying for some years to get a British Court to issue an injunction banning Ms.

Percy from the site. However, although the MoD ostensibly owns the site (they requisitioned the hill during the war), they do not occupy it, and they refuse to say who does; courts in the past have refused to grant an injunction against trespassers unless the occupier of the land applied. The NSA, not "officially" occupying the land, didn't want to appear in open court, hence Ms. Percy's irritating picnics continued. The MoD is now having another crack at an injunction, this time in the High Court. Amongst other issues the Court will effectively have to rule on whether Britain has sovereignty over foreign bases on our soil. But the Court will have to reach its decisions with no official information about the base, its operations, its inhabitants, even other bases or establishments with which it might come into contact— because Malcolm Rifkind, the Defence Secretary, has issued a public interest immunity certificate preventing the disclosure of any relevant information to the Court, or anyone else. So British Courts aren't allowed to know about these activities on British soil. Max Madden, MP for nearby Bradford West, asked to look around the base; he was told it "wasn't appropriate." **MPs from both sides of the Commons have asked questions about the NSA** in Parliament; no answers have been forthcoming. The question has to be "Does the Government know what's going on inside these bases?" and if it doesn't know, how on earth can it control it?

What I can tell *you* that a *British Court* can't hear, is that the **NSA and the British GCHQ** (the Government Communications Headquarters) **are working together and are both upgrading their operations to monitor British and European telecommunications.** In recent years, developments in "neural network" computer software have allowed the automation of telephone and telex monitoring. For instance it is believed that *all* overseas phone/telex calls are machine monitored for specific "key words," with up to a third of internal calls suffering the same treatment. Now improved technology and increased funding will allow a massive expansion of this activity. As well as phone calls and telex messages, faxes will now be intercepted, but the real step forward for **Big Brother** has to be the full-time monitoring of all digital traffic, first between the new digital cell phones, but especially between computers, i.e. as E-mail or on the Internet. This new development of an ongoing project is known as **Steeplebush 2**, but don't tell anybody 'cus that's a secret.

What isn't secret, and what plants all this firmly in the flesh of reality rather than paranoia, is that the Government has finally done the "decent" thing and placed GCHQ's spying on its own citizens on a legal footing. The Intelligence Services Act 1995 allows GCHQ to "monitor or interfere with electromagnetic, acoustic, or other emissions" without a warrant, or Home Office permission, or even a Court order of course. Over in the States it's also no secret that the American Government has for some years now been frantically pressuring computer manufacturers to manufacture chips and software that *cannot* hold a code that the Government cannot read. [Remember that clipper chip. . .the backdoor key?] The Yanks are still fighting against the civil liberties lobby to get the legislation through. Little things like the American Constitution apparently mean nothing to the American Government. [Even the foreigners recognize the importance of the protections established in our Constitution, and that the politicians and agencies are trying to ignore or change it, to permit them even more surveillance and control in our personal lives.]

And they just told us the Cold War was over! Instead, it looks like there's a new enemy for the Western powers to fear, subvert, and destabilize . . .their own people. [Bold emphasis added.]

Grolier's Defines the NSA

The *Grolier's 1994 Multi-Media Electronic Encyclopedia* defines the National Security Agency (NSA) as follows:

> The **largest and most secret** of the intelligence agencies of the U.S. government, the National Security Agency (NSA), with headquarters at Fort Meade, Maryland, has two main functions: to protect U.S. government communications and to intercept foreign communications. It protects government communications by enciphering [encoding/encrypting] messages and taking other measures to ensure their secrecy. In its foreign intelligence function, the NSA marshals a vast corps of intelligence analysts who use sensitive electronic equipment to monitor, decipher, and translate the communications of foreign governments. It could follow space rocket launchings in the former USSR and can overhear conversations between aircraft pilots and ground-control personnel in remote areas of the globe. The NSA was established in 1952 as a separately organized agency with the Department of Defense. It replaced the Armed Forces Security Agency. [Emphasis added.]

The NSA's Biometric Consortium is "Big Brother"!

The NSA is behind biometric research at corporations, universities, and various other government research labs.

The "stock" definition of *Biometric Consortium* appeared in *The 1997 Advanced Card and Identification Technology Sourcebook,* p. 105, as well as their E-mail and website addresses. Please note that the address given as the Consortium's address is located at the NSA at Fort Meade, Maryland.

Biometric Consortium
R221, DIRNSA
Fort Meade, MD 20755-6000

(301) 688-0278; fax (301) 688-0289
E-mail: jpcamb@alpha.ncsc.mil

Joe Campbell, Senior Electronic Engineer

The NSA's new "Biometric Consortium," Human Identification Division, has two Internet addresses, as follows:

(http://www.alpha.ncsc.mil)

and

(http://www.vitro.bloomington.in.us:9090/BC/)

The Biometric Consortium was formed in 1993 to provide **a central organization for the U.S. government's interest in biometric technology**. The group has representation from over 50 civilian and defense agencies [now it is over 200]. Its main goal is to stimulate the development of reliable, reasonably priced biometrics through the establishment of testing standards, test beds, and education. The Consortium can be seen at its new location on the worldwide web. [Emphasis added.]

NSA Is Behind the National ID Card

The NSA is a major supporter of the Biometric Consortium, both in encouragement and funding, and they are behind all the efforts to identify us nationwide! NSA funds the FBI's NCIC 2000 program. . .which, in turn, funds all state DMV's to promote the new drivers' licenses/voter registrations ("motor/voter" national ID cards). It's just one big web, and the NSA is the spider!

In 1993, the National Security Agency created yet another sister organization (see the next chapter for other "sisters" of the NSA) at its main facility in Fort Meade, Maryland. . .

one that specializes in the biometric identification of people. It was named the "Biometrics Consortium." Mr. Joe Campbell, Senior Electronics Engineer, is in charge (the full address, phone/fax numbers, website, and E-mail addresses were printed above).

According to NSA's "party line/hype," the Biometrics Consortium was formed in 1993 for precisely the same reasons given in the above article from *Advanced Card and Identification Technology Sourcebook*. With those stated goals in mind, just why is our government so intensely interested in "biometrics"? And what does the term mean, anyway? I've told you about some of the current methods routinely used, but I need to fill in the gaps with a more comprehensive study.

The term *biometrics* is defined as "automated methods of **verifying or recognizing the identity of a living person** based on physiological or behavioral characteristics" [bold emphasis added]. Physiological characteristics are: fingerprints, hand geometry, eye retinal patterns, and facial features.

In addition to the physiological characteristics, there are reliable behavioral characteristics that are unique to you and no one else. They include: signatures, voice patterns, and computer keyboard keystroke dynamics. Why would the government want to act as **a central clearing house** for these identification methodologies? Well, it should be obvious by now that **the government wants to positively identify you so it can positively CONTROL YOU!**

So, there you have it! Not only is the NSA already storing nearly all available personal information on us in its databases that's been *collected, consolidated, and centralized* from various civilian and military networks globally (including credit reporting agencies, the US Postal Service, driver's license bureaus, and others), they now are funding, controlling, and orchestrating many new "civilian and defense" programs designed to "stimulate the development" of better ways to **positively identify us.** It should be obvious that **no one will be able to escape their system.** Note above how the NSA informs us of their reason for creating this new agency in the first place: Indeed, it was formed "to provide a **central organization** for the US Government's interest in biometric technology." What this actually means (in all practical reality) is that the NSA is now planning to consolidate, take charge of, and orchestrate **all identification matters** in the United States. **Remember, the key word here is CENTRALIZE.** In other words, **the NSA will control all identification data on everyone from its databases at Fort Meade!** It is my sincere opinion that in the future, NSA will be "centralizing" this data on a global scale; in fact, we know that they already are involved in much intelligence-gathering on foreign soil, all of which is collected and funneled into the main database at Fort Meade.

Various dictionaries define the word *centralize* as: "To bring to a central point or under central control . . . to converge, to consolidate, to come together as one, to focalize, to streamline, to unify, to join, to confederate, **to nationalize**" [emphasis added]. In addition, the word *central* is defined as "constituting or being near a center." Therefore, we should understand clearly from this that it is the stated **GOAL of the "almighty" NSA** to become the **principal identification authority in America!** Look out, America, here comes the satanically enslaving **New World Order! Big Brother isn't coming . . . he's already here!**

More Information About the Biometrics Consortium

If we haven't proven our case that the NSA owns the Biometric Consortium, it won't be difficult to do. The "U.S. Government Biometric Consortium's" website offers pages and pages of (colorful, if you have color capability) information. One of their pages is a list of "Full Members," which at the time this was published consisted of 40, including the US Postal Service, Federal EBT Task Force (electronic money), Federal Highway Administration, NSA, and Social Security Administration. Other groups/organizations/businesses are referred to as "Associate Members." (There are now 200 and the BC is growing daily.) The "Full Member" list of government entities is as follows:

Air Force
ARPA
Defense Commmissary Agency
Defense Protective Security Service
Department of State
DISA
Federal Bureau of Prisons
FDA
Marine Corps
NIST
Office of Senate Security
Secret Service
Special Technologies Laboratory
US Postal Service
Army
Bureau of Engraving & Printing
Defense Logistics Agency
Department of Energy
Department of Transportation
Electronic Systems Center
Federal EBT Task Force
INS
Naval Surface Warfare Center
NRL
ORD
Security Policy Board
US Customs Service
Army Research Laboratory
DEA
Defense Nuclear Agency
Department of Justice
Department of Treasury
FBI
Federal Highway Administration

IRS
Navy
NSA
Rome Labs
Social Security Administration
US Food and Drug Administration

(Most of the above are self-explanatory, but in case you aren't familiar with all of the abbreviations, check the section, "Acronyms and Abbreviations" in Bamford's book, *The Puzzle Palace,* previously cited.) Obviously, this list does not include all the commercial entities, banks, businesses, etc., all of which want to be in on enhancing the biometric connections for the identification of their customers and constituents.

I have noticed that conspicuous by its absence in the above list of government agencies, is FEMA. At present, I don't know the implications of this omission. However, I do know that FEMA likely will play a major role in the control of people and events in this country (using the information in the NSA computers) as it shifts to global operations. . .under the New World Order. I will have to do further research on FEMA's participation (probably hidden) in the Biometric Consortium. (See the next chapter for more information on FEMA.)

The Biometric Test Center

A Biometric Test Center has been established at San Jose State University, San Jose, California. They openly announce that **"NSA is the sole source of funds to date."** However, they invite funding from any "unbiased" source.

The US Government Biometric Consortium is chartered as a Working Group under the Security Policy Board.

Self-described Mission and Function Statement

The website pages describe the Mission of the Biometrics Consortium as follows:

▶ Promote the science and performance of biometrics

▶ Create standardized testing databases, procedures, and protocols
▶ Provide a forum for information exchange between Government, private industry, and academia
▶ Address the safety, performance, legal, and ethical issues surrounding biometrics
▶ Advise and assist member agencies concerning the selection and application of biometric devices

The Function as stated is: "The Consortium plans to pursue the following over the next few years:"

▶ Develop standardized test methods for evaluating various biometric systems
▶ Develop standardized methods for reporting test results and describing biometric performance
▶ Establish a national test facility
▶ Evaluate various biometric techniques of interest to Consortium members

Much information about the Consortium's activities have been taken from the Internet and reduced on the pages that follow.

Biometric Security: Government Applications and Operations

Among the many pages of information available, there is an extremely comprehensive paper (many pages) that has been prepared for the NSA/Biometric Consortium website. I will be quoting from it quite extensively, and there may be a certain amount of overlap with what I already have shared with you; but the new information gleaned will make the overlap insignificant. They begin by giving us an Abstract.

The information age is quickly revolutionizing the way transactions are completed. Everyday actions are increasingly being handled electronically, instead of with

The Biometric Consortium

Chair: **Dr. Joe Campbell**

Vice Chair: **Ms. Lisa Alyea**

Recording Secretary: **Mr. Tom Whittle**, P.E.

Support: Tracor Corporation

🛑 **This information resides on a DOD interest computer.** 🛑

Important conditions, restrictions, and disclaimers apply.

Introduction | BC Meetings | Working Groups | National Biometric Test Center | Government Activities | Publications | Periodicals | Events | Research | Databases | Examples of Biometric Systems | Related Sites | Employment | And now for something completely different... | Finding What You Want | Join the Biometric Consortium's LISTSERV

Last updated 7 August 1997

Introduction

Biometrics: Automatically recognizing a person using distinguishing traits (a narrow definition)

- Biometric Security: Government Applications and Operations (CardTech/SecurTech Government 1996)
- Update on the US Government's Biometric Consortium (CardTech/SecurTech 1996)
- Update on the US Government's Biometric Consortium (CardTech/SecurTech 1995)
- Security Policy Board (SPB) and SPB Statement by The White House Press Secretary
- National Security Council (Asst. to the President for National Security Affairs)

Biometric Consortium   http://www.vitro.bloomington.in.us:8080 - BC

Biometric Consortium Meetings

- BC9, 8-9 April 1997, Holiday Inn, Crystal City, VA
  - Business Meeting (13 slides), Joe Campbell, US DoD (Frames and Java required)
  - Progress Report (3 slides), Lisa Alyea, US DoD (Frames and Java required)
- BC8, 11-12 June 1996, San Jose State University
  - Business Meeting (17 slides), Joe Campbell, US DoD
  - Estimating Performance Characteristics of Biometric Verifiers (11 slides), Kathleen Diegert, Sandia National Laboratories

Working Groups

Testing and Reporting Group: Carl Pocratsky and Lisa Alyea
(Test Center Director: Capt. John Colombi, PhD)
> Responsible for establishing testing standards, developing performance testing protocols, designing a test facility, deciding upon the format for the reported results, providing a mechanism for the dissemination of final reports, and defining a repository for reported information.

Vulnerability Group (no vendors): Anonymous
> Same responsibilities as the Testing and Reporting Group, but as viewed from the standpoint of internal or external vulnerabilities of biometric devices.

Database Group: Dr. Jim Wayman
> Responsible for defining standards for each particular type of database, collecting databases into one central location, and disseminating database information to those that require it for testing purposes.

Ground Rules Committee: Winnie Lehman and Tim Bergendahl
> Responsible for disseminating information about the Consortium, promoting external relations and contacts, encouraging internal interaction, defining Consortium operating procedures, and addressing any legal or ethical issues that affect the Consortium.

Research and New Technologies Group: Dr. Alan Higgins
> Responsible for keeping abreast of the latest research and innovations in the field of biometrics, as well as providing a repository for such information.

National Biometric Test Center

Government Test Center Director: Capt. John Colombi, PhD
San Jose State University Test Center Director: Dr. Jim Wayman

The National Biometric Test Center (located at San Jose State University's Biometric Identification Research Institute)

Biometric Testing Factors

Government Activities

- Electronic Signatures (FDA: 21 CFR Part 11: Electronic Records)
- Agencies scan biometrics for potential applications, *Federal Computer Week*, 20 January 1997
- Automated Fingerprint Identification System (AFIS), CBD, 26 Sep 1996, PSA#1688 SOL RFP-7046
- Fingerprint Capture Devices, CBD, 17 May 1996, PSA#1597
- Standards for the Electronic Submission of Fingerprint Cards to the FBI
- H.R. 2202 Immigration Bill/Senate Bills S. 269 and S. 1361
- Draft Authentication Module Interface Standard
- Integrated Automated Fingerprint Identification System (IAFIS)
- National Crime Information Center (NCIC) 2000 Newsletter (here is an alternate link)
- INS Passenger Accelerated Service System (INSPASS)
  - INSPASS Update
  - INSPASS
  - INS Automation Blasted, *Government Executive*
  - Customs upgrade trims travelers' wait, *USA Today*
  - Securing America's Borders (DoJ)
  - Inspection (AIT)
- Electronic Benefits Transfer: Use of Biometrics to Deter Fraud in the Nationwide EBT Program. GAO Report Number OSI-95-20, September 1995. Raw text, Adobe Acrobat PDF, GAO
- For Support of Health and Welfare Data Center (California Budget, Subcommittee #5, Governor's Line-Item Vetoes)
- U.S. Prisons to Use Biometrics (Oct 1994)
- Federal Information Processing Standards Publication 190: Guideline for The Use of Advanced Authentication Technology Alternatives
- Information Security and Biometrics at the National Security Agency under the High Performance Computing and Communications Program
- Los Angeles County Stops Fraud with Automated Fingerprint Matching System (AFIRM)
- Illinois Department of Public Aid: I-SCAN Project (Retinal Scanning)
- Connecticut's Digital Imaging of Fingerprints for Welfare Benefits
  - Biometrics in Human Services User Group Newsletter, V1, N1 (see above for official Word version)

Other suggestions?

 Publications

- Who knows who you are?, *InfoWorld*
- The Body as Password, *Wired*
- IBM's Advanced Identification Solutions
- Laboratory Evaluation of the IriScan Prototype Biometric Identifier, Sandia National Labs, April, 1996
- Biometric identification looms on landscape of network log-ins: High-end technology is becoming more affordable, *PC Week*, 26 March 1997
- Brave New Whorl: ID Systems Using the Human Body Are Here, but Privacy Issues Persist

Biometric Consortium   http://www.vitro.bloomington.in.us:8080/BC

- Digital identification: It's now at our fingertips and sidebar Novell, NIST push standards for biometrics, *EE Times*
- Biometry: human-tracking system goes global, *EE Times*
- Touching Big Brother: How biometric technology will fuse flesh and machine
- MOSCOM and Chemical Bank to Commence Voice Verification Trails (3/21/96)
- Biometric References Database
- Speaker Verification References (BibTeX format)
- Speaker Recognition Tutorials
- Testing with The YOHO CD-ROM Voice Verification Corpus (ICASSP-95)
- Protecting Privacy and Information Integrity of Computerized Medical Information
- Identification vs Society
- Human Identification in Information Systems: Management Challenges and Public Policy Issues

Other suggestions?

Periodicals

- ACM Special Interest Group on Security, Audit and Control
- *Automatic I.D. News*
- Biometric Digest
- *Biometric Technology Today, The Biometrics Report,* etc.
- *EE Times*
- *Infosecurity News*
- IEEE Transactions on ...
- *IEEE Transactions on Speech and Audio Processing*
- *IEEE Transactions on Pattern Analysis and Machine Intelligence*
- *PIN's Advanced Card & Identification Technology Sourcebook,* Ben Miller's annual publication
- Security Management (ASIS)
- *Speech Communication*
- National Institute of Justice's Headlines & Technology News Update

Other suggestions?

 Events

Biometric Consortium Meetings (by invitation only)

- BC10 Meeting: late 1997-early 1998
- To propose a presentation, please click here and tell us about it.
- Every BC presentation should address these key points.

Biometric Conferences and Seminars

- IEEE Image and Multidimensional Digital Signal Processing Workshop 98, Alpbach, Austria, 12-16 July 1998
- Association for Biometrics Conference (in association with the Department of Trade and Industry),

London, 4 December 1997
- Workshop On Automatic Identification Advanced Technologies, Stony Brook, NY, 6-7 November 1997
- 31st Asilomar Conference On Signals, Systems, And Computers; Asilomar Conference Center, Pacific Grove, CA, 2-5 November 1997
- Speech Technology in the Public Telephone Network, Rhodes, Greece, 26-27 September 1997 and Speaker Recognition in Telephony (COST250)
- CardTech/SecurTech '97 Government, Arlington, VA, 15-16 September 1997

Past Events

Other suggestions?

Research

- Biometric Systems Laboratory (Italy)
- Chip Architecture for Smart CArds and secure portable DEvices (with biometrics)
- European Cooperation in the field of Scientific and Technical Research (COST)
- MIT Media Lab's Vision and Modeling Group
- NIST's Visual Image Processing Group (fingerprint, face, etc.)
- DNA
  - Cloning and Ethics
    - Animals As Inventions: Biotechnology and Intellectual Property Rights
    - Biotechnology & Science
    - Cloning Humans
    - Cloning Sheep (Dolly), *Phil Inquirer*
    - Cloning Sheep (Dolly), Byte This
    - Cloning Rhesus Monkeys, CNN
    - Cloning Rhesus Monkeys, *Wash Post*
    - First Adult Mammal Cloned, Yahoo's large index
    - *Nature* Web Special: Cloned Sheep
      Nature, the "international weekly journal of science," has created a web page to accompany the ground-breaking letter it published in the February 27, 1997 issue: "Viable offspring derived from fetal and adult mammalian cells," by I. Wilmut, et al. The letter is available, as well as a *Nature* Opinion piece, and short articles of commentary by Axel Kahn of the INSERM Laboratory of Research on Genetics and Molecular Pathology at the Cochin Institute of Molecular Genetics, Paris, and Colin Stewart of the NCI-Frederick Cancer Research and Development Center, Frederick, Maryland. (Note that the site is free, but registration is required.)
    - Shaping Genes: Ethics, Law and Science of Using New Genetic Technology in Medicine and Agriculture
    - Unraveling the Code of Life
  - DNA Fingerprinting in Human Health and Society
  - Yahoo's Human Genetics
- Face

- ○ The Face Recognition Home Page
- ○ Facial Analysis
- ○ Facial Animation
- Fingerprint
  - ○ "Automated Systems for Fingerprint Authentication Using Pores and Ridge Structure," *Proceedings of SPIE*, Automatic Systems for the Identification and Inspection of Humans (SPIE Vol 2277), San Diego, 1994, p. 210-223. (802 kB PostScript)
  - ○ Cal Tech
  - ○ Carleton U/DEW Engineering
  - ○ The FBI Fingerprint Image Compression Standard
  - ○ An Introduction to Wavelets: FBI Fingerprint Compression
  - ○ FBI Fingerprint Compression Standard WSQ Software for UNIX Sun under SunOS 4.1.1 (uncertified)
  - ○ FBI Fingerprint Compression Standard WSQ Software for Windows 3.1 (uncertified)
  - ○ Free Software to Measure the Spatial Frequency Response (MTF) of Fingerprint Scanners
  - ○ The Human Identification System Project
  - ○ ImEdge Technology
- Handwriting
  - ○ Document Understanding and Character Recognition (DIMUND)
  - ○ Handwriting Recognition Group
  - ○ International Graphonomics Society
  - ○ OSCAR
  - ○ Script & Pattern Recognition Research Group
  - ○ The UNIPEN Project
- Voice
  - ○ CAVE - The European CAller VErification Project
  - ○ NIST Speaker Detection Evaluation
  - ○ Speech Research (links at UCSC)

Other suggestions?

Databases

- FacE REcognition Technology (FERET) (facial)
- FBI's Operational Capability Demonstration (OCD) data set (fingerprints)
- Linguistic Data Consortium (voice)
- Manchester Faces Image Database
- NIST Standard Reference Data
- NIST's fingerprint CD-ROM
- Oregon Graduate Institute (voice)
- YOHO (voice)
- See the Research sites above for additional databases

Other suggestions?

Examples of Biometric Systems

- Face
    - Cambridge Neurodynamics
    - Identification Technologies International
    - Intelligent Vision Systems
    - Miros, In-your-face security, *PC Week* Labs Review, 26 March 1997
    - Keyware Technologies
    - MIT Media Lab's Photobook
    - NeuraWare Face Recognition Systems
    - Siemens Nixdorf's FaceVACS
    - USC's Elastic Graph Matching
    - Viisage
    - FaceIt at Visionics and Rockefeller U
- Fingerprint
    - Live Scan Vendors
        - 3M
        - American Biometric Company
        - Biometric Identification Inc.
        - Central Research Laboratories
        - Digital Biometrics
        - Fingermatrix
        - IDeas International
        - Identicator
        - Identix
        - Security Print
        - Sony; I/O Software
        - Startek Engineering
        - Ultra-Scan
        - Vitrix
    - The FBI's IAFIS and NCIC 2000 Programs
        - Lockheed Martin
        - Mitretek Systems
        - Harris (and Criminal Justice Products)
        - Also see the IAFIS and NCIC 2000 links
    - Large-Scale AFIS Systems
        - Cogent Systems and HP
        - North American MORPHO Systems
        - NEC
        - Printrak International
        - TRW (uses Cogent Systems)
        - Unisys (uses NEC)
    - Various
        - AND Identification - System integrator
        - Biometric Tracking, L.L.C. - Smart card and biometric plug-in
        - Cambridge Neurodynamics
        - Comnetix - Fully integrated criminal justice software solutions
        - Cross Check - Imaging
        - Fingerprint Technologies - Australian consortium of companies
        - Harris/AuthenTec FingerLoc - Fingerprint chip
        - Jasper Consulting - Fingerprint identification solutions
        - Mytec - Fingerprint as security key

- National Registry Inc. (NRI) - Finger image identification; Your fingerprint is your password, c|net
- PrintScan International - Software for fingerprint recognition
- Security Print - Anti-Fraud Use of Fingerprint
- Thomson-CSF Semiconducteurs Spécifiques FingerChip(tm) - Fingerprint chip
- Veridicom - Fingerprint chip; 'Fingerprint Chip' Touted for ATMs, PCs, *NYT*

  ○ Related
    - AFIS and Live Scan Links
    - CJ Tech News
    - FingerPrint USA's Fingerprint Links
- Hand
  ○ Recognition Systems' ID3D
- Handwriting
  ○ AEA's Chequematch and Countermatch
  ○ CADIX
  ○ CIC
  ○ PenOp
  ○ Security & Identification's Automatic Signature Verification using Acoustic Emission
- Iris
  ○ British Telecom; Keeping an eye on Iris and Personal Secure Access to Networked Applications - the use of Iris Recognition for User Validation
  ○ IriScan
  ○ Sensar
- Vein
  ○ Security & Identification's Veincheck
  ○ Veincheck
- Voice
  ○ BI Voice Verification
  ○ Brite Voice Systems
  ○ ImagineNation's Vault
  ○ iNTELiTRAK's Voice Verification Gateway for WWW Servers and CITADEL GateKeeper Adds New Dimension to Network Security by Introducing Secured-Server, Two-Key, Biometric System; ITT Industries' SpeakerKey Provides Core Technology
  ○ Keyware Technologies
  ○ ITT's SpeakerKey and FAQ
  ○ MOSCOM Corporation
  ○ Qvoice's Star Trek Deep Space Nine Voice Print
  ○ Sensory ("Voice Password on a Chip")
  ○ Sprint Voice FONCARD
  ○ T-NETIX's SpeakEZ
  ○ Veritel and Veritel Canada
  ○ Voice Control Systems' SpeechPrint ID
  ○ Speaker Recognition (comp.speech Q6.6)
  ○ Speaker (and Speech) Recognition (comp.speech links)
- Various
  ○ "biometric" search at IBM
  ○ CardTech/SecurTech Exhibitors
  ○ NCSA CBDC Links to Biometrics Vendor Sites

Other suggestions?

Biometric Consortium   http: www.vitro.bloomington.in.us:8080 BC

Related Sites

- Biometric Groups
    - Association for Biometrics (AfB), UK and the former AfB site - excellent reference materials!
    - Commercial Biometrics Developer's Consortium (CBDC)
    - Financial Services Technology Consortium (biometric fraud prevention)
    - International Association for Identification (IAI)
    - Security Industry Association (SIA)
- 1997 Automated Fingerprint Identification System (AFIS) Committee
- Australian Biotechnology Association
- Automatic Identification Technology Commerce and Education - About Biometric ID
- Consultants & System Integrators
    - Julian Ashbourn's Technology Corner
    - Fingerprint Technologies
    - FingerPrint USA
    - Q&A Consulting
- DARPA's Internet for Security Professionals
- EAGLES' Assessment of Speaker Verification Systems
- East Shore Technologies (check the EST Challenge)
- EDI HotLinks (standards, etc.)
- Federal Security Infrastructure Program (for secure applications: tokens, keys, and authorization)
- Justice Technology Information Network (JUSTNET)
- 20G4 Multi-technology Automated Reader Card (MARC) Project
- NIST's Computer Security Resource Clearinghouse
- Physical Security Equipment Action Group
- Privacy
    - Electronic Privacy Information Center
    - Personal Information Goes Public, SA
    - Privacy in the Digital Age, c|net
    - Privacy International
- Protecting Human Subjects
- Rainbow Security Book Series (e.g., "Orange Book")
- The Smart Card Cyber Show (with museum)
- Speaker Verification API (SVAPI)
    - SVAPI Notes
    - Quintet Signature Verification API (QAPI)
- Standards
    - American National Standards Institute
    - International Standards Organization
- Twins
    - Gilia Angell's TWINSource
    - Twin Pages in the World Wide Web
- University Biometric Curricula
    - Purdue's Automatic Data Collection (biometrics)
    - San Jose State University's Biometric Identification Research Institute
- UPS is Testing NETDOX
- US Postal Service's Electronic Postmarks

- Warning: 666 is Coming!
- Yahoo's Biometric Links (updated each visit)

Other suggestions?

Employment

- Biometric Employment Opportunities
  - Visionics
  - Cross Check
- Biometric Resumes
  - Students

Other suggestions?

And now for something completely different...

- Hilgers' Links to Biometry
- CSIRO Biometrics Unit
- Biometrie und Populationsgenetik
- Carolina Biological Supply Company

Other suggestions?

Finding What You Want

- MetaCrawler. Easy to use keyword/phrase **search**.
- Yahoo. The huge web **catalog** organized by topic.
- AltaVista Advanced Search. Use powerful Boolean search criteria to focus a search.
- Lycos Multimedia. Search for photos, art, videos, music, and sounds.
- c|net's Search. Specialty searches and catalogs.
- Search the US Patent Office.
- Deja News. Search the USENET Newsgroups (discussion forum).
- Four 11 and Switchboard. Find e-mail & postal addresses and phone numbers.

Join the Biometric Consortium's Electronic Discussion Group (LISTSERV)

The Biometric Consortium's LISTSERV is for US Government employees. It is a free electronic mailing list for sharing discussions about all things biometric, ranging from research questions to meeting announcements.

To request a subscription to the Biometric Consortium's LISTSERV, send e-mail to LISTSERV@PEACH.EASE.LSOFT.COM. Leave the subject line blank and write "INFO BIOMETRICS" (without the quotes) in the body of your message. Do not include anything else in the

Biometric Consortium   http://www.vitro.bloomington.in.us:8080 - BC

message (it is not read by a human).

If your subscription is approved, you will be able to send messages to the BC LISTSERV's posting address BIOMETRICS@PEACH.EASE.LSOFT.COM.

All LISTSERV commands (e.g., "SET BIOMETRICS DIGest" for daily delivery of all the LISTSERV traffic) should be sent to LISTSERV@PEACH.EASE.LSOFT.COM. If you need help using the BC's LISTSERV (e.g., searching and getting old postings from our LISTSERV archive), please consult the LISTSERV General User's Guide. If the Guide doesn't answer your question, please send e-mail to the BC list owner BIOMETRICS-request@PEACH.EASE.LSOFT.COM.

Thanks to Tracor Services Corporation and NSWC Crane for hosting the Biometric Consortium's page!

Tom (WhittleTJ@aol.com), Joe and Lisa (bc@alpha.ncsc.mil) welcome your comments.

You're visitor number **17118** since 6 November 1995.
This URL is <http://www.biometrics.org:8080>.

Note: the inclusion of any items on this web site does not constitute their endorsement by the US Government, the Biometric Consortium, or any of its members.

pencil and paper or face to face. This growth in electronic transactions has resulted in a greater demand for fast and accurate user identification and authentication. Biometric technology is a way to achieve fast, user-friendly authentication with a high level of accurary. This presentation will highlight some of the benefits of using biometrics for authentication. Emerging applications, both within the Government and industry, will be discussed. Also presented will be an overview of the US Government Biometric Consortium and how this group is bringing together technologists from Government and industry to work together on improved standards.

The next section in their paper is called Overview, and it is possibly more than you want to know, but for those who are interested in details, I am duplicating it in its entirety.

Biometrics are automated methods of recognizing a person based on a physiological or behavioral characteristic. Examples of human traits used for biometric recognition include fingerprints, speech, face, retina, iris, handwritten signature, hand geometry, and wrist veins. Biometric recognition can be used in *identification* mode, where the biometric system identifies a person from the entire enrolled population by searching a database for a match. A system also can be used in *verification* mode, where the biometric system authenticates a person's claimed identity from his/her previously enrolled pattern. Using biometrics for identifying and authenticating human beings offers some unique advantages. Only biometric authentication bases an identification on an intrinsic part of a human being. Tokens, such as smart cards [in which they also are involved heavily], magnetic stripe cards, physical keys, and so forth [or any combination of the above], can be lost, stolen, duplicated, or left at home [the next step, of course, is the biochip implant—to coin a current slogan, "You can't leave home without it!"].

Passwords can be forgotten, shared, or observed. While all biometric systems have their own advantages and disadvantages, there are some common characteristics needed to make a biometric system usable. First, the biometric must be based upon a distinguishable trait. [I reported earlier in this chapter about the check printing company that was incorporating a photo, in digital format, for your personal checks. No one could see your picture, not even you, but when you cash the check, it is fed into a machine that reads the digitized photo and prints it on a screen for visual verification.] For example, for nearly a century, law enforcement has used fingerprints to identify people. There is a great deal of scientific data supporting the idea that "no two fingerprints are alike." Newer methods, even those with a great deal of scientific support, such as DNA-based genetic matching [just another form of biometrics], sometimes do not hold up in court. Another key aspect is how *user-friendly* is the system. Most people find it acceptable to have their pictures taken by video cameras or to speak into a microphone. In the United States, using a fingerprint sensor does not seem to be much of a problem. In some other countries, however, there is strong cultural opposition to touching something that has been touched by many other people. While cost is always a concern, most implementers today are sophisticated enough to understand that it is not only the initial cost of the sensor or the matching software that is involved. Often, the life-cycle support cost of providing system administration support and an enrollment operator can overtake the initial cost of the hardware. Also of key importance is accuracy. Some terms that are used to describe the accuracy of biometric systems include *false-acceptance rate* (percentage of imposters accepted), *false-rejection rate* (percentage of authorized users rejected), and *equal-error rate* (when the decision threshold is adjusted so that the false-acceptance rate equals the false-rejection rate). When discussing the accuracy of a biometric system, it is often beneficial to talk about the equal-error rate or at least to consider the false-acceptance rate and false-rejection rate together. For many systems, the threshold can be adjusted to ensure that virtually no imposters will be accepted. Unfortunately, this often means an unreasonably high number of authorized users will be rejected. To summarize, a good biometric system is one that is low cost, fast, accurate, and easy to use. [Emphasis added.]

Examples of Biometric Applications

Again, I will be duplicating this entire section; thereafter I will be highlighting from the sections on "Current Applications" and "Planned Applications."

There are many examples of biometrics being used or considered in Federal, State, local, and foreign government projects. One use is to provide robust authentication for access to computer systems containing sensitive information used by the military services, intelligence agencies, and other security-critical Federal organizations. Physical access control to restricted areas is another key application. There are many law enforcement applications, mostly for fingerprint recognition, at the Federal, State, and local levels. Other law enforcement applications include home incarceration and physical access control in jails and prisons. Perhaps one of the most extensive applications of biometrics is for entitlements [funds received in some way from the local, state, or federal governments]. Fraud in entitlement programs is estimated by the General Accounting Office at over $10 billion per year. Pilot programs in several states have demonstrated dramatic savings by requiring biometric authentication when someone is applying for entitlement benefits. There are also significant applications for biometrics in the commercial sector. Some of the biggest potential applications include the use of

Fingerprints have long been used as an identifying attribute of every person. Why use fingerprints? Fingerprints offer an infallible means of personal identification. This is the essential explanation for their having supplanted other methods of establishing a person's identity who are reluctant to reveal themselves. Thus, fingerprints present a reliable way of singling out a person.

In detective novels and movies, we often find the authorities poking on fingerprints trying to identify the enemies. Institutions like the National Bureau of Investigations keeps a record of fingerprints who have filed for clearances. As the filers increase in number, a need for a computerized system of filing seems to arise, thus the need for a database. A database is a repository (or collection) of data which may later on be updated and or queried. However, as the number of entries in the database increase, the demand for a time-efficient, and at the same time space-efficient database management scheme blooms. This need calls for a fast query mechanism while storage requirement (due to overheads and data storage requirement) is kept at tolerable l evel.

In the previous years, relational databases answered the needs of database users. This had been primarily due to the straightforward approach to database design and implementation that relational approach offered. However, as time progresses, databases will eventually have to be updated due to new requirements (or specifications) and modifications to relational databases may prove to be tedious tasks.

In the recent times, the development of another way of thinking developed, called the **object-oriented approach** . This new way of thinking does not merely pertain to ordinary programming but also brought a new frontier to database techno logy --- **object-oriented databases (OOD)**. Thus database designers now have a choice between relational and object oriented approaches to database design and implementation.

Object-orientation allows a great deal of maintainability (as contrasted to relational databases' less flexibility for modification). This means that current databases' requirement for modifiability (for easy update) can now be answered through object-o riented databases.

The HIS is an identification and forensics tool. It offers a computerized method of identifying the owner or possible owners of a given fingerprint. It also provides a database that contains records of a number of individuals, including copies of their fingerprints.

The HIS is aimed for large-scale databases (databases that contain a huge number of personal records). It is developed for use of investigation bureaus, the National Investigation Bureau in particular, which until now uses manual operations, both in fi ling and searching the database.

The HIS is composed of three (3) parts: the database server, the client program, and the recognition identification classification engine.

The database server (called the   HISS, Human Identification System Server   ) is developed using a utility called the Scaleable Heterogeneous Object REpository (SHORE). This utility provides tools that enable the administrator to ma intain the database. Th e database server is running on a UNIX platform, that is, it is programmed under the UNIX operating system environment (as contrary to the commonly used DOS environment). The database server also follows the object-oriented paradigm. This is a new way o f thinking or looking at things where operations are treated as messages being passed from one entity to another, as contrary to the conventional procedural approach, where operations are looked at as series of steps to take or perform.

When an ordinary person (other than the HIS Administrator) uses the HIS, he/she does not see the HISS or the classifier. Instead, it uses the "client program" of the HIS. This part serves as the user's way of communicating with the HIS. We call this c lient program as   MOLE (More Or Less automatic Extractor). This part is created under the Windows□ environment (as contrary to the HISS' UNIX environment). This is because it is easy to create a graphical user interface (GUI) under Windows□. This GUI serves as the connecting line between the user and the system. The MOLE allows a user to query the database, that is, to search the database, given a set of information. It provides a graphical display of a query form and allows the user to see the pair matches being performed by the HIS.

The technology offered by the HIS is the use of an object-oriented database management system running under UNIX, an Artificial Neural Network-based classifier and a fast and efficient query search engine.

The group is using the **Scalable Heterogeneous Object REpository** , or **SHORE**. SHORE is a persistent object system under development at the University of Wisconsin that represents a merger of object-oriented database and file system technologies. Click   here for a more detailed documentation of the   **SHORE** project.

The Classifier accepts a fingerprint image and generates a partial score for that image and gives a classification score for a set of ten (10) fingerprints. Each person is identified through the classification score of his/h er fingerprints. This informa tion shall be kept by the HIS Database for query use. The Classifier is currently undergoing implementation. The Classifier, the HIS Database, or the whole   **HIS** project for that matter, is implemented on a UNIX platform, since the   **HIS** aims to be a distributed systems software.

After the completion of the Classifier and the HIS Database, the subprojects shall be merged to produce the complete   **Human Identification System** (I), which offers human identification security, not only for investigation bureaus but inte rested corporations (and other establishments) as well.

*Last modified **May 29, 1996***
*Please mail us for **comments or suggestions** about our project and/or homepage. Write us at :*
shoreadm@asti.dost.gov.ph

The Washington Post

MONDAY, MAY 6, 1996

SCIENCE
TECHNOLOGY

At Banks of Future, An Eye for an ID

By Kevin McManus
Washington Post Staff Writer

The cash machine of the near future may not care about your PIN or your plastic. But it will take a quick peek at your face—specifically at the fibers, furrows, crypts, blood vessels and other minutiae of your iris.

For just over a decade, scientists have known how to delineate the characteristics that make the iris of every eye as unique as a fingerprint. But it was only in 1992 that John Daugman, then a Harvard University researcher in computational neuroscience, developed a method for digitally encoding a photographic image of an iris.

Daugman's technique has now been incorporated into an automated teller machine developed by Sensar of Princeton, N.J. Sensar, a subsidiary of the David Sarnoff Research Center Inc., made its own key contribution to the ATM: a video camera that can sense a human from a few feet away and quickly zero in on either eye.

This focusing feature enables the ATM unobtrusively to photograph an iris of a customer who simply stands facing the machine. The 256-byte code representing the image is then compared with representations in a database, and if it matches the record on file for that individual's iris, the customer can proceed with a transaction. In a recent demonstration in a Sensar lab, the scanning and matching procedure took only a few seconds. Sensar says several banks will start test-

- Another identification device being tested at the National Security Agency uses infrared light to create a three-dimensional image of a user's face. Again, the information is fed into a computer and compared with records in a database.

ing its ATM in late 1996. Should it perform well, it may give iris scanning the advantage over other "biometric" technologies that use the human body—or parts of it—as an identification standard.

Each of these competing technologies has at least one drawback sensitive enough to prevent its inclusion in a broadly applied system such as an ATM, according to biometric researchers.

- **FINGERPRINT.** Forget the ink pad. Modern fingerprinting techniques involve optical scanning and digitized images. Typically, a subject presses a fingertip against a glass plate. This delivers a copyable image, but it also may foul the plate with skin residue and dirt. Another disadvantage: Some fingertips have been scarred or worn smooth by heavy labor.

- **HAND GEOMETRY.** A subject puts the entire hand (or, for some devices, only the index and middle fingers) into an optical reader. Tests suggest scanners can quickly recognize hands that have already been digitally "enrolled" in the system. But biometrics experts believe many people won't want to stick their hands inside the machine. Also, hand and finger shapes can change because of injury and other factors, and have not been shown to be as unique as fingerprints.

- **VOICE RECOGNITION.** Devices turn an acoustic signal into a digital code, which represents a pattern of resonant frequencies

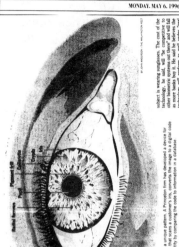

unique to each person's voice. Drawbacks include the size of the code required and the fact that an individual has to "perform" to prove his identity. Typically, he is asked to recite numbers or words based on a prompt from the machine to prevent the use of a tape recording to defeat the system. Also, people's voices can change due to illness or other factors.

- **FACE RECOGNITION.** A portion of the subject's face (usually the upper two-thirds) is photographed and the image is reduced to a digital code. The main shortcomings: People who look alike can fool some scanners, and face shapes can change with aging and weight fluctuation. Also, with two-dimensional scanners, a photograph can pass as a live subject, and with three-dimensional scanners, the size of the code is unwieldy.

- **RETINA SCANNING.** One Louisiana firm, EyeIdentify Inc., controls patents enabling it to dominate the market for this technology. Since 1976, EyeIdentify has made devices that "re-cognize" the unique pattern of blood vessels on a subject's retina (the inner layer of tissue at the back of the eye) and match it against a database of other codes. But a subject must place his face within a few inches of the scanning device.

The National Security Agency is a center

for biometric research because of its interest in protecting government buildings and data processing systems. At its Fort Meade headquarters, the NSA runs a laboratory where a half-dozen scientists evaluate identification systems. One of the researchers, Joseph P. Campbell Jr., chairs a group called the Biometrics Consortium, whose 200 members include researchers from business, academia and government. The group's homepage is: http://www.vitro.bloomington.in.us:8080/BC/

Campbell says he knows of no technology that qualifies as the "perfect biometric," suitable for any application. But he and Dave Murphy, technical director of the NSA lab, acknowledge that iris scanning has many attractions, including the iris's immutability (its pattern apparently doesn't change after the age of about 18 months), the compactness of the digital code describing it, and the unobtrusiveness of the scanning device.

Campbell and Murphy have identified three drawbacks: the difficulty of scanning very dark eyes; the cost of Sensar's ATM device (between $4,000 and $5,000); and the possibility that the technology could have a higher error rate when used by large population.

Kevin McManus is a former vice president contends that the scanner can pick up depending information from dark irises—even when the

subject is wearing sunglasses. The cost of the technology, he said, will "be competitive to other biometric systems out there" and will fall as more banks buy it. He said he believes the technology will perform as well under "real world" conditions as it has in Sensar's lab, where it has never recognized a subject who had no prior code on file.

McQuade said "six or seven banks have expressed interest in the Sensar ATM, but only one, Huntington Bancshares of Columbus, Ohio, was willing to be identified as a potential customer.

"It's unobtrusive, quick and, we think, highly reliable," said Bill Randle, a senior vice president at Huntington. He added that the Sensar scanner will be used not only in the bank's ATMs but also in "virtual branches" where customers talk to bank officers remotely, via an instant bank's lobby.

The first scientist to suggest that each iris was unique was Alphonse Bertillon, a French physician who studied the subject in the 1880s. Development of iris-scanning technology began around 1982, when American ophthalmologists Leonard Flom and Aran Safir set out to patent the idea that the iris could be used for identification. Using photos of identical twins' irises, Flom and Safir documented what they called the "random morphogenesis" of the iris. Their technique for documenting the appearance and location of crypts, filaments, freckles, pits, rings and other minutiae in the iris was awarded a patent in 1987. In 1992, Daugman, who is now a senior research fellow at Cambridge University, figured out how to turn an iris image into a 256-byte "iris code."

Courtesy of The Washington Post.

biometrics for access to Automated Teller Machines (ATMs) or for use with credit or debit cards. Many types of financial transactions are also potential applications; e.g., banking by phone, banking by Internet, and buying and selling securities by telephone or by Internet. Fraud on cellular telephone systems has increased dramatically and is estimated by some sources at over $1 billion per year. Biometrics are being considered to reduce this fraud. Telephone credit card fraud is also a significant problem that may benefit from the use of biometrics. There are also commercial applications for computer access control, access to web site servers, access through firewalls, and physical access control to protect sensitive information. [Author's note: As we learned from personal interviews with the developers of LUCID 2000™, *et al,* the "firewall" is a device created to keep the separate entities from interfering with one another's business activities, i.e., the bank records from the insurance records, from the medical records, etc., etc. Of course, there would not be a need for firewalls if they didn't plan to "centralize" or consolidate everything in one place on the same smart card, MARC card, driver's license, biochip, *et al.*]

Here are some of the Current Applications for biometrics, some of which are common knowledge and some of which may surprise you.

INSPASS — Immigration and Naturalization Service's Passenger Accelerated Service System designed to provide prompt admission for frequent travelers from foreign countries. It uses hand geometry for biometric verification. You just slide your INSPASS card through the reader and stick your hand in the guide—fast and simple. Currently in operation at John F. Kennedy Airport in New York and Newark International Airport in New Jersey.

Thermal Faceprint

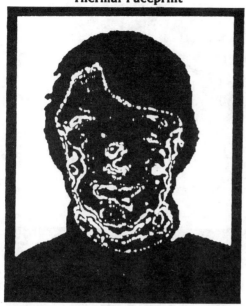

Automatic I.D. News, July, 1995, ran an interesting article on the new thermal faceprinting, "A defaced face can't beat the heat: Thermal faceprints are hot new ID method/Thermal faceprints provide new kind of secure automatic ID."

Captions under the two photos (one of the visual face and the other of the thermal scan) read: "System displays unique thermal facial characteristics which it uses to identify a face in six second."

John Burnell, News Director for *Automatic I.D. News,* writes:

"A 'hot' new technology that never forgets a face is the newest form of personal automatic identification. If you're one in a million, there are 5,000 people in the world just like you—except that your face releases heat in a pattern as unique as your fingerprint. . . .

"The system uses an infrared video camera to take a thermal picture, called a thermogram, of a face. Software processes the image and makes the recognition based on analysis of the vascular system, facial tissue, and skin heat emission. . . . Perspiration, bruises, swelling, and even plastic surgery or disguises won't change an individual's heat emission pattern.

"The applications for this technology are endless. We envision a day when consumers won't need cards at ATMs, high-level telephone communications can be fully secured, and newborns can be protected before leaving the hospital through the creation of private family records. . . . Ear and nose temperatures aren't included in the analysis because they are highly sensitive to temperature changes. The infrared camera is insensitive to light and produces accurate images in total darkness from up to four feet away, although the range could be extended. . . . the technology is more accurate than other biometric identification techniques. . . and is more user friendly because it only requires looking into a camera. . . .

" . . .TRS will pursue eight applications during the next five years: access control, computer security, identification credentials, credit card security, communications security, private records, and law enforcement support."

BENEFIT SECURITY
ard

Al Gore
1234 5678 9012 3

UNITED STATES DEPARTMENT OF JUSTICE
Immigration and Naturalization Service (Form I-833 Card)

INSERT THIS SIDE

INS PASS

This card is not valid for use as a passport or visa.

MARC

CHARLES R. WESTINGHOUSE
20/123456789   TAMC

RANK	SERVICE	STATUS	DATE OF BIRTH	BLOOD TYPE
1LT	USA	AD	19690615	O-POS

CANPASS — Canadian version of INSPASS, except the biometric used by Canada is fingerprint, rather than hand geometry. Currently in use at Vancouver International Airport.

PORTPASS — Similar to INSPASS, but is used to monitor vehicles at border crossings, as opposed to travelers at airports. It uses voice recognition rather than hand geometry. Presently used at a Canadian crossing, and planned for use at Mexican crossings soon. One version requires the vehicle to stop; another version, known as the Dedicated Commuter Lane, **uses a radio frequency tag (RFID) affixed to the vehicle in order to obtain the biometric as the vehicle is moving.** [Talk about your high-tech!]

PRISONS — The federal Bureau of Prisons is using hand geometry units to monitor the movements of prisoners, staff, and visitors within certain Federal prisons. Visitors and staff, as well as prisoners, are required to enroll and must carry at all times their magnetic striped card on which positive biometric information is embedded. According to them, "Staff are enrolled to reduce the possibility of mistakenly identifying them as an inmate or for positive identification in the event of a disturbance." [That's pretty bad when you can't tell the staff from the prisoners without a smart card.] The system also allows for the tracking of prisoners' movements. By the end of 1995, around 30 Federal prisons were to have the hand geometry monitoring system installed.

AFIRM — Automated Fingerprint Image Reporting and Match. In 1991, Los Angeles County in California installed the first AFIRM system. AFIRM was needed to reduce fraudulent and duplicate welfare benefits. The biometric used is fingerprints. L.A. County claims to have saved $5.4 million dollars in the first six months, and the savings have been growing ever since. AFIRM is expected to be in statewide operation in California by some time in 1997.

SPANISH NATIONALS (TASS) — Spanish National Social Security Identification Card. The TASS program is a smart card initiative employing fingerprint technology to eliminate enrollment duplication and provide secure access to personal information upon retrieval. The program is an ambitious one, in that it will combine pension, unemployment, and health benefits all on one card. [I guess if Bill and Hillary couldn't push the universal health card off on U.S. citizens, they decided to try it on Spanish nationals.]

COLOMBIA LEGISLATURE — Uses hand geometry units to confirm the identity of the members of its two assemblies immediately prior to a vote. [Emphasis added.]

Many Federal, State, and local government agencies have purchased biometric systems. The Defense Advanced Research Projects Agency (DARPA), Drug Enforcement Agency (DEA), Department of Defense (DoD), Department of Energy, Department of Public Safety, Department of State, Federal Bureau of Investigation, Federal Reserve Bank, Hill Air Force Base, the Pentagon, and the US Mint have approximately 250 biometric devices with 13,000 enrolled users for access control applications.

Now, for some of the Planned Applications:

DRIVER'S LICENSE — California, Colorado, Florida, and Texas have efforts underway to establish biometric-based screening of drivers. California, Colorado, and Texas already record fingerprint images on drivers' licenses, and Florida has it under consideration.

EBT — Electronic Benefits Transfer. I have given thorough coverage to EBT's, so I will not discuss it much further. However, because of the success in fraud prevention in Los Angeles County's AFIRM program, fingerprint identification is under consideration "to eliminate what could amount to extensive losses from the abuse of lost or stolen cards." [You see, even before the proposed systems are in place, they already are considering the possibilities of "lost or stolen". . . injectable biochips, here we come!]

IAFIS — The FBI's Integrated Automated Fingerprint Identification System "is designed to electronically replace the horrendously outdated, mostly manual fingerprint identification system that requires paper-based fingerprint cards, postal submissions of the cards, and labor-intensive searches." Paper cards would be replaced with electronic entries. Requests and searches would be conducted electronically. Their goal is to reduce the response time to a requesting agency from the current 10 weeks to only 24 hours.

NCIC 2000 — National Crime Information Center 2000 offers new and improved capabilities for the National Crime Information Center Biometric information, such as that contained in the signature, face, and fingerprint, will be used in an automated system. Patrol cars will have the capability to capture fingerprints and eventually relay the information to local, State, and/or Federal Automated Fingerprint Identification Systems (AFIS's). [The goal is to have the system improved and fully operational by the fall of 1999. . .which is why I suppose it is called NCIC 2000.]

Space for a Database

You may have realized that computers with enough capability to handle all that is proposed will consume monumental space, even with the size of the hardware growing constantly smaller. That's easy! Just spend some more of our money. The NSA has constructed a new building at the modest sum of $45 million. The project consists of a two-story building with approximately 100,000 square feet of net usable space for supercomputers, operational, and maintenance areas. The

NSA's new $47 million supercomputer facility at Ft. Meade, Maryland. Opened October, 1996. Internet photo.

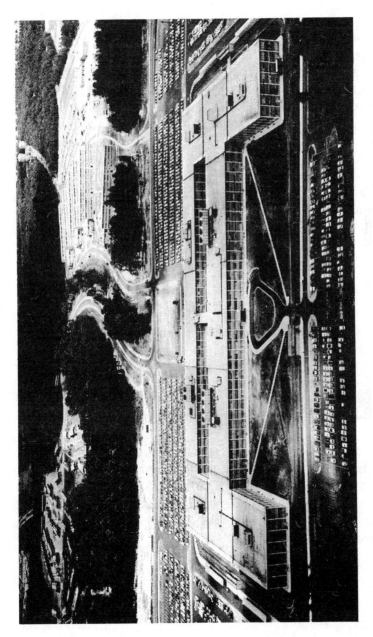

National Security Agency headquarters (circa 1957 when the NSA opened), Ft. George G. Meade, Maryland. Photo Credit: Department of Defense.

facility was turned over to NSA on October 15, 1996, and was scheduled for completion in January, 1997.

Indeed, resting today in the cavernous subterranean expanses below the National Security Agency's Headquarters/Operations Building is the **greatest concentration of highly advanced computers the world has ever known!** The NSA's enormous basement, which stretches for city blocks, holds the largest and most advanced computer database site in the world in a 1996 list that's available from the Internet. Yes, **this list ranks the NSA as number one out of 194 of the most powerful computing sites on earth**. A copy of this list is available by writing the following E-mail address on the Internet:

gunter@interactive.net

The NSA: "666-Beast" Computer Facility

Contrary to the previously held popular belief that the "666-Beast Computer" resides in Luxembourg, Europe, it really resides here in America at NSA! This unbelievably sophisticated place is the land where computers literally talk back and forth with one another and where, using what is called "brute force," they are able to spit out solutions to complex statistical problems in **nanoseconds** rather than years.

In 1983 the NSA went global. It put into operation an enormous worldwide computer system of networked databases code named **PLATFORM**. PLATFORM tied together 52 existing but separate computer database systems used throughout the world. Of course, since 1983, many more have joined NSA's network.

The National Security Agency is the Mother of America's Computer Industry

The National Security Agency has been a silent but very powerful partner in America's computer growth from the very beginning! Yet, because of its policy of secretive anonymity,

NSA's role has been almost totally hidden behind quiet grants and funding to the computer industry. Despite the anonymity, however, NSA's involvement in creating the computer industry has been enormous. Cray, IBM, RCA, Sperry Rand, Philco, General Electric, Burroughs, Texas Instruments, Sematech, and many other corporations too numerous to list, all have benefitted handsomely from NSA grants and contracts for the development of advanced computer systems and peripheral functions. In fact, several years ago, the NSA boasted of its role in the development of the computer industry by stating the "NSA certainly hastened the start of the computer age."

T3E Cray Supercomputer. Courtesy of Cray Computers.

In 1976, for example, Cray Research of Minneapolis, Minnesota, created and delivered to NSA the first of two "CRAY-1" $15 million computers. Cray Research was founded by Seymour Cray, an electronics engineer who also founded the Control Data Corporation in 1957. Mr. Cray's "CRAY-1" was capable of crunching anywhere from **150 to 200 million calculations PER SECOND!** Now that sounds like it would fit the description of a supercomputer! But as incredible as it seems, the CRAY-1 utilizes 20-year-old technology. Today's Cray supercomputers, the most advanced in the world, can crunch mind-boggling numbers up to **60 billion calculations per second (60 GFLOPS)!** For example, the NSA presently employs the latest **CRAY Model T3E-LC1024** supercomputer. The CRAY T3E-LC1024 is the most complex and sophisticated machine in the world. For more information on CRAY computers, call the factory at (612) 452-6650, or use the Internet to write Cray's E-mail at:

(crayinfo@cray.com)

Supercomputers will be contributing greatly to our surveillance and enslavement as we move further down the slippery slope toward the New World Order.

Remember, all this R & D in the computer industry has been subsidized or underwritten by the NSA. NSA's supercomputers utilize the latest **GFLOPS** and *PETAFLOPS* computing technology. This existing state-of-the-art technology would seem fantastic enough without further improvement. But soon, supercomputing **TERAFLOPS** technology will be capable of performing an unbelievable **trillion operations per second**. Without NSA funding, however, none of these technologies would exist. Is it any wonder with that kind of investment that this technology is doubling every 18 months? It's a case of more is better, but only if it's smaller and faster. Indeed, NSA money has been responsible for the development of virtually all of this technology, either directly or indirectly, from the very beginning. The NSA is even bold enough to admit this in one of their documents that can be down-loaded from its Internet website as follows:

> NSA has been a silent partner with private industry from the earliest days of postwar computer development.
>
> Many commercial computer lines have sprouted from earlier designs for NSA use. A good example of this computer industry/government partnership was HARVEST, a cooperative project in the 1950's between NSA and IBM [note the very early NSA/IBM connection here] to build a new, state-of-the-art second-generation general-purpose processor. To be successful, HARVEST had to have a super high-speed memory and high-speed tape drives, beyond anything then in existence. Developed over a five-year period, the most innovative new component of this advanced processor was TRACTOR, the high-speed tape drive system. HARVEST went on line in 1962, and it was finally retired in 1976. **Since the beginning of the computer age, a partnership between NSA and the American computer industry has existed.** This partnership has fostered the development of computers for cryptologic processes. [Emphasis added.]

Actually, quite a bit of information is presently available on the Internet regarding the kinds of advanced supercomputers the NSA now uses. But suffice it to say at this point, most of NSA's high-dollar, sophisticated supercomputing technology is based on something called **nanotechnology.** Nanotechnology is the technological method of creating **ultra-small micro mechanical devices** on an **atomic scale.**

How can this be possible!?! In the Bible we are told that in the last days knowledge would increase, with the implication that it would increase exponentially. If nothing else proves that we are in the last days, surely this would. Presently, technology is doubling every 18 months, and it would appear that this time is decreasing daily. Science is now capable of engineering computer chips and other mechanical devices **down to nearly the size of a single atom.** Dictionaries define *atoms* as "the smallest particles of chemical elements that can exist alone or in combinations." Just imagine what Lucifer, the Antichrist, will be able to do with all this advanced technology during the Tribulation Period. He will be able to "watch" and control **everyone** and **everything** on earth . . . He does not have the ability that God has to be omnipresent, so this technology will provide him with the ability to be "technically" omnipresent. This will result in the most com-prehensive form of **electronic surveillance and enslave-ment** imaginable. I call this concept of electronic control **CYBERIA,** a new kind of **Russian Siberia in Cyberspace**. There is more detailed information on E-Money and the cashless society in my book *The Mark of the New World Order.*

The National Security Agency Even Manufactures Some of Its Own Computer Chips

The NSA even has its own "special processing" manufac-turing facility for making its own highly classified computer chips. NSA states in one of its published documents available on the Internet that "NSA has exacting requirements for **special computer chips**. Because of the difficulty of satisfy-ing its needs on the commercial market, and because of **the highly classified nature of some of the chips**, in **1990** NSA opened a facility to **fabricate otherwise unobtainable** devices to support the needs of the DOD" [emphasis added]. What kinds of chips are these? The NSA designed and made the Clipper Chip, the Skipjack, and the Capstone Chip. (Coin-cidentally(?), "Capstone" is the term for the all-seeing eye on top of the Masonic pyramid on the back of our dollar bills.) We also know something about a so-called private corporation closely affiliated with them, **Sematech Corporation in Austin, Texas**. Sematech is making some of the most advanced chips on earth. It is a research and development (R & D) lab that is a consortium of very large electronics and defense companies, such as Motorola, Texas Instruments, etc. **Sema-**

tech is affiliated with the government's Advanced Research Projects Agency (ARPA—subsequently DARPA) in Virginia. In fact, Sematech gets most of its funds from ARPA, which is essentially a "back-door" funding organization of the NSA. Note how they all work together for the goals of Big Brother! The NSA is, indeed, developing a computer system of Orwellian proportions.

New ARPA/Sematech 0.25 Micron-sized Computer Chips will be Capable of Storing One Billion Bits of Data!

Sematech Corporation in Austin, Texas, now manufactures and markets computer chips that are **0.35 microns in size**. That's equivalent to about 1/200th the size of a strand of human hair. If that capability alone were not enough to boggle one's mind, Sematech is now perfecting the manufacturing of even smaller chips that will be about **0.25 microns in size.**

In 1988, **Mr. Robert Noyce** began leading Sematech in the development of these advanced technologies. Mr. Noyce is none other than the founder of **Intel Corporation,** as well as the physicist genius **who invented the original silicon-chip integrated circuit**. His invention brought about the entire PC revolution and led to the extensive use of microchips in all of today's consumer products. With a guy like this running the show, what do you think Sematech may be capable of producing in the future? I'm sure that what is considered science fiction today, will be tomorrow's standard technology (for a little while, at least, until the next "better and smaller" innovations overtake it and render it obsolete).

Rumor has it that Sematech's new chips will be capable of storing approximately **one billion bits of data!** That's called a **"GIGA"** or one billion pieces of data. The newer personal computers presently available commercially typically are capable of storing one gigabyte (one billion bytes) or more of data on their huge hard disks. Such hard disk storage capability is incredible enough, but just imagine **a single**

chip that is capable of storing one billion bits of information. What an almost unbelievable accomplishment!

ARPA Helped Finance
Sematech Corporation's Research

As indicated above, **Sematech Corporation was funded by the illustrious Advanced Research Projects Agency** of the DOD, which is indirectly tied to NSA. In other words, **ARPA and NSA** were right there helping Sematech with all the money it could handle in order to get quantum computing science rolling. An interesting thing about Sematech, however, is the fact that one of its major "partners" is **Texas Instruments Corporation.** Coincidentally(?) Texas Instruments is a very large **manufacturer of biochip transponder RFID microchip implants for animal identification.** Do you see how all of this ties together? It's just one huge Big-Brother conspiracy designed to bring forth Satan's evil, communistic/socialistic New World Order of electronic enslavement.

Project Lucifer: IBM's Demonic
Connection to NSA

During the late 1960's, IBM board chairman, Thomas Watson, Jr., set up a cryptology research group at IBM's research laboratory in Yorktown Heights, New York. Led by Horst Feistel, the research group concluded its work in 1971 with the development of a **very advanced new CIPHER CODE named "LUCIFER"** (the dictionary defines *cipher* as "an arithmetically computable code"). No one really knows with any degree of certainty why the name Lucifer was chosen for this computer program, but the fact remains that it was! I find this particularly interesting given the fact that everyone knows the name Lucifer is just another name for the devil, Satan! In fact, as I informed you earlier, **many dictionaries define "Lucifer" as "used as a name for the devil."**

After Lucifer's creation, IBM immediately sold it to **Lloyd's**

of London Insurance Company for use in their **cash-dispensing system**, which IBM also developed. **Lucifer** was very successful in this banking application.

The "Lucifer" Cipher was Transformed into a "Highly Marketable Commodity"

Spurred by the success of Lucifer, IBM turned to Walter Tuchman, a 38-year-old engineer with a doctorate in information theory, then assigned to IBM's Kingston development lab. A 16-year veteran of IBM, Tuchman was asked to lead a data security products group that would **transform Lucifer into a "highly marketable commodity."** The Lucifer Cipher was ready for market in 1974.

Aided by Carl Meyer, a German-born electrical engineer who had earned his doctorate from the University of Pennsylvania, Tuchman soon discovered that Lucifer would require "considerable strengthening before it could withstand massive commercial use." The team then spent the following two years improving the Lucifer Cipher by giving it more complex functions. The strengthening process involved intense "validation," whereby experts would bombard Lucifer with sophisticated "cryptanalytic" attacks. Finally, in 1974, "the Lucifer Cipher was ready for market."

During the same year, the US National Bureau of Standards (NBS) decided to search for a cipher encryption method *that could serve as a government-wide standard* for the storage and transmission of data. IBM submitted their Lucifer Cipher code to NBS for their consideration for government-wide adoption.

The NSA Was Enormously Interested in the Lucifer Project

According to James Bamford, author of *The Puzzle Palace: Inside the National Security Agency, America's Most Secret Intelligence Organization,* the 1983 bestseller previously cited in this book:

> The NSA had taken an enormous interest in Project Lucifer from the very beginning. . . .
> **The NSA had even indirectly lent a hand in Lucifer's development** [emphasis added].

According to Alan Konheim, a senior employee at IBM's Yorktown Heights lab, **"IBM was involved with the NSA on an ongoing basis."**

Here is the information you will need to obtain a copy of *The Puzzle Palace:* Published by Penguin Books USA, Inc., 375 Hudson Street, New York, NY 10014, Phone 1-800-253-6476 (ISBN 0-14-006748-5).

External "Clean-up" at the NSA

Recently, the NSA has attempted to clean up its "super-secret" illusive image by forming a new public-affairs/public-relations office at their headquarters facility in Fort Meade, Maryland. The NSA even has published a small new slick-looking brochure of general information designed for public consumption, which is available to virtually anyone who calls and asks for it. The brochure may be obtained by calling NSA's public affairs office in Fort Meade, (301) 688-6311. Their new global Internet website is located in *cyberspace* at:

www.nsa.gov:8080

This should help you in doing your own research on NSA.

Warning! Don't be entrapped by the NSA's new smoke-screen attempt at public relations! Big Brother simply is trying to clean up his image with a slick new marketing campaign. Isn't poison always marketed with positive, glowing sales hyperbole telling how it will help alleviate vermin and pestilence? And, of course, that's true in many cases. But **poison** also is capable of killing all other living things it touches. Therefore, who is to say that the *poisonous NSA databases* won't someday touch all of our lives in a similar negative way? This chapter is so long because we wanted to give great detail about this monstrous "all-seeing" National Security Agency.

LUCID 2000™—A Brief Look

Dr. Jean-Paul Creusat, designer of the LUCID 2000™ system, granted me a lengthy interview in which he provided the details about how this system came to be created and how it is planned to operate in the near future. This is not one of the "secret projects". . . in fact, it is publicized widely. Dr. Creusat is a fine gentleman with the best of intentions and impeccable credentials and experience. But LUCID 2000™ inevitably will be tied with the NSA supercomputers, so I am including a very brief overview at this point.

In the July/August, 1994 edition of *The Narc Officer* magazine, page 69ff, an article appeared titled: "Year 2000 & 'L.U.C.I.D.© System': A Milestone to Curtail Terrorists and International Organized Crime." He gives an introduction spelling out all the horror stories we have heard in the last few years, and how they have increased more recently, about drug deals, money laundering, organized crime, terrorists, *et al.* After laying the foundation for the need for such a high-tech identification system, Creusat espouses the opinion that the "future universal intelligence Super Highway" will be the "LUCID 2000™ System."

> Born from the inspiration of the intricate geometrical structure of the DNA chain (the famous double helix), where the genetic blueprint of life is contained in one molecule, L.U.C.I.D.© System will contain the equivalent capacity of millions of individual data integrated within one translucent device. . . .The model proposal will be molded impartially within official cards or documents such as:
>
> Health care
> Driver's license
> Identification
> Credit cards and bank cards
> Passport or refugee documents, and
> Social Security

L.U.C.I.D.© will be capable of storing and **updating "up-to-the-minute personalized information** from an individualized master data bank" [emphasis added].

This is where the aforementioned "firewall" allegedly will be used, to prevent cross-contamination (my choice of words) between entities whose information is on the card and to limit who has access to which part (supposedly to protect the privacy of your many assorted transactions and prevent unauthorized exchange of information).

Next, we are given the "curtail the terrorists and international organized crime" speech, i.e. "Threat to the World Security," "Challenge to World Governments," and "Global Threat to the Quality of Life." In this section (page 70), he defines Major Drug-Producing Countries and Major Drug-Transit Countries, then identifies the countries involved in either or both of these. Next he defines and identifies Major Money Laundering Countries, followed by a report on alliances between terrorists and international organized crime. Creusat defines and provides examples of "Criminal organization," and gives quite a breakdown on terrorists, including definitions for the terms *terrorism, international terrorism,* and *terrorist group.*

Since this publication is specifically designed for law enforcement use worldwide, Creusat included in the article an extensive listing of terrorist groups currently associated with international organized crime. The listing provides the name of the terrorist group, and any aliases under which they may have operated, the origins of the group, the area(s) of operation, and who is supporting their activities. Now, for law enforcement, this is a wonderful collection of information to have available; however, in my opinion and by their own admission, the use of LUCID 2000™ will not end there. It quickly will filter down to the private sector keeping track of all the transactions (buying, selling, political activity, protests, etc.) in your life, and no one but them determines *what* will be collected or *how it will be used. Your purchases and phone service already are being profiled. . . where do you think most of your junk mail originates, or how your credit card company or phone company can notify you of "unusual" purchases on your card?*

He gives an extensive look at worldwide "safehavens" for terrorists and international organized crime, followed by the locations considered to be safehavens. On page 74, Creusat says, "There are a number of major criminal organizations, two of which have a worldwide grasp and are directly impairing world security: The Colombian drug cartels and the Chinese criminal groups organized around Triad secret societies." Then he describes ten groups, with brief comments on their activities.

Dr. Creusat sees the LUCID 2000™ System as a "universal application to the Criminal Justice System and the *future antagonist to terrorist and international organized crime.*" Creusat concludes:

> Properly employed L.U.C.I.D.© would curtail the new breed of international organized crime challenging governments throughout the world. The System Proposal will create a climate that makes it *more difficult and expensive* for such criminals to operate. [Notice that even he does not kid himself into expecting this to be a cure-all for international crime and terrorism. The fact is, those groups can afford the skilled individuals to evade these restrictions, probably better than LUCID 2000™'s supporters. The criminal element has no sense of morality, therefore, it has no compunctions about doing whatever it takes to achieve its ends.]
>
> As the information age progresses, the most successful institutions and entities will be those that first perceive and exploit the potential of new technologies. This proposal is intended to advance the prospect that cooperating world governments, operating on behalf of their citizens and against international criminals, will enjoy the full benefit of available technology [interpret

that as exchange of information, networking, or just plain Internet] **to create the best possible tracking system** for the present and to develop a framework that may be adapted as new technologies continue to emerge. [Emphasis added.]

There you have it . . . this program wouldn't be very effective if the database *didn't* contain as much information as could be collected on **everybody**, because until they run the subject through the computers, they have no sure way of knowing who might be involved, drug dealers, criminals, or terrorists . . . it might even be a US citizen (big surprise!), so they want that database to be as comprehensive and all-inclusive as they can get it—which means making the facilities and hardware large enough to hold all the information they will be collecting, then loading it up with everything they can find on anybody, via the US Postal Service, Social Security, welfare benefits, sales and purchases profiles, driver's license data, religious affiliation, *et al.* Now, if you project this information forward to the time when a dictator wants to take over our country, or merge us into the New World Order (same thing!), it will be a relatively simple task, as he will know where to locate all the dissenters and protesters. He will have control through the international military, and easily can dispatch such Constitutionalists to the large federal prison facilities that have been built on the perimeters of major airports. As you can see in my scenario, one thing leads to the next, and the next, and the next. It truly is a "slippery slope."

In the September/October edition of *The Narc Officer,* page 54ff, the article is titled "L.U.C.I.D.© & The Counter-Terrorism Act of 1995." This article includes an Abstract, an Introduction, Future Trends in the World Security, L.U.C.I.D. System Specific Objectives, but probably the scariest is their admission about linking and Internet use.

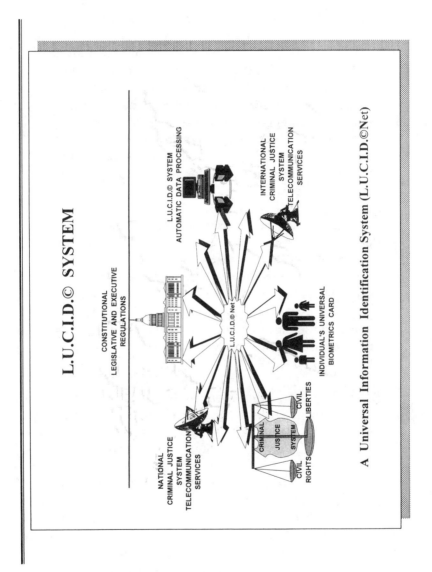

Courtesy of The Narc Officer *magazine.*

Connect the Existing Data Elements to the L.U.C.I.D.© System via L.U.C.I.D.© Net

The data elements from the networks of federal, state, and local government agencies; public and private non-profit organizations; NCIC, NCB-INTERPOL, Triple I, and Department of Justice and the NLETS **identification management systems will feed the Universal Computerized Identification Clearinghouse Resource Center** [who fits the decription in that title better than the NSA?] **through an instantaneous tracking system via cyberspace.** L.U.C.I.D.© Net will be designed to take advantage of the current infrastructure of popular and **readily available commercial equipment that operate under** the Transmission Control Protocol/**Internet Protocol**, TACP/IP protocols.

Developed under **ARPA sponsorship [NSA],** the current **Internet** grew out of the original **ARPANET** project, initiated at UCLA in 1969. . . . ARPANET was transferred to the Defense Communication Agency (now the Defense Information Systems Agency—DISA). . . [emphasis added].

This article also addresses: Interactive Information via Cyberspace from Distant Biometrics Sensors and/or Biometrics Card Sensors; the Future Universal Biometrics Card (a "Smart Card," undoubtedly similar in construction and purpose to the military MARC card); Security and Confidentiality of the Universal Information Identification System through L.U.C.I.D.© Net.

As universal access to the Internet implies equal and reasonable opportunity for the individual to be connected, the question was raised in a front-page article in the January 23, 1995, edition of *U.S. NEWS:* **"Is anything Safe in Cyberspace?"** I guess we all know the answer to that. In the same edition, Vic Sussman treated the crucial subject of "Policing Cyberspace."

Probably the most helpful information in this second article

is Creusat's listing of "Key Words." Though not as comprehensive as the list in *The Puzzle Palace,* it tells about those
that are of most importance to the LUCID 2000™ project.
Please take note of the ones with NSA connections (see
next chapter on sister organizations) and how many are based
on information retrieved on individual citizens, rather than
"international crime and terrorist" organizations.

Key Words

National Crime Information Center (NCIC) 2000;
Integrated Automated Fingerprint Identification System
(IAFIS); National Instant Criminal Background (NICB);
Interstate Identification Index (III) or Triple I; National
Central Bureau (NCB)—Interpol; Computerized Crim-
inal History (CCH); National Strategy Information Center
(NSIC); Omnibus Counter-Terrorism Act of 1995, H.R.
896 and S. 390; Counter-terrorist Center (CTC); Bulletin
Board Service (B.B.S.); National Law Enforcement Tele-
communications System [(NLETS); Advanced Research]
Projects Agency (ARPA); ARPANET; Defense Information
Systems Agency (DISA); Biometrics Sensors: Biometrics
Card Sensors; L.U.C.I.D.© System Universal Biometrics
Card; DNA genotyping and Human Leukocyte Antigen;
Iris scan; "Smart Card"; Computer Emergency Response
Team (now known as the Cert Coordination Center);
Capstone Chip; Clipper's Skipjack; Tessera PCMCIA card;
"Password Sniffer"; International Criminal Police Organi-
zation (ICPO)—INTERPOL.

In brief, the terms *Capstone Chip* and *Clipper's Skipjack* (both
of which were designed and made at NSA's chip-manufacturing
facility), which are mentioned near the end of the above list,
are examples of those "backdoor keys" we mentioned earlier,
so that access can be gained—by the government and who
knows who or what else—to your so-called privacy-protected,
encrypted information and transactions. The connection to
NSA or its sister organizations is quite evident, as documented

in the book by Daniel C. Lynch and Leslie Lundquist, titled, *Digital Money: The New Era of Internet Commerce,* pages 95-98, the sections dealing with Capstone, Clipper, and Skipjack.

Declassification of NSA Documents

Under the Freedom of Information Act everything older than 25 years supposedly is to be declassified and made available to anyone seeking information on a particular subject. This is operating on the premise that anything 25 years or older has little if any remaining value as sensitive data. Again working on their image, the NSA issued a press release on April 2, 1996, titled, "The National Security Agency Releases Over 1.3 Million Pages of Declassified Documents." Of course, this was to promote good will and enhance their image with the general public. They still will not release any documents which might reflect badly on their activities in those early days, and other documents are "released" with black marked out lines of the things they still don't want made available for general distribution or disclosure. Mainly what has been released so far are the communications by the KGB and other entities that took place during the Cold War era. There is a massive list of documents which you may research at NSA's location on the Internet, with instructions how to obtain something you may desire to see first hand.

Suing the NSA

Much unnecessary to-do has been made in some publications about a lawsuit brought against the NSA. I began to investigate this suit, its ramifications, and its ultimate disposition. The Clerk's Office of the U.S. District Court, Washington, DC, gladly made available all documentation pertaining to said action. The suit was filed in the United States District Court on February 20, 1992, and was brought by petitioner John S. Akwei. His statement justifying the suit read: "Prevented from obtaining gainful employment by defendants [NSA], who utilized National Security Agency offices and resources to control and at their will illegally discontinue my employment."

After hearing his detailed list of allegations, the Court determined that there was not "any identifiable legal cause of action. Accordingly, it will be dismissed as frivolus pursuant to 28 U.S.C. s/s 1915(d). It is this 6th day of March, 1992, hereby ORDERED that this complaint is dismissed. Stanley Sporkin, United States District Court."

Of course, I certainly wouldn't put it past the NSA to do something like this, or even worse, but that was not the case in this suit. If you read the plaintiff's allegations, you readily will understand why this was determined to be a frivolous lawsuit and ultimately dismissed. It appears that he had a bigger case of paranoia than any genuine, legitimate, provable complaints.

In addition to this action, the NSA has been sued several times during its 40-year history, including a suit filed by Jane Fonda and Tom Hayden in the 1970's.

If you wish more details, contact Amy Gordon, ITS, Inc., Document Retrieval & Research Services, in Washington, DC, Phone (202) 857-3837.

Lucifer's Evil Spirit is Alive & Well in the New Global Economic & Communications System

Lucifer is, indeed, alive and well on planet earth! The Bible tells us that he will enslave the world by controlling our buying and selling in the last days. Without his "666" I.D. "mark," we will be unable to transact business globally. And just in case you conclude that you never need to transact any business globally—you'll just do business locally—don't kid yourself. . . globally means everywhere on the globe, including your little community, no matter how isolated it may seem by today's standards. One easily can see this diabolical plan unfolding if one is a "born-again" believer in the Lord Jesus Christ! With Christ's Holy Spirit resident in us, we can envision easily how Satan's plan is unfolding in many respects. One can see it in the global computer industry, the New-World-Order socialist UN-led global government; the World Wide Web of the Internet; the imminent cashless electronic commerce system in the form of various electronic funds transfer programs called EBT; and the loss of constitutionally guaranteed privacy rights, due to the computerization and **networking/linking** of all private, corporate, city, county, federal, and international government databases with the **National Security Agency's** supercomputers.

The LUCID 2000™ I.D. Mark: Without it, You're Out of Business!

We are being told today that the major problem encountered in making electronic transactions via networked databases is ensuring that all users of the system are, indeed, who they say they are and being able to securely guarantee your monetary transaction out in cyberspace. In other words, all users must be positively identified. We also are told that what must become mandatory by the year 2000 are more advanced, high-tech forms of positive identification. System users first must be verifiably **identified biometrically** before being permitted access to the new Internet-connected electronic bartering system. Without positive and secure individual identification, fraudulent activities may result, they say. **Enter the Mark-of-the-Beast system: LUCID 2000™**! Satan's LUCID 2000™ System of international identification will perform this function. Without the **LUCID 2000™ Mark**, no one will be able to access "electronic money or credits," or any other government "benefits" (i.e., welfare, IRS, Social Security, health, "entitlements" funds, and other agencies), anywhere in the world. Satan's Mark-of-the-Beast in everyone's **right hands** will be **mandatory!** (And you can see how quickly this "danger" of Smart Cards being "lost or stolen" can progress to RFID implants that you *can't* lose.) Furthermore, rejecting the Mark literally **will cost you your life!** Indeed, rejecting the MARK will sentence you to death in the New World Order!

For more information on this subject, please refer to my first book, *The Mark of the New World Order,* and watch the bookstores for my forthcoming publications, *Big Brother's Supercomputers* and *America's Identity Crisis and the Coming International I.D. Card.* The NSA's "Little Brother/Sister" organizations are inextricably linked like a spider web.

NSA: Lucifer's "Beast" Computer

As mentioned earlier in this chapter, many Christians have speculated and talked about a "666 Beast" computer system in Europe being the *major* database system the Antichrist will use to control people. However, my thorough investigation of this matter reveals that this is not true . . . it cannot possibly be the system. Yes, there is a huge "classified" computer system in Belgium that is owned, controlled, and operated by the European Community (EC), but it is **far inferior** to NSA's equipment and capability. Accordingly, my educated, well-investigated opinion is that the NSA will become "The 666 Beast" computer system. The NSA is behind virtually everything.

I will close this chapter by repeating a portion that I quoted earlier, by Senator Frank Church about the "Big Brother" activities of the intelligence gathering agencies, NSA in particular (see page 477 of *The Puzzle Palace). It definitely bears repeating!*

> At the same time, that capability at any time could be turned around on the American people and no **American would have any privacy left,** such [is] the capability to monitor everything: telephone conversations, telegrams, it doesn't matter. **There would be no place to hide.** If this government ever became a tyranny, if a dictator ever took charge in this country, the technological capacity that the intelligence community has given the government could enable it to impose total tyranny, and there would be no way to fight back, because

the most careful effort to combine together in resistance to the government, no matter how privately it was done, is within the reach of the government to know. Such is the capability of this technology. . . .

I don't want to see this country ever go across the bridge. I know the capacity that is there to make tyranny total in America, and we must see to it that this agency and all agencies that possess this technology operate within the law and under proper supervision, so that we never cross over that abyss. **That is the abyss from which there is no return** [emphasis added].

The National Security Agency's Sister Intelligence Agencies: Lucifer's True Worldwide Computer Web!

Because, following extensive research, it is my opinion that the National Security Agency (NSA) is at the very heart of the accumulation of the myriad of facts available on each individual, and corporate, bank, military, or governmental agency—at any level—I have been extensive in the discussion and documentation in the previous chapter. Like an octopus whose tentacles reach out and grab, then draw in to itself, the NSA is drawing in an ever-increasing database on *everyone and everything*. **It's all for one and one for all in the NSA's computerized New World Order!**

The U.S. Intelligence Community—Defined

In Jeffrey T. Richelson's outstanding book, *The U.S. Intelligence Community* (Third Edition, 1995, Westview Press, Boulder, Colorado), he deals very thoroughly with as many of the NSA's sister intelligence organizations as I have seen anywhere in one publication—I highly recommend this valuable book, the Contents of which is reprinted in part on the next two pages. Perhaps "sister" organizations could be more accurately defined as "Little Brothers," who collect and funnel information to the Big Brother computers at the NSA.

CONTENTS

Courtesy of Jeffrey T. Richelson, The U.S. Intelligence Community.

Courtesy of Jeffrey T. Richelson, **The U.S. Intelligence Community.**

Richelson has this to say about the intelligence community in the United States:

The Intelligence Community

The U.S. intelligence community has been precisely defined in a number of government directives and regulations. One of those regulations stated that:

> The CIA, the NSA, DIA, the [National Reconnaissance Office, the Bureau of Intelligence and Research of the Department of State, the intelligence elements of the military services, the FBI, the Department of the Treasury, the DOE, the Drug Enforcement Administration, and the staff elements of the Director of Central Intelligence constitute the intelligence community.

Recent additions to the community are the Central Imagery Office [replaced by NIMA 10-1-96] and the Defense HUMINT Service. Also worthy of consideration are the Defense Mapping Agency, the intelligence components of the unified commands, and the intelligence elements of the Department of Commerce. These intelligence elements, along with those mentioned directly above, can be grouped into five categories:

- national intelligence organizations,
- Department of Defense intelligence organizations,
- military service intelligence organizations,
- the intelligence components of the unified commands,
- and civilian intelligence organizations.

Presently, all of these are under the auspices—or are working in conjunction with—the NSA.

Just try to grasp the magnitude of eavesdropping and spying that is going on today throughout the world, even if we stopped with only those revealed by Richelson. Yet, we can't stop there because that is only just the beginning—we must consider all the nongovernmental agencies out there collecting information, developing profiles on our buying habits, and telephone calling habits, our health and insurance, our travel, our banking activities, etc., etc. In order to enable you to keep these separate in your minds, I have labeled them as *direct* and governmental or nongovernmental *indirect* intelligence organizations. Later in this chapter I will expand on this information, but for now, here is a brief explanation of how I define the two terms:

> **Direct Intelligence Organizations** — Designed for intelligence-gathering purposes only.
> **Indirect Intelligence Organizations** — All other private and governmental organizations with a specified purpose *other than* intelligence gathering (i.e., the IRS who gathers plenty of information on folks, but the purpose[?] allegedly is to collect income tax, not just information). These groups indirectly and ultimately download data into the *direct* intelligence organization's database.

One more definition you should recognize is for the "Black Chambers Projects," or some variation on that name. Basically, it's all that super secret stuff, particularly secret funding of projects it wants to keep under wraps.

The NSA, either directly or indirectly, is affiliated with many external, national, and international governmental organizations and private corporations that have a working agreement to exchange information on citizens. (Although I suspect—with a few notable exceptions—that most of the information "exchanging" is going in one direction . . . toward the expanding of the NSA database.)

Sister Organizations of the NSA (Little Brothers)

In this chapter, I will address the many major groups linked with the NSA, identifying them either as "direct" or "indirect" suppliers of gathered information. As I promised previously, I will define more extensively "direct" organizations as those whose primary purpose is to intercept, decode, and report on intelligence for government use and security. I define "indirect" organizations as those who collect infinite amounts of data on individuals for governmental use (i.e., IRS, Postal Service, Department of Motor Vehicles, Voter Registration, Social Security, *et al*) and/or nongovernmental use (such as credit bureaus, insurance companies, banks, *et al*), but whose data we now find channeled into the NSA supercomputers.

On the Internet (http://www.odci.gov/ic/usic/chart.gif) a circular chart is presented (see next page) showing the participation of the governmental organizations under the directorship of the Director of Central Intelligence (DCI). As I explained to you previously, the DCI also serves as head of the CIA, but seems to have less control over intelligence-gathering activities than the head of the NSA. You will note that the CIA is listed as an independent agency, while the Departments of State, Energy, and Treasury are listed as indirect agencies, meaning nonmilitary/security spying groups, but all spokes in the intelligence wheel are under the DCI. As I proceed, I will tell you a little about each of these, without going into too much detail because of space constraints. There are 12 of them (excluding the NSA which already has been covered extensively), plus many other direct and indirect foreign and/or national agencies to investigate, documenting their tie-in with the NSA or other groups with whom information is exchanged/shared.

Investigation confirms that there is little or no difference between them, even though their names and publicly announced goals vary widely. Virtually all government databases already have been—or soon will be—linked together fully at the local,

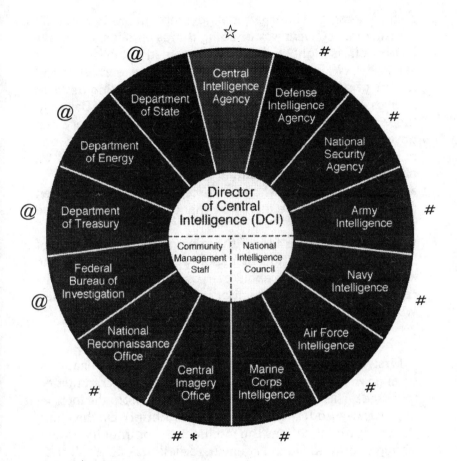

☆ Independent Agency

\# Department of Defense (DoD) Elements

@ Department Intelligence Elements (Other than DoD)

* Effective October 1, 1996 the CIO was replaced by the
   National Imagery & Mapping Agency (NIMA)

state, federal, and international government levels. After all, it's the most *efficient* way of doing things, and it should save us tax dollars, right? Even privately owned databases are for sale, i.e. TRW, Equifax, the US Postal Service, and other collectors of personal information, thereby becoming *de facto* sources of information for the government databanks. Basically, the federal government has turned most civilian, military, and government databases—at virtually every level—into one huge networked, interconnected NSA system that **will be shared** with the United Nations, Russia, Interpol, Europol . . . actually, with anyone who asks, *except YOU!* The term often used today to describe this phenomenon is **shared database resources**.

Now, let's study a few of these computerized sources of intelligence information that soon will allow Big Brother to know nearly everything about everyone, so that he more easily can track, control, and monitor us in the communistic New World Order.

The US Government's Thirteen

First, let's start with the government's own organizational breakdown pie chart of the so-called "Intelligence Community" (pictured). This information was downloaded from the Internet at (http://www.odci.gov/ic/usic/contents.html). On the chart, the government defines the intelligence community as consisting of only 13 federal agencies (as follows), but I will show later that these 13 are barely the tip of the iceberg. There are so many organizations involved in either direct or indirect spying, information gathering, and surveillance—both overt and covert—that I am confident no one has an exhaustive list . . . they just keep popping up!

- Central Intelligence Agency
- Defense Intelligence Agency
- National Security Agency
- National Reconnaissance Office
- The Central Imagery Office (Effective October 1, 1996,

replaced by the NIMA)
- Army Intelligence
- Naval Intelligence
- Marine Corps Intelligence
- Air Force Intelligence
- Department of State/Bureau of Intelligence and Research
- Department of Energy
- The Treasury Department/Office of Intelligence Support/ Financial Crimes Enforcement Network (FINCEN)
- The Federal Bureau of Investigation/National Crime Information Center/Interstate ID Index/Criminal Justice Information Services Division (formerly known as The National ID Center)

Now, let's break down the above information into categories a little easier to examine. I'll also add a few that were not listed above, for a more complete picture.

National Intelligence Organizations:
- National Security Agency (NSA), the largest intelligence database in the world!
- Central Intelligence Agency (CIA)
- National Reconnaissance Office (NRO)
- Central Imagery Office (CIO—effective October 1, 1996, replaced by NIMA)

Civilian Intelligence Organizations
- Department of State Intelligence (DSI)
- Department of the Treasury Intelligence (FINCEN)
- Department of Commerce Intelligence (DCI)
- Drug Enforcement Administration Intelligence (DEA)
- Department of Energy Intelligence (DEI)
- Federal Bureau of Investigation (FBI)/National Crime Information Center (NCIC 2000)
- Department of Transportation Intelligence (DOT)
- Federal Emergency Management Agency (FEMA). Discussed extensively in my book *The Mark of the New World*

Order; expected to play a major role in the control and re-location of US citizens, our goods, supplies, etc., in conjunction with the United Nations' military apparatus (or some other name with the same implications) to enforce compliance with the dictates of the New World Order after our takeover.

- National Law Enforcement Telecommunications System Projects Agency (NLETSPA)
- Multi-Jurisdictional Task Force (MJTF)

Defense Department/Military Intelligence Organizations

- Defense Intelligence Agency (DIA)
- Defense Human Intelligence Service (HUMINT)
- Defense Mapping Agency (DMA)
- Army Intelligence Organizations (AIO)
- Navy Intelligence Organizations (NIO)
- Air Force Intelligence Organizations (AFIO)/Air Force Systems Command (AFSC)
- Marine Corps Intelligence Organizations (MCIO)
- Military Unified Command Intelligence Organizations (UCIO)
- Atlantic Command
- Central Command
- European Command
- Pacific Command
- Southern Command
- Space Command
- Special Operations Command (those black helicopters)
- Strategic Command
- Transportation Command
- Defense Information Systems Agency (DISA)
- Defense Advanced Research Projects Agency (DARPA/ARPA)

Communications and Other Signals Intelligence (SIGINT) Sources of Data

- Space Collection/Space Surveillance
- Airborne Collection
- Ground Stations Collection
- Covert Listening Posts
- Surface Ships
- Underseas Collection/Ocean Surveillance
- Nuclear Monitoring
- Measurement and Signature Intelligence (MASINT)

US Government Intelligence Agreements: Liaison Arrangements Regarding Sharing Intelligence Data with Foreign Nations

In the list that follows, note the "sharing" agreements with Communist nations.

- Australia
- Canada
- United Kingdom/United States Security Agreement (UKUSA)
- Israel
- Norway
- Red China (Communist)
- Soviet Union/Russia (Communist)
- Japan
- United Nations (Communist)
- International Criminal Police Organization (ICPO/INTERPOL)

Other Government and Civilian Intelligence Organizations That Feed Information to Various State and Federal Government Computers and the National Security Agency

- All state departments of motor vehicles
- All credit bureaus (TRW, Equifax, *et al*)
- The US Postal Service's National Change of Address Center in Tennessee

- All state and county welfare agencies
- Eventually, all banks and other financial institutions
- All point-of-sale retail establishments
- All gasoline retailers
- All major highway and interstate freeway databases, via the IVHS/ITS system
- The Social Security Administration
- Telephone companies
- Utility companies
- Etc., etc., etc.

Politics and Intelligence Secrecy

As early as January, 1950, President Truman was instigating directives discouraging any publicity about the intelligence-gathering agencies of the United States government. (Remember, this was before the so-called Freedom of Information Act, so they were exerting their full power and influence to see to it that John Q. Citizen had no idea of the extent to which his own government was spying on foreigners, as well as nationals. Of course, the McCarthy era should have been a wake-up call!) National Security Council Intelligence Directive No. 12 (NSCID No. 12) was signed in Washington, DC, on January 6, 1950, and reads as follows:

Avoidance of Publicity Concerning the Intelligence Agencies of the U.S. Government

Pursuant to the provisions of Sections 101 and 102 of the National Security Act of 1947, as amended, and in accordance with Section 7 of NSC 50, the National Security Council hereby authorizes and directs that the following policy be established, since any publicity, factual or fictional, concerning intelligence is potentially detrimental to the effectiveness of an intelligence activity and to the national security:

(1) All departments and agencies represented by membership on the Intelligence Advisory Committee shall take steps to prevent the unauthorized disclosure

for written or oral publication of any information concerning intelligence or intelligence activities. The head
of each department or agency will determine his channel
for granting such authorization as may be necessary.

(2) The sense of the above directive shall be communicated to all other executive departments and
agencies as an expression of policy of the National
Security Council.

(3) In cases where the disclosure of classified information is sought from the Director of Central Intelligence
(DCI), and he has doubt as to whether he would comply,
the question will be referred to the National Security
Council.

—Source: Truman Library

Ever since about 1950 when President Truman established
this organization, each President has added his special touch
to the secrecy of these information gatherers' activities. In
the previous chapter, I have included a photo of the Reagans
exiting the NSA headquarters; he was the first President to
visit the NSA facility. Also pictured is President Bush at the
NSA. Not to be outdone, President Clinton adds the following
information on the White House web site, titled "Intelligence
for the Twenty-First Century."

Intelligence for the Twenty-First Century

". . .we face a host of scattered and dangerous challenges. . .ethnic and regional tensions. . .the potential
for terrorism and for criminals to acquire [nuclear,
chemical, and biological weapons]. . .we have to work
together. . .so that we can meet the challenge of doing
this work even better with even more public support and
confidence in its integrity and long-term impact. That
is my commitment to you as you renew your commitment to America, in a world fraught with danger, but
filled with promise that you will help us to seize."

—President Clinton's Remarks to the

Staff of the CIA and Intelligence Community
Central Intelligence Agency
July 14, 1995

This NSC Fact Sheet notes that it was last updated on September 25, 1996. I will include excerpts below of pertinent portions, but you may obtain it in its entirety from the Internet at (http://www.whitehouse.gov/WH/EOP/NSC/factsheets/intel.html). Basically, it tells us how Clinton is making the intelligence community a bigger and better place, not to mention a lot more expensive!

Since the beginning of his Administration, President Clinton has been committed to **preserving and expanding** the central role of the United States in the post-Cold War world. A major part of the task has involved having the best possible information and intelligence to make decisions about the present and future. A strong, motivated, **integrated,** highly professional Intelligence Community is essential to that effort [emphasis added].

A Record of Accomplishment: A Higher-Quality Intelligence Community

• President Clinton has undertaken a number of actions, including requesting increased intelligence funding in 1997 to improve the quality of intelligence and to guide the Intelligence Community into the twenty-first century. [Author's note: The NSA already has supercomputers that far exceed "state-of-the-art." In addition to being number one worldwide in computer power, they measure the computers at their headquarters **by the ACRE!** So I guess this increased funding must be for people to program, encrypt, and run them.]

• The Report of the Commission on the Roles and Missions of the Intelligence Community and the Aspin Brown Commission, which validated or recommended a number of initiatives, both represent the President's

commitment to building an Intelligence Community for the future.
- President Clinton appointed John Deutch [since replaced by George J. Tenet] as the Director of Central Intelligence because of his view of the importance of the Intelligence Community.
- The Senate Intelligence Committee reported in its 1996 Intelligence Authorization report, "the work of U.S. intelligence agencies *against terrorism* has been an example of **effective coordination and information sharing.**" [Emphasis added.]

The fact sheet points out that Clinton's priorities include information for not only military or political business, but for private persons and groups, such as "specific transnational threats, such as weapons proliferation, terrorism, international crime, and drug trafficking."

What's even scarrier is what they tell you they plan to do with their personnel...in fact, the potential for internal surveillance is unlimited under this plan.

Personnel:

- Recognizing that personnel is the most important resource of the Intelligence Community, CIA and DOD have expanded training and assignment possibilities. [There's where some of that additional funding is going!]
- The intelligence community will initiate a program for 100 high-potential officers in FY 97 to *encourage assignments outside parent agencies* [**interpret that INFILTRATE**] to broaden perspectives and increase expertise. [You can rest assured that's not all that will increase...undoubtedly they will be contributing to the filling of the databases in all those NSA supercomputers.] **The program will grow to 900 officers in five years**, and participation will become a requirement for promotion to the senior Executive/Intelligence Service... [emphasis added].

I already have mentioned "information sharing." Here is what they have to say about law enforcement coordination: ". . . intelligence and law enforcement communities have significantly increased cooperation and coordination of policies, operations, and activities. Senior level management . . . meet regularly and frequently . . . and clearly communicate to their subordinates the *overriding requirement to work together. . . . regular sharing of information . . . [is] now the rule,* not the exception" [emphasis added].

Under the heading, Counterintelligence, we find: "The Clinton Administration created the National Counterintelligence Center to serve as a resource and clearing house for the interagency community."

Through one of those infamous Presidential Decision Directives, which permits pushing through a President's personal agenda without benefit of Congressional vote, Clinton, ". . . through Executive Orders, laid down the guidelines [for the National Security Policy]. . . . establishing the first nationwide standards for clearances, personnel security and **reciprocity** [reciprocity — some more of that "sharing" stuff]. [Emphasis added.]

Another item under Clinton's list of accomplishments is the creation of the National Imagery and Mapping Agency (NIMA), to replace the Central Imagery Office. The establishment of NIMA came at the "strong recommendation of the Director of Central Intelligence, the Secretary of Defense, and the Chairman of the Joint Chiefs. . . . This new agency would *coordinate the production and use of satellite and other imagery* for intelligence and mapping" [emphasis added]. More sharing!

Next they established new guidelines to allow them to co-mingle with those "who have committed human rights abuses or other criminal acts, ..." They give this excuse: "These guidelines do not prohibit relationships with human rights violators or criminals who provide valuable information. Rather, they recognize that *intelligence agencies, like law enforcement,* must deal with unsavory individuals and require that asset background be weighed along with the value of intelligence provided and the reliability of the source" [emphasis added]. In other words, stoop as low as you must . . . the end justifies the means.

Here is what they write about encryption of electronically transmitted messages/information:

Encryption:

The President and the Vice President are seeking to create *a new policy for commercial encryption* to *strengthen the security of electronic information worldwide* while also protecting law enforcement and intelligence concerns. This system, *called key management,* would allow information to be protected by strong encryption, **while permitting encryption key recovery and access by authorized individuals** within a framework of **rigorous privacy safeguards**.

Yeah, right! Remember when I previously mentioned terms such as "clipper chip," and others? They are providing themselves with a back door key to *your* encryption with "key recovery," while setting up their own systems to prevent similar intrusion into *their* encrypted information. The sooner they can get us all on total electronic dependence, the sooner they can learn what little is left to learn about us that they don't already know! Although, with all the database sharing that is occurring, it is probably very little.

On July 15, 1996, by another of those handy little Executive Orders, Clinton established a "one-year Critical Infrastructure Protection Commission. The Commission will recommend ways, *both executive and legislative* [How about that! They're finally going to include the legislature in the process!], to strengthen the security of the nation's physical and information infrastructure, including telecommunications, financial institutions, power, and vital human services." *As if they didn't already have the biggest "infrastructure" in the world.* And note the inclusion of "financial institutions" into their infrastructure, as well as "power" (which I believe includes utilities, gasoline, and other sources of energy) and other "vital human services." As I've told you so many times before, *they plan to control everything!* By this one Executive Order (July 15, 1996), a Commission has been established to recommend ways to include in their infrastructure everything essential to the personal life of the individual—utilities, financial activities, vital human services (which undoubtedly would include health needs, food, transportation/trucking/rail freight/airlines, *et al*)—"to strengthen the security of the nation."

Until Clinton receives the report of the Commission, he has directed the FBI to work (share) with other federal agencies, as well as state and local governments, to provide security for our "critical physical and cyber assets." Those could be called "Cyberia" assets.

Strategic Assessment 1996: Elements of U.S. Power—A Book

Chapter Six of this book is titled "Intelligence" and includes the following sections: Introduction, Instruments, Collection, Analysis and Reporting, Covert Action, Conclusion. Because of the length (15 pages, 8½" × 11"), I have not duplicated it here. Also, much of the information would be redundant because of the points that I already have covered. However, it is an excellent overview of how things came to be, as well as what is going on now in the intelligence community. It is accessible on the Internet at the following address:

http://www.ndu.edu/ndu/inss/sa96/sa96ch06.html

"Direct" Sister Organizations (Government)

Now, let's dig a little deeper into the sister organizations of the NSA who are engaged primarily in the monitoring, gathering, and analyzing of information, subsequently incorporating the information into shared databases. However, before we leave the NSA and concentrate on its sisters, I want to quote once more from the FAS report on the NSA titled

"Organization and Functions," concerning its secrecy and security: "The most detailed insight into NSA organization is found in the **NSA Employee's Security Manual**, posted on the Internet on 6 April 1994 (grady@netcom.com in igc: alt.pol.org.ns), which provided building locations for the security offices of each of the groups, among other interesting tidbits."

Central Intelligence Agency (CIA)

As an introduction to and abbreviated history of the CIA, read the following report by *Grollier's, Inc.* (1996).

Central Intelligence Agency

The Central Intelligence Agency (CIA) is one of several organizations responsible for gathering and evaluating foreign intelligence information vital to the security of the United States. It is also charged with coordinating the work of other agencies in the intelligence community —including the **National Security Agency** and the Defense Intelligence Agency. It was established by the National Security Act of 1947, replacing the wartime Office of Strategic Services.

The CIA's specific tasks include: advising the president and the National Security Council on international developments; conducting research in political, economic, scientific, technical, military, and other fields; carrying on counterintelligence activities outside the United States; monitoring foreign radio and television broadcasts; and engaging in more direct forms of espionage and other intelligence operations.

Throughout its history, the CIA has seldom been free from controversy. In the 1950's, at the height of the cold war and under the direction of Allen Welsh Dulles, its activities expanded to include many undercover operations. It subsidized political leaders in other countries; secretly recruited the services of trade-union, church, and youth leaders, along with businesspeople, journalists,

academics, and even underworld leaders; set up radio
stations and news services; and financed cultural organizations and journals.

After the failure of the CIA-sponsored Bay of Pigs
Invasion of Cuba in 1961, the agency was reorganized.
In the mid-1970's, a Senate Select Committee and a
Presidential Commission headed by Nelson Rockefeller
investigated charges of illegal CIA activities. Among
other things, they found that the CIA had tried to assas-
sinate several foreign leaders, including Fidel Castro of
Cuba. It had tried to prevent Salvador Allende from
winning the 1970 elections in Chile and afterward had
worked to topple him from power.

Between 1950 and 1973, the CIA had also carried on
extensive mind-control experiments at universities,
prisons, and hospitals. In 1977, President Jimmy Carter
directed that tighter restrictions be placed on CIA clandestine operations. Controls were later also placed on
the use of intrusive surveillance methods against U.S.
citizens and resident aliens. [Author's note: Ways around
this restriction since have been discovered and put into
use by the major intelligence gatherers. As you will recall
from the previous chapter, NSA trainees now are "practicing" on us, by monitoring our private communications.]

Late in the 1970's, however, fears arose that restraints
on the CIA had undermined national security. The
agency's failure to foresee the revolution in Iran (1979)
gave new impetus to efforts at revitalization. President
Ronald Reagan and his CIA director, William J. Casey,
loosened many of the restrictions, but such activities as
the mining of Nicaraguan harbors in 1984 as part of the
covert campaign in support of the Contra rebels and the
still-unclear role of the CIA in the Iran-contra affair
focused renewed public attention on the agency.

Following Casey's death in 1987, Reagan appointed
William Webster, director of the Federal Bureau of
Investigation, to be the CIA director. His reputation for

integrity helped restore the agency's image, but intelligence failures during the Gulf War (1991) tarnished his tenure. He was succeeded by Robert M. Gates (1991-93) and James Woolsey (1993-94).

In 1994, in the worst spy scandal in CIA history, a career officer, Aldrich H. Ames, was arrested by the Federal Bureau of Investigation and admitted spying for the USSR and Russia for nine years. Woolsey resigned under fire and, after disclosure in 1995 of clandestine CIA links to U.S. government-proscribed death squads in Guatemala, was succeeded by Deputy Secretary of Defense John Deutch, who immediately retired much of the agency's hierarchy. [Emphasis added.]

Of course, the effect of such a move is to *concentrate the power* in the hands of fewer people, and therefore, fewer safeguards. As I told you previously, Deutch has been replaced by George Tenet, formerly Deputy DCI and President Clinton's second nominee to fill the position. Tenet served as Acting DCI for some months until his unanimous confirmation in the Congressional hearings, and subsequently was sworn into office on July 11, 1997. Whereas Deutch was a member of the Council on Foreign Relations (CFR) and the Trilateral Commission (TC), as well as a director of the CITICorp bank (major promoter of smart cards), it appears—surprisingly—that Tenet is a member of neither.

John M. Deutch

Deutch was sworn in on May 10, 1995, as DCI and head of the CIA, and he has lasted about two years. He holds a Ph.D. from MIT, where he joined the faculty in 1970. He has served in a myriad of government assignments. I find it ironic, considering his position as DCI and head of the CIA, that he is a member of the Commission on Protecting and Reducing Government Secrecy. Talk about your oxymorons! Or maybe it's a paradigm shift. Mr. Deutch was born in Brussels, Belgium, and became a naturalized citizen of the United States in 1945.

George J. Tenet (DCI)
Director of Central Intelligence
Director of the CIA
Effective July 11, 1997
Courtesy of CIA

On July 3, 1995, Tenet was sworn in as the Deputy DCI, serving under Deutch. The *Washington Post* reported on March 20, 1997: "President Clinton yesterday nominated George J. Tenet, who has been deputy CIA director since 1995, to head the spy agency and predicted he would win easy Senate confirmation."

Although at the writing of this article Tenet was yet to be confirmed, the *Post* also reported, "Tenet will be confirmed, Clinton told reporters, 'because he's well-known to the Senate and well-respected by Republicans as well as Democrats.' . . . he emerged as front-runner almost immediately from a short list of contenders. . . ."

Tenet is a 44-year-old family man and former White House and congressional staff member who has been running the CIA as acting director for several months, and his chances for congressional confirmation appeared to be excellent, as he was perceived to be a man of integrity by those with whom he has worked. This has proven to be the case by his subsequent unanimous approval.

On the Internet (http://www.odci.gov/cia/public_affairs/speeches/dci_speech_073197.html) we find the following transcript of Tenet's acceptance speech at his swearing-in ceremony:

Remarks by DCI George J. Tenet at Swearing-In Ceremony by Vice President Gore

I am honored, Mr. Vice President, by the opportunity that you and the President have given me to lead our country's Intelligence Community—particularly as this year marks the 50th anniversary of the founding of the Central Intelligence Agency. As I assume this position, I haven't the slightest doubt what you, the President, and the American people expect from me and the exceptional men and women that I will lead. In pursuit of our mission, you must know that first and foremost:

• That the Intelligence Community is working to protect the lives of Americans everywhere.

• That we are working to protect our men and women in uniform and to ensure that they dominate the battlefield whenever they are called and wherever they are deployed.

• That we are protecting Americans from threats posed by terrorists, drug traffickers, and weapons of mass destruction. [Author's note: This is the one that concerns me most, as it portends the loss of our privacy and freedom in exchange for our "protection and safety."]

• That we are providing our diplomats with the critical insights and foreknowledge they need to advance American interests and avert conflicts.

• And, that we are focusing not just on threats but also on opportunities—opportunities to act before danger becomes disaster [Author's note: Prevention is good, but "innocent until proven guilty" is now obsolete if they are planning to catch the criminal before a crime even is committed.] and opportunities to create circumstances favorable to American interests.

These are issues on which we simply cannot **afford to fail**.

In short, Mr. Vice President, we will meet these challenges head on with the highest standards of personal integrity and professional performance. We can and will take the risks necessary to protect our country, but we also pledge to never act recklessly. We are accountable to you, the President, and to the American people for all that we do.

A special part of the privilege you have given me is the opportunity to lead the men and women of the Intelligence Community. They are simply unmatched in their dedication, drive, and devotion to duty. They bring not only their expertise to work, but a deep conviction that national security is neither a nine-to-five job nor just a career, but a public service of grave importance.

Working with them every day has driven home for me a vital point: as important as sophisticated technology is to our work, intelligence is primarily a human endeavor. And so, for me, our people must always come first.

My goal for our people is a simple one: That they should consistently be the nation's premier experts in their field—whether they are engaged in analysis, operations, or scientific and technical pursuits.

If we—your intelligence team—tackle these challenges with energy, decisiveness, conviction, and integrity—we will live up to the high expectations that you, the President, and the American people rightly have for your intelligence service. We will be the best intelligence service in the world. As Director of Central Intelligence, I will aspire to nothing less.

Implicit in all that I have said are four commitments that will guide me every day that I serve in this office:

• **To the President, you, Mr. Vice President**, and all others who rely on our Nation's intelligence capabilities—We will deliver intelligence that is clear, objective, and without regard for political consequences. Getting it right in circumstances that require accurate information and sound judgment will always be my highest priority.

- **To the Congress**—you can count on my honesty and candor. What distinguishes our intelligence service from all others is the link with the American people that comes through strong Congressional oversight—it is vital to maintaining the trust and faith of our citizens. And I will not violate this trust.

- **To the men and women I will lead** over the next several years—We will be partners. I've told you that I want leaders who will take care of their people. This starts with me. I will care about your work at all levels, be there when you need me, and stand up for you when times get tough. Together we will ensure that American intelligence is the nation's first line of defense in a world that still holds plenty of surprise and danger.

- **To the American people I would say**—Your intelligence service is committed to protecting your country from all those who would threaten it. We will honor the trust that you have placed in us, and we will serve you with fidelity, integrity, and excellence. [Emphasis added.]

He concludes his speech by thanking many of those employers and co-workers who personally have assisted him in reaching this point in his career, as well as providing a brief family history and acknowledging the loving support of his family members.

The Position

To reiterate, the CIA is led by the Director of Central Intelligence (DCI), who manages the CIA in addition to serving as head of the Intelligence Community. Their mission and goals

Figure 2-1. Organization of the Office of the DCI/CIA.

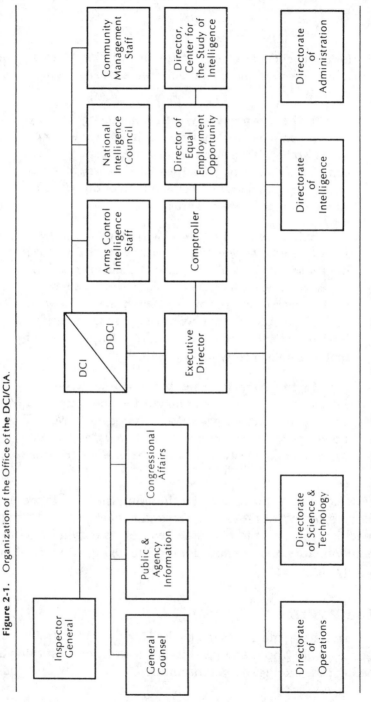

Courtesy of Jeffrey T. Richelson, The U.S. Intelligence Community.

—as stated in a National Performance Review, Phase II Initiatives, An Intelligence Community Report, September 1995, located on the Internet at
(http://www.odci.gov/ic/npr/sep95/sep95.html#annexb)
are as follows:

> The DCI has three principal responsibilities; serving as the head of the US Intelligence Community, the principal advisor to the President for intelligence matters related to national security, and head of the CIA. The DCI is responsible for providing timely and objective intelligence — independent of political considerations and based on all sources of information available to the Community — to the President, heads of executive departments and agencies, the Chairman of the Joint Chiefs of Staff and senior military commanders, and where appropriate, to the Senate and House of Representatives. The DCI is also responsible for performing "such other functions as the President or the National Security Council may direct."

Isn't it interesting that they can furnish data collected to all those political appointees and military bigwigs, *but only where THEY deem appropriate* is such information made available to the duly-elected representatives of the people, our Congress and Senate.

The principal Deputies of the DCI are: Deputy Director of Central Intelligence, Executive Director for Intelligence Community Affairs, Executive Director (who runs the CIA on a daily basis), The National Intelligence Council, Deputy Director for Administration, Deputy Director for Intelligence, Deputy Director for Operations, Deputy Director for Science and Technology, and the Inspector General.

The organizational chart (left) is from Richelson's book, *The U.S. Intelligence Community.*

The CIA Seal

Note the Masonic Phoenix Bird/US Eagle at the top of the CIA's Seal/Insignia

Truman's Executive Order 10111 established the CIA seal.

"It is described in heraldic terms as follows:

Shield: Argent, a compass rose of sixteen points gules

Crest: On a wreath argent and gules an American bald eagle's head erased proper.

"Below the shield on a gold color scroll the inscription 'United States of America' in red letters, and encircling the shield and crest at the top with the inscription 'Central Intelligence Agency' in white letters.

"All on a circular blue background with a narrow gold edge. The interpretation of the CIA seal is as follows:

"The American Eagle is the national bird and is a symbol of strength and alertness. The radiating spokes of the compass rose depict the coverage of intelligence data from all areas of the world to a central point."

I find that final statement particularly enlightening, and by all indications they certainly are living up to their stated expectations.

CIA Headquarters Buildings

The original headquarters building was designed in the mid-1950's by the New York firm of Harrison and Abramovitz, designers of the United Nations Building. The facility is located about eight miles from downtown Washington, DC.

Satellite photo of the CIA Headquarters Building, Langley, Virginia.
© *1995 VARGIS, LLC.* • *All Rights Reserved.*

As the population of the Agency increased, it was determined another building had to be constructed. It is joined to the west facade of the original building and includes two six-story office towers, connected by a four-story core area. It is a steel/glass structure, as compared with the precast concrete construction of the original building.

Entrance to CIA facility at Langley, Virginia. Photo courtesy of the CIA.

CIA Headquarters. Photo courtesy of the CIA.

Original CIA Headquarters Facility.

The new building was completed and occupied in March, 1991. The original building consists of 1,400,000 square feet and the new building contains 1,100,000 square feet of space. Building and grounds comprise 258 acres.

Entrance to CIA headquarters building, Langley, Virginia. Note the Great Seal of the United States with occultic "all-seeing-eye" pyramid and inscription: "Novus Ordo Seclorum" — New World Order. (See closeups next pages.) Photo courtesy of the CIA.

Close-up view of the Masonic "Great Seal"
which adorns the entrance of the CIA building.
Observe the same design as on the reverse
of the dollar bill.
Photo courtesy of the CIA.

"Etched into the wall of the original building's central lobby is a biblical verse which also characterizes the intelligence mission in a free society. It reads:

"And ye shall know the truth and the truth shall make you free.

—John VIII-XXXII"

What a difference 40 years makes!. . .the new building sports the Masonic pyramid and all-seeing eye (see closeup above)!

Federation of American Scientists (FAS) — Watchdog of the Intelligence Community

The FAS had so much information to share on the NSA, let's examine some of their findings about the CIA, as well. *The Oregonian,* Tuesday, May 20, 1997, ran this article about the activities of the FAS.

Scientists sue to reveal CIA's spy budget

The Federation of American Scientists sued the Central Intelligence Agency on Monday to force it to reveal one of Washington's worst-kept secrets: the size of the budget for U.S. espionage.

The amount, or "black budget," is hidden inside false accounts and classified compartments within the Pentagon's budget. It has been reported to be about $29 billion a year, give or take a billion.

The CIA spends about $3 billion a year. The agency's director and the secretary of defense allocate most of the rest to military intelligence services such as the **National Security Agency**, which conducts electronic eavesdropping, and the National Reconnaissance Office, which builds spy satellites.

Intelligence spending is officially a state secret, and it has been since the CIA was created 50 years ago. But the veil of secrecy has slipped somewhat.

The Federation of American Scientists, founded in 1945 as a research group concerned with national security policy, has decoded some of the secret sections of the Defense Department's budget where intelligence spending is hidden. But the number remains officially classified. [Emphasis added.]

Under the name of the FAS Intelligence Reform Project, an immense amount of information is available about most of the intelligence community's activities, and the information that follows, as we close out our examination of the CIA, was obtained from the FAS website on the Internet.

FAS Intelligence Reform Project

The FAS reported a listing of Congressional Hearings related to intelligence and/or espionage that occurred or were begun in 1996. John Deutch and the CIA were prominent in these activities. The following listing is to give you an idea of what concerns Congress seriously enough to appoint

committees and subcommittees to investigate them. Hearings
were conducted on:

> International Organized Crime (1-31-96)
> Current and Projected National Security Threats to
>   the United States and Its Interests Abroad
>   (2-22-96)
> Economic Espionage (2-28-96) — Senate
> Combatting International Terrorism (3-5-96)
> International Crime (3-12-96)
> Worldwide Demand for Nuclear Weapons Materials
>   (3-20-96)
> Russian Organized Crime (4-30-96)
> Economic Espionage (5-9-96) — House
> National Information System Security (5-22-96) —
>   "Information Security: Computer Attacks at
>   Department of Defense Pose Increasing Risks"
> Iran/Bosnia Arms (5-30-96)
> Security in Cyberspace (6-5-96)
> Olympics and the Threat of Terrorism (6-11-96)
> Foreign Information Warfare Activities Against the
>   United States (6-25-96)
> Bosnia (7-24-96)
> Impact of Encryption (7-25-96)
> Bosnia (8-1-96) — a second committee
> Intelligence Analysis on the Long-Range Missile
>   Threat to the United States (12-4-96)

FAS Reports on CIA Locations

The FAS tells us about the "CIA/NSA CSSG Special Collection Service." This is a joint facility—just another connection between the NSA and this sister ("Little Brother")
organization.

Located at 11600 Springfield Road, Beltsville, Maryland,
it has three buildings (identified as west, south, and east) and
the floorspace analysis indicates that all areas are used by
the Special Collection Service, listed as "occupant."

With a "connection" that is not quite so clear, the FAS also lists a facility at 8101 Odell Road, referred to as the Beltsville Annex, but the occupant is listed as the State Department.

State Department
Beltsville Communications Annex

This facility presents a bit of a puzzle. It is located right next door to the joint CIA/NSA *"CSSG" Special Collection Service facility* on Springfield Road, although there does not appear to be an obvious direct physical connection between the two. While the Beltsville Communication Annex is listed in the State Department telephone directory as State Annex SA-26, there is no indication on the sign at the site of this affiliation, which is contrary to typical State Department practice. It is also reported that SCS personnel [agents] use Consular Service and Diplomatic Telecommunications Service as "cover" when "forward deployed," so it would stand to reason that they might operate from a "State Department" facility when in the United States in order to maintain the plausibility of their cover. Of course, the robustness of their cover would be even further enhanced if the facility actually *were* a State Department facility. So in this case, we are left with a Scottish "not proven" verdict.

Other CIA facilities listed by the FAS include the National Photographic Interpretation Center (NPIC), located at the Washington Navy Yard (see aerial photo).

The National Photographic Interpretation Center is managed within the CIA Directorate of Science and Technology (DS&T). NPIC is a joint CIA/Defense Department center whose product is disseminated to its parent agencies, which, in turn, incorporate it into all-source intelligence reports. NPIC also produces imagery interpretation reports, briefing boards, videotapes for national-level consumers, and provides support for the military.

Washington Navy Yard.

NPIC employs some 1,200 image interpreters and archivists. NPIC, designated the **Southwest** station, is connected to other facilities in Washington through a high-capacity fiber-optic cable system.

Another CIA facility reported by the FAS is called "Blue U," located at 1000 North Glebe Road, Arlington, Virginia. The so-called "Blue U" was a Directorate of Operations CIA training facility for such clandestine trade-craft skills as photography, letter-opening, and lock-picking (see aerial photo).

CIA — Glebe Road.

CIA — Rosslyn, Virginia.

Although they don't reveal the activity, the FAS reports another CIA facility in Rosslyn, Virginia (see aerial photo).

Another facility is identified as the CIA Vienna Technology Park at 901, 801, and 1021 Follin Lane. Yet another is located at Tysons Corner; they also maintain a facility known as the Federal Intelligence Document Understanding Laboratory. In addition, there is "Area 51 — Groom Lake, Nevada." This is believed to be the UFO research base, known simply as "Area 51." Similar UFO research activities are believed to

CIA Headquarters Floorplans

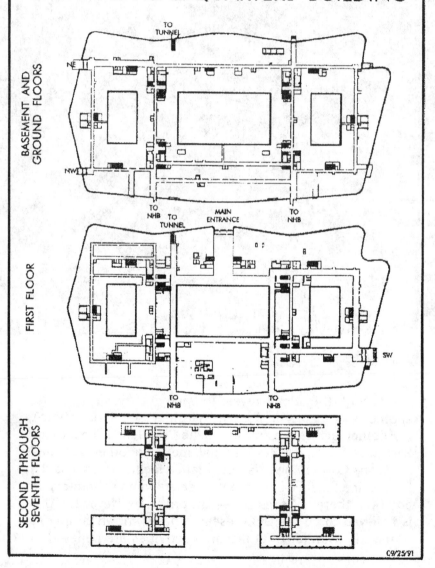

LEGEND

■ – ELEVATORS / ESCALATORS
▨ – WAVEGUIDES

STAIRS
■ – EXIT ON 1ST FLOOR
▤ – EXIT ON 2ND FLOOR
▦ – EXIT ON 4TH FLOOR
■ – EXIT ON GROUND FLOOR

ORIGINAL HEADQUARTERS BUILDING

BASEMENT AND GROUND FLOORS

TO TUNNEL

NE

NW

TO NHB
TO TUNNEL
MAIN ENTRANCE
TO NHB

FIRST FLOOR

SW

TO NHB
TO NHB

SECOND THROUGH SEVENTH FLOORS

C9/25/91

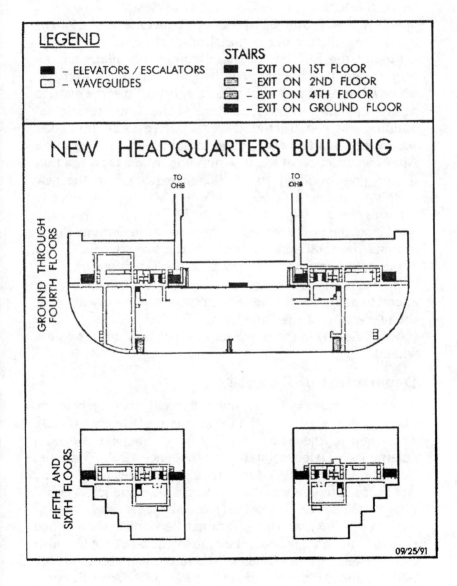

be occurring at the Pine Gap facility in Australia—pictured previously. (Of course, this doesn't include any of their operations outside our national borders.)

Finally, the FAS has provided some floor plans for the original and new buildings of the CIA headquarters offices, which I described previously. But they bring up some matters of discrepancies in the reporting. At the time the original building was constructed, it was reported to be 1,000,000 square feet; building and ground combined totaled 219 acres. After construction of the new building, it was reported that the original building was 1,400,000 square feet, the new building contains 1,100,000 square feet, with the building and grounds comprising 258 acres. The FAS very astutely points out: "Note the discrepancies in the area of the Original Building and the total acreage between the two sources." They make no attempt to offer any possible explanations.

Now that we have covered the CIA and the NSA, let's move ahead to address the other eleven spokes in the wheel under the leadership of the Director of Central Intelligence (DCI) (not necessarily in the sequence in which they appear on the wheel).

Department of Defense

Let's continue our examination of intelligence agencies by taking a quick recap of the Department of Defense (DoD). According to the wheel, the following agencies are DoD "elements": Defense Intelligence Agency (DIA), National Security Agency (NSA), Army Intelligence, Navy Intelligence, Air Force Intelligence, Marine Corps Intelligence, Central Imagery Office (CIO—now the National Imagery and Mapping Agency—NIMA), and the National Reconnaissance Office (NRO). Other groups under their jurisdiction, but not included in the wheel, are the Defense Information Systems Agency (DISA), and its many related programs, Defense Support Program (DSP), ARPA/DARPA, and others.

Under the provisions of EO 12472 (another one of those infamous Executive Orders), the DoD was assigned the following National Security Emergency Preparedness (NS/EP) telecommunications responsibilities. I will just highlight them here, but take notice of how widespread is their reach. Of course, there is what seems to be the inevitable NSA connection. "Ensure that the Director, NSA, provides the technical support necessary to develop and maintain adequate plans for the security and protection of NS/EP telecommunications."

DoD NS/EP telecommunications assets include the following systems and capabilities:

Advanced Research Projects Agency (ARPA—subsequently DARPA) Network
Defense Data Network (DDN)
Defense Switched Network (DSN)
Defense Message System (DMS)
Defense Satellite Communications System (DSCS)
Direct Communications Link (Washington-Moscow Hotline)
Future Secure Voice System (FSVS)
Joint Chiefs of Staff Alerting Network
National Military Command System
Washington Area Wideband System
Worldwide Military Command and Control System

The 13 agencies in the wheel all are linked by computer and have shared databases. The NSA is believed to be the clearinghouse and head of computer databases, surveillance, identification of individuals (and all the implications of that ability), tracking of criminals, espionage, *et al.* With its "Big Brother/Beast" acres and acres of computers, it is the greatest collector of information in the global community, and it gets most of it from the "Little Brother" sister organizations. Additional foreign links in the information/identification system include Interpol, Pine Gap, Australia, (as well as England, Germany and Japan), NCIC—Moscow and China, the United Nations (UNCJIN—United Nations Crime & Justice Information Network).

New Zealand's GCSB

At this point it is time to introduce to you another excellent book: *Secret Power, New Zealand's Role in the International Spy Network,* by Nicky Hager, 1996, Craig Potton Publishing, New Zealand. Intelligence authority, Jeffrey T. Richelson, author of *The U.S. Intelligence Community,* wrote one Foreword, which he begins:

> The world of signals intelligence is one that govern-
> ments have traditionally tried to keep hidden from public
> view. The secrecy attached to it by the United Kingdom
> and its allies in the Second World War, particularly code-
> breaking operations, carried over into the Cold War.
> Whether their adversaries were attacking them with
> weapons or diplomatic strategies, the concern was the
> same—that revelations about methods and successes
> would lead an adversary to change codes and ciphers
> and deny the codebreaker the ability to read the foe's
> secret communications.

Next Richelson enlightens us about the UKUSA Security Agreement of 1948, formalizing close cooperation between five countries—the United States, the United Kingdom, Canada, Australia, and New Zealand. Although the treaty has never been made public, it has become clear that it provided not only for a division of collection tasks and sharing of the product, but for common guidelines for the classification and protection of the intelligence collected as well as for personnel security. (As we will discover shortly, when it was determined that an area was not covered by any satellite "footprint," immediate steps were taken to seal the breach. The old adage, "The sun never sets on the British empire," is becoming accurate once again.)

Naturally, the secrecy factor does not escape Richelson. He writes:

> That signals intelligence became more noticeable did
> not, for many years, alter the attitudes of the authorities

about the necessity for strict secrecy. In the United States the National Security Agency [NSA], established in 1952, was officially acknowledged only in 1957. For years, what were well known to be US operated signals intelligence stations have been officially described as facilities engaged in the research of "electronic phenomena" or the "rapid-relay of communications." It took the US over 20 years after the Soviet Union obtained detailed information on a US signals intelligence satellite even to acknowledge the existence of such satellites. . . .

. . .What the public does know, it knows largely because of the efforts of industrious researchers who have collected and analysed obscure documents and media accounts. . . .These researchers have included Desmond Ball in Australia, Jame Bamford *(The Puzzle Palace)* in the United States, and Duncan Campbell in the United Kingdom.

Nicky Hager's *Secret Power* earns him a place in that select company. . . . His expos of the organisation and operations of New Zealand's Government Communications Security Bureau (GCSB) is a masterpiece of investigative reporting and provides a wealth of information.

David Lange, former Prime Minister of New Zealand, also has contributed a Foreword to Hager's book. Among his remarks are the following:

Life at the time was full of unpleasant surprises. State-sponsored terrorism was a crime against humanity *as long as it wasn't being practiced by the allies, when it was studiously ignored.* In the national interest it became necessary to say "ouch" and frown and bear certain reprisals of our intelligence partners. We even went to the length of building a satellite station at Waihopai. But it was not until I read this book that I had any idea that *we have been committed to an international integrated electronic network. . . .*

> . . . But it is an outrage that I and other ministers were
> told so little, and this raises the question of to whom
> those concerned saw themselves ultimately answerable.
> [Emphasis added.]

The entire text of each Foreword is available at these websites,
respectively, courtesy of the FAS.
Lange: (http://www.fas.org/irp/eprint/sp/sp_f1.htm).
Richelson: (http://www.fas.org/irp/eprint/sp/sp_f2.htm).

Let's learn a little of what Nicky Hager has to say in his
book (a copy of his Table of Contents is reprinted here for
your information). In Chapter 4 he introduces the role of the
UKUSA in fighting the Cold War. He tells about the origin
of the agreement then continues, "The UKUSA agreement
served to establish a post-war alliance between the United
States, Britain, Canada, Australia, and New Zealand *for covertly
intercepting and analysing radio communications from countries all around the world.* It built into a permanent force, a
worldwide electronic spy system . . . .

"In the 1990s, radio officers with earphones have largely
given way to satellite interception and the immense computer
capabilities of the ECHELON system, but UKUSA is still the
basis of it all [emphasis added]."

In Chapter 10, Hager discusses the "new world order" that
was brought about by the invention and worldwide distribution
of the flintlock muskets, as the European nations "carved
up the world into their respective empires. In the 1990s
military technology is much deadlier than the once-dominant
flintlocks, but the causes of war and military repression have
not changed substantially: . . . . In the 1990s, however, intelligence capabilities are often as much a source of power and
influence as military forces." Hager defines the ECHELON
system as "the 21st-century electronic spy network."

> Each station in the UKUSA intelligence network has
> a special secret codename that identifies the intelligence
> collected there. The GCHQ Hong Kong station's intelli-

CONTENTS

Courtesy of Nicky Hager, Secret Power.

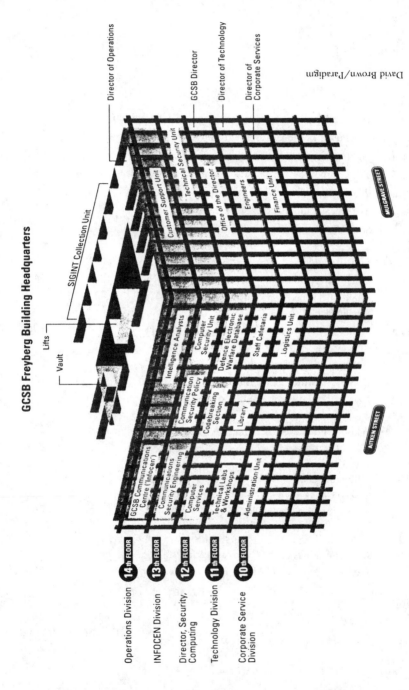

GCSB Freyberg Building Headquarters

Director of Operations

GCSB Director

Director of Technology

Director of Corporate Services

David Brown/Paradigm

MULGRAVE STREET

AITKEN STREET

SIGINT Collection Unit

Customer Support Unit

Technical Security Unit

Office of the Director

Engineers

Finance Unit

Lifts

Vault

Intelligence Analysts

Computer Security Unit

Communication Security Policy

Defence Electronic Warfare Database

Codebreaking Section

Library

Staff Cafeteria

Logistics Unit

GCSB Communications Centre ('Infocen')

Communications Security Engineering

Computer Services

Technical Labs & Workshops

Administration Unit

14th FLOOR — Operations Division

13th FLOOR — INFOCEN Division

12th FLOOR — Director, Security, Computing

11th FLOOR — Technology Division

10th FLOOR — Corporate Service Division

The layout of GCSB headquarters in Wellington: inside the most secret building in New Zealand. Courtesy of Nicky Hager, Secret Power.

gence was codenamed GERANIUM. The NSA Yakima station, set in the midst of canyons and desert next to an Indian reservation, produces intelligence called COWBOY. Intelligence from the Waihopai station was given an inexplicable yet strangely apt codename: FLINTLOCK. Intelligence collected at the station for the UKUSA alliance is identified by this word and by Waihopai's station designator, NZC-333.

In the ECHELON system the codenames are used to identify the Dictionary [a dictionary determines which "flag" words monitored will be recorded and analyzed] at each station. The Waihopai computer contains the FLINTLOCK Dictionary and the GCSB also has keywords placed in other Dictionaries, such as the COWBOY Dictionary at Yakima.

Unlike much of the work of the UKUSA radio interception stations, *Waihopai (and its sister stations) are targeted not on some enemy's military communications, but on all the ordinary telephone calls, faxes, telexes and Internet and other e-mail messages sent by individuals, groups, businesses, and governments around the world.*

. . . Around the world UKUSA stations like Waihopai *now work as an integrated collection system:* GCSB staff automatically receive some intelligence from other stations in the network; and **NSA intelligence staff** sitting at Fort Meade outside Washington DC **have an automatic, 24-hour flow of raw FLINTLOCK intelligence fed into their computers.** . . .

The Waihopai station is targeted on Intelsat civilian satellite communications in the Pacific. . . [emphasis added].

Hager also says: "Internet users are continuously intercepted. They do not have to be specifically targeting you; the Dictionary picks out any messages containing one of the agencies' keywords."

Appendix A in *Secret Power* is a "Who's Who in New Zealand

APPENDIX A

WHO'S WHO IN NEW ZEALAND FOREIGN INTELLIGENCE ORGANISATIONS

SENIOR GCSB STAFF IN 1996

Director	Ray Parker (F)
Director of Operations	Warren Tucker (A)
Director of Technology	Mike Spring (F)
Director of Information Systems Security	John Brandon (A)
Director of Corporate Services	Tony Fryer (F)
New Zealand Liaison Officer (Washington)	John Willson (A)
New Zealand Liaison Officer (Canberra)	Keith Smith (F)
Officer in Charge, Tangimoana	Barry Keane (F)
Officer in Charge, Waihopai	Colin Waite (F)

Unit Managers:		
	K Unit (SIGINT production)	Glen Singleton
	C Unit (SIGINT collection)	Bruce Miller (N)
	L Unit (customer support)	Leon Crosse (F)
	N Unit (network services)	Bob Ohlson (N)
	TS Unit (computer services)	Robert Walter
	D Unit (technical services)	Roy Anderson
	S Unit (technical security)	Brian Nokes (F)
	E Unit (COMSEC engineering)	Ian Howie (F)
	R Unit (computer security)	Malcolm Shore (F)
	M Unit (COMSEC)	Chris Farrow (N)
	P Unit (protective security)	Mike Loughran (F)
	A Unit (administration)	Heather McKenzie
	F Unit (finance)	Chris Carson
	L Unit (logistics)	Ian Juno (A)

Senior Executive Officers:		
	Information Security	Peter Ross (A)
	Information Systems	David Hilling
	Legal	Hugh Wolfensohn (N)
	Office of the Director	Brian Gore (A)

Nearly all of these staff were previously high-ranking New Zealand military officers (F stands for ex-Air Force, A for ex-Army and N for ex-Navy). One of the four information security units was disestablished and the staff moved into another unit in January 1996.

Courtesy of Nicky Hager, Secret Power.

Foreign Intelligence Organisations," and I have duplicated it for your information. I highly recommend you obtain a copy of this meticulously researched, thorough book.

The Secrets of Pine Gap and Canberra

I have reduced five pages by the above title from the Internet and inserted them following this page. Even though the type is small, it still is readable, and I suggest you do so. Others have found this same information and it has been duplicated in books and Internet transmissions worldwide. However, I want to make it clear that I **do not** concur with much of what is said. This is a New Age group who believes that UFO's and ET's are a proven fact. But regardless of their own particular purpose for this investigation, they have uncovered some pertinent information concerning the events going on in Australia and have arrived at some very plausible conclusions. Should you care to access it for yourself, it is located, among other sites, at website:

(http://www.newage.com.au/ufo%2Falien/pine.html).

They quote from an article written in French by Lucien Cometta and later translated into English by Dr. John Francois Gille, who moved from France to Albuquerque, New Mexico (I'm guessing probably because of the reported UFO activity in the vicinity).

Here are a few paragraphs which I want to "highlight" for you.

> The United States has three major bases in Australia. One is in South Australia (Nurranger, near Woomera, T.N.), another in New South Wales, and the third (and by far the largest) is located within about 230 km (143 miles) of the geographical center of the continent, not far to the west of Alice Springs (Northern Territory), at the foothills of the southern slopes of the MacDonnell Range. This base is completely underground, with barely visible entrances to the surface. This "Top Secret" base is entirely financed by the United States Government,

The Secrets of Pine Gap and Canberra

INTRODUCTION

According to John Lear   and several other researchers the U.S. government may have made a 'pact' with a non-human race as early as 1933. According to some this 'race' is not human as we know it, yet it claims to have it's origin on earth several thousands of years ago. Some sources allege that this predatory race is of a neo-saurian nature. This has led others to suggest that the dinosaurs which ruled the surface of the earth in prehistoric times may not have become entirely extinct as is commonly believed, but that certain of the more intelligent and biped-hominoid mutations of that race developed a form of intellectual thought equal to or surpassing that of the human race, and then possibly went into hiding. For instance one branch or mutation of the supposedly extinct sauroid race, Stenonychosaurus was according to paleontologists remarkably hominoid in appearance, being 3 1/2 to 4 1/4 ft. in height with possibly greyish-green skin and three-digit clawed fingers with a partially-opposable 'thumb'.

The opposable thumb and intellectual capacity is the only thing preventing members of the animal kingdom from challenging the human race as the masters of planet earth. For instance the ape kingdom possesses opposable thumbs yet it does not possess the intellectual capacity to use them as humans do. The dolphins possess intellects nearing that of humans but do not possess opposable thumbs or even limbs necessary to invent, etc. Could their be an 'animal' which possesses both of these characteristics? The cranial capacity of Stenonychosaurus was nearly twice the size of that of human beings, indicating a large brain and possibly advanced though not necessarily benevolent intellect. According to researchers such as Brad Steiger, Val Valerian, TAL LeVesque and others this may actually be the same type of entity or entities most commonly described in 'UFO' encounters, as well as the same type of creatures depicted in early 1992 in the nationally viewed CBS presentation 'INTRUDERS'. According to Lear and others the government may have established a 'treaty' with this race, which they later learned to their horror was extremely malevolent in nature and were merely using the 'treaties' as a means to buy time while they methodically establish certain controls upon the human race with the ultimate goal of an absolute domination.

It is also alleged by certain deep-level intelligence agents that the Illuminati, or the 'Cult of the Serpent', is willfully wor

From Dr. Jean François Gille, who moved to Albuquerque, New Mexico from France, comes a translation of a French document that exposes the relationship between several factors in the matrix of world affairs. The article, titled - 'PINE GAP BASE: WORLD CONTEXT', was written by Lucien Cometta and later translated into English by Dr. John Gille:

"In order to understand the case of the Pine Gap US base (near Alice Springs, Australia) better. I feel compelled to give some explanations beforehand. I hope these explanations will help to increase the general awareness of the extraordinary importance that facility has for mankind as a whole.

"The majority of people, all over the world, are not lingering in doubt as to whether UFOs and ETs are real. They know they are real. Here in early 1989, no one questions their existence. The case for UFOs and ETs aroused passions, controversies and grandstanding for many years. Some of it has not been quite rational. The matter being relatively settled, public opinions should cool down. It is with a serene and clear mind that we ought to be thinking of our future relationship with the peoples from space. However, the public mind is not at peace. It vaguely feels that the government are hiding "something real big", and it wonders where our leaders are going to lead mankind.

"During the process of research and study of UFOs and aliens, researchers who do not take the explanations of the scientific establishment at face value have discovered unsettling facts; these facts have started the lifting off (of) the lid of the coverup. The value and prestige of their sources of information do not leave any doubt about the truthfulness of these reports; the main outlines are summarized below.

PINE GAP

"The United States has three major bases in Australia. One is in South Australia (Nurranger, near Woomera, T.N.), another in New South Wales, and the third (and by far the largest) is located within about 230 km (143 miles) of the geographical center of the continent, not far to the west of Alice Springs (Northern Territory), at the foothills of the southern slopes of the MacDonnell Range. This base is completely underground, with barely visible entrances to the surface. "This 'Top Secret' base is entirely financed by the United States Government, and is officially known as the Joint Defense Space Research Facility.

"When the JDSRF was first initiated, its aim was scientific research for the supposed development of a space defense technology. It is now known that since its inception, its primary purpose was research into electromagnetic propulsion.

"What exactly is Pine Gap? As strange as it may seem, even Australian Federal Parliament members do not know. Among the Cabinet members, only a small number of 'initiates' have a vague idea of what this is all about. The only information source available to the public is the cross-checking done by private researchers such as Jimmy Guieu, following statements made by the United States or Australian magazines (always very short and terse paragraphs), and anything the locals may notice.

"It is said that under Pine Gap is the deepest drilling hole in Australia - about 5 miles (more than 8,000 meters). Such a hole is likely used as an underground antenna able to recharge the batteries of submarines in the Pacific and Indian Ocean through ELF broadcasts. Such a gigantic antenna could be used to generate the gigantic stationary wave around the Earth.

"Some say that Pine Gap has an enormous nuclear generator to supply energy to a new type of transceiver. It seems too that there is a high-powered, high-voltage plasma accelerator which may be put to use to transmit electric current, or even to produce a 'death-ray', or quite simply to feed a plasma gun. All this is not as incredible as it sounds: it is now known that the US base of West Cape, near Exmouth Gulf in Western Australia (Harold E. Holt USN Communication Station), has an older type of the transceiver used at Pine Gap which is used to send electric current to submerged US submarines who trail a wire antenna. It is known that electric currents transmitted in this way are referred to as plasmo-dynamic cells.

"Several times, locals have seen WHITE DISKS about 30' in diameter in the process of being unloaded from large US cargo planes at the airports serving Pine Gap. Those disks had the USAF emblem on them. It seems likely that disks are assembled and based at Pine Gap. The number of disks seen at night leaves no doubt in anyone's mind. An amazing quantity of furniture has been delivered by plane from the United States. The locals also say that an enormous amount of food is stocked in warehouses of what could well be a true multi-leveled underground city.

"On the other hand, Pine Gap is well known as one of the most important control centers for spy satellites which circle the globe. An article published in late 1973 claimed that the Pine Gap installation, along with its sister installation in Guam, were used to control the photographic missions of the large American satellites in orbit above the Earth.

"Pine Gap has enormous computers which are connected to their American and Australian central counterparts, which collect all the information secured in these countries, not only about finance and technology, but on every aspect of the life of the average citizen. Those computers at Pine Gap are also evidently connected to similar mainframes in Guam, in Krugersdorp South Africa, and at the Amundsen-Scott US base at the South Pole.

"Let us say, incidentally, that the employees (more than 1200) of the US base in South Africa all claim to be members of the US consular mission in that country. It may be worthy of note that the Amundsen-Scott base at the South Pole is located on a sensitive magnetic spot of our planet, that it holds exactly the same assets as Pine Gap, and that all the information about most of the average citizens of Western Europe is stored there in memory banks tens of meters under the icepack.

"A statement made by the Australian premier about 1987, assuring that 'France must disappear from the Pacific, from the Kerguelen Ridge, and from Antarctica' sheds light on the importance of this polar base for the Anglo-Saxon world.

"The most disquieting fact about Pine Gap may be that the employees working on the base, and especially those earmarked for duty on electromagnetic propulsion projects, have undergone brainwashing and even implantation of intracranial devices. Those employees have turned into unconditional slaves of their master, whoever he is. Rather scary, isn't it?

"The true point of the brainwashing of those individuals, along with the ruthless attempts to implement the coverup of really advanced military technology, will become clear at the end of this article.

"For me, it all began with the construction of the new Parliament building in Canberra, which cost billions of dollars. Australia has only 18 million inhabitants, yet it apparently treated itself to a building far beyond its means...supposedly to accommodate its government even if the old Parliament building was perfectly fine.

"This new building, enormous, immense and magnificent would easily fit the needs of the USSR or of the United States, which both have hundreds of millions of citizens to rule. That building puzzled me, and I started to talk about it until the day I bumped into an Englishman who told me that the Australian premier, Bob Hawk, was a Rhodes scholar, and as such he worked toward the setting up of a One World Government, and that this new Parliament building likely had something to do with it.

"Sometime after, I stumbled on a pamphlet published by the Human Rights Organization, which talked about a group of about a hundred people well-placed in high finance, politics, the judiciary branch and big business. This group was called the 'Club of ROME'. According to this pamphlet, the CLUB OF ROME was pledged to a consortium which controls all international finance. A number of other groups similar to the CLUB OF ROME are equally pledged to that finance consortium, AND ARE INFILTRATING THE VARIOUS POLITICAL AND RELIGIOUS GROUPS WITH THE INTENTION TO MAKE PROGRESS TOWARD THE INSTITUTION OF A WORLD DICTATORSHIP.

"The whole thing looked a little bit too preposterous to be true, it seemed to me. Nevertheless, a friend of mine gave me an audio cassette taped at a lecture given by Peter Sawyer, a former high-ranking Australian civil servant, which exposed a certain number of facts he had noticed while in office. He talked, in particular, of a telephone exchange in Canberra called 'Deacon Center'. This exchange, built in concrete with 4 (ft. ? - Branton) thick walls, cost hundreds of millions of dollars. It is outfitted with numerous computers, arrayed on four levels. When he tried to find out why such equipment was needed in a country of only 18 million, he discovered that those computers were connected to all the banks, to every post office, to all telephones, and to all of the police stations and customs houses; to every arrival and departure desk for air or sea travelers; and also and above all, to the other data centers collecting data on private citizens... in the United States as well as in Europe.

"That facility on Deacon street is therefore a Center where all the data pertaining to every citizen of the Western World end up being stored. All financial, economic, political and military information, as well as the information on every inhabitant of those countries. As a matter of course, all people living in Australia are put on file, kept up with and labeled.

"Peter Sawyer discovered also that the president of the ROCKEFELLER FOUNDATION came for a lengthy stay in Australia to supervise in person the construction of 20 luxury residences in Canberra (the Australian government footed the bill), in the wonderful setting of a National Park, where, legally, nobody is allowed to build.

"The investigations lead by Sawyer exposed, first, that the new Parliament building is meant to accommodate the world government-to-be; and, second, that the 20 luxury residences will be allocated to the different foreign members of that government... Why choose Canberra as the headquarters of the new world government? Simply because Australia is a peaceful country, with very few natives likely to turn rebellious, and, above all, it's an English speaking country. No other English speaking country can offer the safety Australia will provide at the time of the taking over by the World Government. In America and Europe, uprisings are more than likely, and South America not only is not English speaking, but its fondness for revolutions and social disturbances is well known.

"Australia is thus the ideal place for such an undertaking. How is the advent of a World Government possible in the near future? It is relatively easy, as we will explain.

"First, who are those 'internationalists' who want to take over the planet? THE ONES WHO WANT TO SET UP A WORLD GOVERNMENT ARE 15 FAMILIES OR SO, WHO ALREADY GOVERN ALL OF INTERNATIONAL FINANCE AND KEEP A TIGHT LEASH ON MOST GOVERNMENTS THROUGH THE ABSOLUTE CONTROL OF THEIR FINANCES AND THEIR DOMESTIC ECONOMY. These finance moguls devised their plan after World War I, and have been working since on an insidious undermining process aimed at economic destabilization all over the West.

"If those financiers are obviously labeled 'capitalists', it is a very deceptive label, though, for, in fact, they never stopped to pull the strings of the progressive parties, as well as those of the conservative parties. Their idea is logical, and lay, quite simply, in the destabilization of the countries of the West on the political, economic and religious levels. IT MAY BE SURPRISING TO SOME THAT THESE 'INNOVATORS' HAD INFILTRATED THE TOP LEVELS OF THE MAIN RELIGIOUS ESTABLISHMENTS, ONLY A SMALL NUMBER OF YEARS WAS NEEDED TO MAKE THEM VIRTUALLY POWERLESS... (Were these establishments 'bought out' through financial contributions? - Branton)

"Economic destabilization is implemented through a slower but most efficient process. This process (already under way) will cause the entire financial system of the West to collapse. The people involved are the same people who cause the price of oil to go up and then, after convincing European neighbors to agree to these price rises, provide that the yield coming from the price rises will be paid to the 'International Reserve Bank', which is entirely at their command. The Reserve Bank hands the money over to a 'holding bank' who lavishly loans the money to Third World countries for usurious rates of interest.

"The holding bank receives the interest paid by the underdeveloped countries, then puts it into another 'holding bank' which, in turn, invests the huge quantity of money on behalf of the Arabs.

"Those investments are made into thriving large businesses. In the meantime, only small interests are sent to Arab countries. "Those who engineered the plan were perfectly aware that the leaders of the underdeveloped countries would be tempted to pocket a good part of the received money.

"I IRB will then tell the Arab countries that the holding bank investments have turned out badly, all their assets had vanished and that no interest will be paid any more. The Arab countries will then have no choice but to put all the securities they own on the market, as well as quite an amount of property bought by the second holding bank. A good part of these possessions will then be frozen, because they will have been bought with the aid of not entirely repaid loans, and they will be part of the assets of the first holding bank, gone bankrupt. The incredible quantity of shares put on the market at the same time will cause a stock market crash of such magnitude that all the national economies of the West will collapse at the same time.

"The planet will find itself in a desperate predicament. Cash will not be worth a damn, and the risks of a global confrontation (planned!) will be high.

ENTER PINE GAP

"At this point, the usefulness of bases like Pine Gap will become obvious. If a Global confrontation is going to break out, those bases will serve as a place of safety for the politicians and their staff, as well as the international financiers, their family and friends.

"If no confrontation breaks out, the financiers will adapt a 'saintly' attitude AND OFFER SUBSTITUTION OF ALL

CURRENCIES BY PLASTIC CARDS, ENSURING 'TRUE EQUALITY' FOR ALL; THE ABOLITION OF ALL OWNERSHIP RIGHTS; and the setting up of a World Government that will 'ensure peace'.

"The masses (consciousness as a group) will be convinced that it is necessary to ensure Peace and Social Justice by any means, including force. THE POTENTIAL ACHIEVED THROUGH THE EQUIPMENT OF THE UNDERGROUND BASES WILL MAKE POSSIBLE THE DISAPPEARANCE WITHOUT A TRACE OF THOSE WHO DO NOT CONFORM AND THOSE WHO 'HINDER THE HAPPINESS OF THE PEOPLE'. Also, it will ensure the swift crushing of any possible uprising. IT MAY ALSO HAPPEN THAT OUR NEW 'MASTERS' WILL END UP TELLING THE PEOPLE THAT THEY HAVE THE ALIENS' SUPPORT, AND THAT WE (ARE) AT THE 'EVE OF THE MILLENNIUM, A GOLDEN AGE'...... IT WILL BE THE WORST DICTATORSHIP EVER KNOWN TO MANKIND.

"......IT IS QUITE CERTAIN THAT OTHER BASES HAVE BEEN BUILT IN THE UNITED STATES AND ELSEWHERE IN THE NORTHERN HEMISPHERE. IT MAY EVEN BE THAT THE US BASES OCCUPIED BY THE GREYS, IN THE US MAINLAND, ARE OF THE SAME TYPE. ONE RUMOR HOLDS THAT A REPRESENTATIVE OF THE GREYS IS FOUND IN EACH OF THE UNDERGROUND US BASES IN THE SOUTHERN HEMISPHERE.

"None of the above has anything to do with science fiction. All of what I said in this text is true, and doesn't give a very rosy picture of the future."

and is officially known as the Joint Defense Space
Research Facility.

When the JDSRF was first initiated, its aim was
scientific research for the supposed development of a
space defense technology. It is now known that since its
inception, its primary purpose was to research into
electromagnetic propulsion. [Author's note: Is it possible
that there is some relationship here with the HAARP
Project?]

It is said that under Pine Gap is the deepest drilling
hole in Australia—about 5 miles (more than 8,000
meters). Such a hole is likely used as an underground
antenna able to recharge the batteries of submarines in
the Pacific and Indian Ocean through ELF broadcasts.
Such a gigantic antenna could be used to generate the
gigantic stationary wave around the Earth.

On the other hand, Pine Gap is well known as one of
the most important control centers for spy satellites
which circle the globe. . . .

Pine Gap has enormous computers which are connected to their American and Australian central counterparts, which collect all the information secured in these
countries, not only about finance and technology, but
on every aspect of the life of the average citizen. . . .

Don't make the mistake of thinking that the European citizens
have been overlooked.

. . . It may be worthy of note that the Amundsen-Scott
base at the South Pole is located on a sensitive magnetic
spot of our planet, that it holds exactly the same assets
as Pine Gap, and that all the information about most of
the average citizens of Western Europe is stored there
in memory banks tens of meters under the icepack.

The most disquieting fact about Pine Gap may be that
the employees working on the base, and especially those
earmarked for duty on electromagnetic propulsion

projects, have undergone brainwashing and even implantation of intracranial devices [Author's note: I have been unable to verify this statement, so for the time being I am regarding it as an unconfirmed rumor.]

Then they raise the question of the new Parliament building constructed in Canberra, apparently of enormous size and *far exceeding* the needs of the Australian government and its 18 million citizens. They estimate that it would fit the needs of the USSR or the US.

> . . . I bumped into an Englishman who told me that the Australian premier, Bob Hawk, was a Rhodes scholar, and as such he worked toward the setting up of a **One World Government**, and that this new Parliament building likely had something to do with it [emphasis added].

Then we are told about the infiltration into various political and religious groups by the *Club of Rome,* with the intent of aiding the progression toward world dictatorship. (See my first book, *Mark of the New World Order* for complete details on this and other similar orders.)

According to this report, Peter Sawyer, a former high-ranking Australian civil servant with access to the information, revealed the establishment of a "telephone exchange" in Canberra called "Deacon Center." It was built in concrete with thick walls, costing hundreds of millions of dollars. According to Sawyer, it has numerous computers, arrayed on four levels. When he tried to find out why such equipment was needed in a country of only 18 million population, **he discovered that those computers were connected to all the banks, to every post office, to all telephones, and to all of the police stations and customs houses; to every arrival and departure desk for air or sea travelers; and also and above all, to the other data centers collecting data on private citizens . . . in the United States as well as in Europe.**

There is much more evidence given for the impending world financial collapse (which is planned, of course), which will prepare the way for our takeover by the New World Order government.

ENTER PINE GAP

At this point, the usefulness of bases like Pine Gap will become obvious. If a Global confrontation is going to break out, those bases will serve as a place of safety for the politicians and their staff, as well as the international financiers, their family and friends.

If no confrontation breaks out, the financiers will adapt a "saintly" attitude AND OFFER SUBSTITUTION OF ALL CURRENCIES BY PLASTIC CARDS, ENSURING "TRUE EQUALITY" FOR ALL; THE ABOLITION OF ALL OWNERSHIP RIGHTS; and the setting up of a World Government that will "ensure peace."

As I warned at the beginning of this section, I don't necessarily agree totally with some of the content in this paper (I think much of it may be science fiction), but the author concludes with the following statement: "None of the above has anything to do with science fiction. All of what I said in this text is true, and doesn't give a very rosy picture of the future." Even with my justifiable reservations, I certainly concur with his analysis of the situation!

I located another reference to this subject on the Internet, stating that the information was taken from George C. Andrews' book, *Extraterrestrial Friends and Foes*. Since the information reads *verbatum* as the above report, I only can assume that Andrews also discovered this information and included it in his book. These five items were covered in this Internet transmission: (1) location and title of the facility; (2) the drilling of a five-mile hole and recharging of batteries of submarines in the Pacific or Indian Ocean through ELF broadcasts; (3) spy satellites; (4) brainwashing and implants of employees; (5) RHIC-EDOM (Radio Hypnotic Intracerebral

Control-Electronic Dissolution of Memory). The fifth one does sound as though it may have possibilities of connection with the HAARP Project. They close by requesting information on any research you may have on RHIC-EDOM. Their E-mail address is (BrazilByct@aol.com).

What Happened to the KGB?

By the way, while we are on the subject of foreign computer links, I should point out that contrary to popular belief, the Russian KGB, reported to be defunct, couldn't be healthier . . . it has just had one of those "phoenix-rise-from-the-ashes-type" rebirths. According to their Internet propaganda, it "was broken up into the SVR, FSK, and a number of other agencies." However, all it did was reemerge as the GRU military intelligence agency.

Now in case you are wondering why I'm bringing up the KGB/GRU at all in this book, it's because we are sharing everything with them, from economic and military intelligence, to UN military service, to the exchange of military officers, to the space station, and much more. So when we are all one global community under the control of the New World Order, we should have plenty of practice under our belts in accepting this international merging of people and governments.

Defense Information Systems Agency (DISA)

As DISA didn't have its own spoke on the wheel, but falls under the DoD, I am going to discuss it here before moving on to the remainder of the 13 spokes.

DISA is an intricate division of the DoD. It is defined in Internet literature as: "DoD agency responsible for information technology and is the central manager of major portions of the Defense Information Infrastructure (DII)." In fact, the web is replete with information on DISA and its numerous tentacles. Its website address is: (http://www.disa.mil/), and the Home Page carries the announcement: "Read Me First!—You are entering an Official US Government System." Information contained in these many pages reveals that Lieutenant General Albert J. Edmonds, USAF, is both the Director of DISA and the Manager of the National Communications System (NCS).

The Mission of DISA is stated as: "To Plan, Engineer, Develop, Test, Manage Programs, Acquire, Implement, Operate and Maintain Information Systems for C41 (Intelligence) and Mission Support Under all Conditions of Peace and War." The NSC assists the President and the Executive Office of the President in exercising wartime and nonwartime emergency telecommunications, and in the coordination of the planning for and provisioning of National Security and Emergency Preparedness (NS/EP) communications for the Federal Government under all circumstances.

Another arm of DISA is the White House Communications Agency (WHCA). Its mission statement incorporates the DISA statement (cited above) and declares that WHCA will be the preeminent provider of information systems providing telecommunications to the President and his White House staff, as well as the National Security Council, US Secret Service, and others.

Also operated by DISA is the DISA Information Systems Center (DISC), however, instead of having a mission to support the President, *et al,* its mission is to support the DISA Director, headquarters, and line organizations worldwide. DISA/DISC Information Resources Division is responsible for operating and maintaining DISA's WWW Internet System, among other duties. DISA has devised a strategy for the Defense Information System Network (DISN), stating their mission is to provide strategic information to the warriors engaged in battle, "and others as required by the DoD, under all conditions of Peace and War." They are located in Arlington, Virginia, and complete details may be obtained from their website: (http://www.disa.mil/DISN/disnhome.html).

On a website for Jet Propulsion Laboratory (JPL), California Institute of Technology (CIT), I ran across the following which ties in perfectly with previous information:

DSP (Defense Support Program)

The DSP program is the U.S. military's early warning system for the detection of long-range ballistic missile launches and nuclear detonations. The system uses a constellation of geosynchronous DSP satellites to provide continual coverage. Initially begun in 1970, over 19(?) DSP satellites have been launched. The satellite bus and instrument payload have been improved over the years, resulting in three different DSP variants. DSP satellites were used during the Persian Gulf War to detect Iraqi Scud missile launches. The DSP system is controlled from Scott AFB, Missouri, with stations at Guam Island, Pine Gap, Australia, and Nurrangar, Australia.

The January 8, 1996, edition of the *Government Computer News* carried an article titled, "Intelligence systems designers combat wartime snafus," by Paul Constance. He begins with a challenging comment: "If the Defense Department had a better intelligence data network, Capt. Scott O'Grady might not have been shot down over Bosnia." The new system that resulted was based on a "means of seamlessly integrating database management...[and] joint communications," among other things.

Just some more fuel for the fire! Merging, joining, integrating...all just another way of saying centralizing the information. Now that we have covered the DoD and some of the sister organizations not mentioned on the Intelligence Wheel, even though their primary purpose always incorporates some form of intelligence gathering, we can get back to the organizations shown there.

Military Intelligence

The four major branches of the military—Army, Navy, Air Force, and Marines—are each a spoke in the intelligence wheel. I'm not sure why the Coast Guard was omitted, but they do have an operation called the Coast Guard Intelligence, and they share facilities in the National Maritime Intelligence

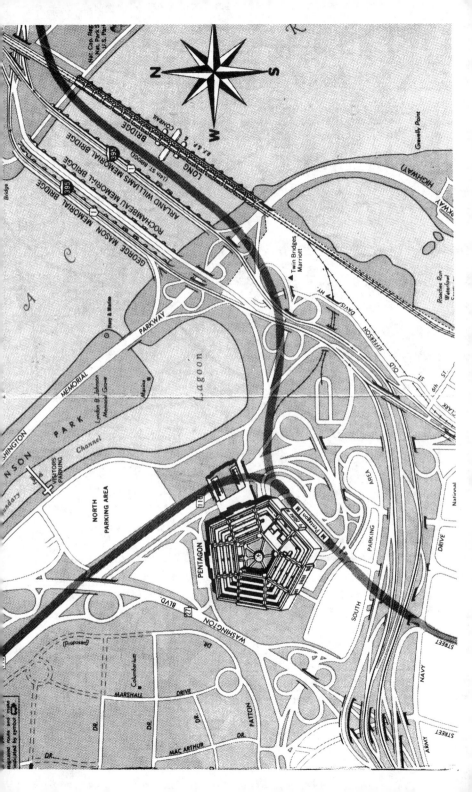

Satellite photo of the Pentagon area. © 1995 VARGIS, LLC. • *All Rights Reserved.*
Previous page: *Washington, DC, area road map.*

Center with Naval and Marine Corp intelligence. The only references to the Coast Guard that I can locate in Richelson's comprehensive book is its appearance in one of the boxes on the Naval Intelligence organizational chart and its reference in the caption of a photo (p. 149) of the National Maritime

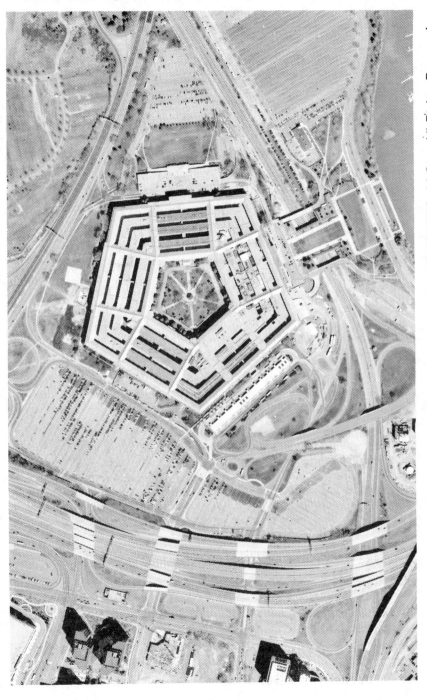

Close-up of aerial photo of the Pentagon and surrounding highways. © 1995 VARGIS, LLC. • All Rights Reserved.

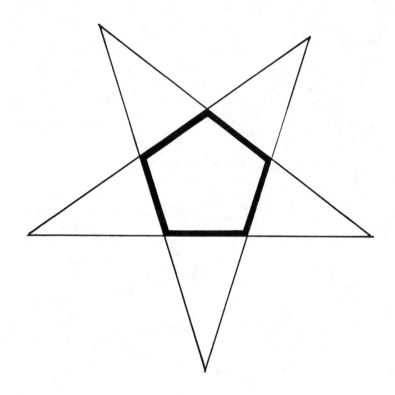

The Pentagon / Pentagram Connection

Note the unique occultic design of the DoD's "Pentagon" headquarters building in Washington, DC. There is a hidden spiritual/Masonic message conveyed by its geometric configuration. Note how a "pentagon" easily can become an occultic/satanic "pentagram" simply by extending the "pentagon's" lines. See diagram of satanic pentagram from Hall's Masonic book, The Secret Teachings of All Ages.

Intelligence Center building and grounds.

As we proceed through this study, I want to encourage you, once again, to get a copy of Richelson's *The U.S. Intelligence Community*. As space constraints preclude my going into great detail about these other direct intelligence gathering organizations, I am going to be intentionally brief. But Richelson's book is very thorough, following the trail of each department in each organization, for those who want to follow it.

He opens Chapter 4, "Military Service Intelligence Organizations," this way:

> Unlike the United Kingdom and Canada, which abolished their military service intelligence organizations with the creation of defense intelligence organizations, or Australia, which restricts its service intelligence organizations to the production of purely tactical intelligence, the United States has maintained elaborate service intelligence organizations.
>
> The continued major role of U.S. service intelligence organizations is partly a function of bureaucratic politics and partly a function of U.S. military requirements. A military force with large service components, each with wide-ranging functional and geographical responsibilities, may be better served in terms of intelligence support by organizations that are not too detached from the service components. Additionally, some strategic intelligence and collection functions may be best performed by service organizations. Thus, some intelligence tasks—such as producing information about foreign aerospace or submarining technology—may be carried out most efficiently by the services most directly affected, in this case the Air Force and Navy, benefiting both the services involved as well as national policymakers.
>
> . . . the past several years has seen the disestablishment and/or **consolidation** of formerly separate intelligence organizations in each of the major services . . . [emphasis added].

Richelson relates that a 1990 report of the Senate Select Committee on Intelligence observed:

> The existence of these multiple organizations raises other important concerns. Over the years, numerous individuals and reports . . . have criticized the Defense

Department for significant duplication of effort; **insufficient integration and sharing of information**;. . .
[emphasis added].

Do you see where this inevitably is leading? **Consolidation?
Insufficient integration and sharing of information?**
They are in the process of preparing to funnel all their intelligence activities into one place, and I am convinced that place
is the NSA . . . only time will tell. However, coupling the fact
that they now have the largest computing capability in the
world with the extensive evidence that is available, it is a
logical assumption. To begin toward that goal, the Assistant
Secretary of Defense issued his *Plan for Restructuring Defense
Intelligence.* The plan instructed each military service to
"consolidate all existing intelligence commands, agencies,
and elements into a single intelligence command within each
Service."

Army Intelligence

Even though the chart is less than complex, when compared
with some of the other organizational charts, it is far reaching,
with many operations contained within the scope of each
category.

From the Internet, the website to gain information on Army
Intelligence is: (http://www.odci.gov/ic/usic/ai.html).

Navy Intelligence

Richelson reports that of all the military services, the Navy
had the most dramatic changes in the early 1990's. The Navy
had seven distinct intelligence divisions/organizations in 1991,
but by January 1, 1993, it had only two. He tells us that of
all the military branches, the Navy has done the best job of
complying with the order to condense intelligence efforts.
For more naval information, the website is:
(http://www.odci.gov/ic/usic/ni.html)
Additional information and many aerial maps of naval
intelligence centers are available on the Internet from the FAS

Figure 4-1. Army Intelligence Organizations.

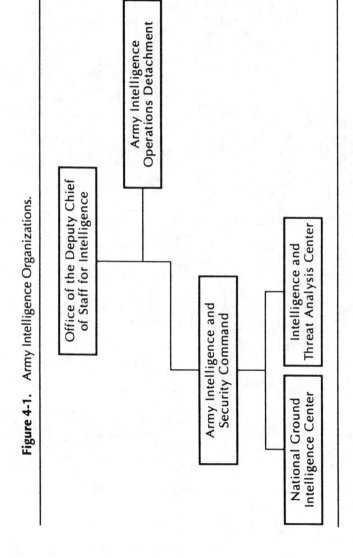

Courtesy of Jeffrey T. Richelson, The U.S. Intelligence Community.

Figure 4-6. Organization of the Office of Naval Intelligence.

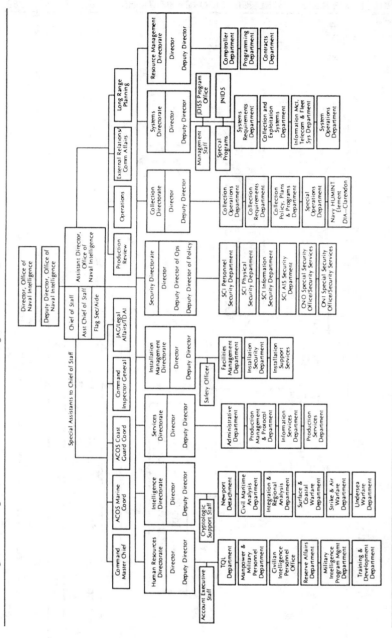

Source: *Office of Naval Intelligence. Courtesy of Jeffrey T. Richelson, The U.S. Intelligence Community.*

group as part of their Intelligence Reform Project (IRP), at (http://www.fas.org/irp/overhead/oni.htm).

Air Force Intelligence

After studying Richelson's information on the Air Force Intelligence organizations, I am left with the impression that their efforts to condense their operations have resulted only in creating different organizations, not necessarily fewer. Of course, they state their mission as ensuring that the Air Force receives the *best* intelligence information. Needless to say, the intelligence arms of the other branches of the military claim exactly the same thing . . . they want the "best" for their own branch of the service. The website address for more information on Air Force Intelligence is:

(http://www.odci.gov/ic/usic/afi.html)

Marine Corp Intelligence

Naturally, this group's mission is to support their own, however, of all the military groups, this one appears to be the most intimidating from an average citizen's standpoint . . . because of the other things mentioned in their authorized activities. In addition to their four intelligence branches, they have one that operates under the title, "Special Activities Support Office." Another one is called, "Counterintelligence and Human Intelligence Branch," with sections for Plans and Policy, Terrorist Threats, and Special Projects. They conduct "liaison with the JCS, the DIA, the NSA, the CIA, the Department of State, and other intelligence organizations." Company A of the Marine Support Battalion Company is located at Fort Meade, MD, home of the NSA.

They provide the least information at their website

(http://www.odci.gov/ic/usic/mci.html)

but the implications of what is given there—if you just read between the lines—is awesome. I don't believe there is any question that the Marines will be used to settle civil disobedience, unrest, and uprisings in the inner cities and elsewhere when everything starts breaking loose in the transition of the

Figure 4-10. Organization of the Air Intelligence Agency.

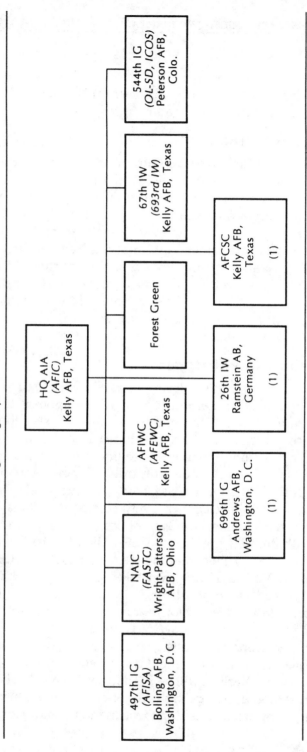

Note: The chart indicates the basic structure for the newly formed Air Intelligence Agency. Organization names are shown followed by their former designations. (1) indicates proposed inactivation. Source: Gabriel Marshall, "FOA Becomes Fact," Spokesman, November 1993, p. 8. Courtesy of Jeffrey T. Richelson, The U.S. Intelligence Community.

Table 4-3. Marine Support Battalion Company Locations.

Company	Location
A	Fort Meade. Md.
B	Edzell, U.K.
C	Guam
D	Galeta Island, Panama
E	Misawa, Japan
F	Rota, Spain
G	Pyong Taek, Korea
H	Homestead, Fla.
I	Adak, Alaska
K	Pensacola, Fla.
L	Guantanamo Bay, Cuba

Source: "United States Navy Plain Language Address Directory," in *United States Military Communications-Electronics Board, USMCEB Publication No. 6, Issue 25, Message Address Directory (Washington, DC: US Government Printing Office, January 30, 1993), p. 145. Courtesy of Jeffrey T. Richelson, The U.S. Intelligence Community.*

takeover of Big Brother and the New World Order. By that time, they likely will be under the administration/authority of some sort of UN military leadership who will "do us a favor" and step in to help us poor citizens restore order to our crumbling world.

One of their stated goals is to "provide pre-deployment training and force contingency planning *for requirements that are not satisfied by theater, other service, or national capabilities*" [emphasis added]. In 1996, *The Register* in Orange County, California, carried an article, complete with photos, showing the Marines from a nearby base practicing maneuvers in a "local neighborhood" created to teach them to control civilian rebellions, riots, terrorism, *et al,* in an urban setting. They also admit that the Marine Corps Intelligence Activity (MCIA) produces a "full range of 'products' to satisfy 'customer' needs in *peace, pre-crisis, or contingency situations . . .*" [emphasis added].

Defense Intelligence Agency

The next spoke in the wheel, the Defense Intelligence Agency, is also a part of the Department of Defense (DoD). Richelson says:

> In addition to the national intelligence organizations within the Department of Defense (DOD)—the National Reconnaissance Office (NRO), the National Security Agency (NSA), and the Central Imagery Office [now NIMA]—there are several department-level agencies with the primary function of satisfying the intelligence requirements of the Secretary of Defense, DOD components, and the military services.
>
> Two of these agencies—the Defense Intelligence Agency (DIA) and the Defense Mapping Agency (DMA)— can trace their origins to the centralization trend that began at the end of the Eisenhower administration. . . .

According to their Internet information, the DIA is the senior military intelligence component of the Intelligence

Figure 3-1. Organization of the Defense Intelligence Agency.

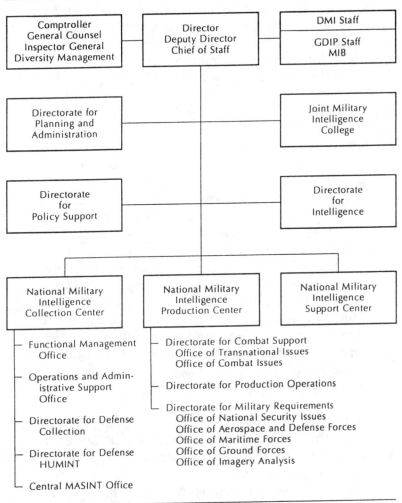

Source: Department of Defense Telephone Directory, April 1994 *(Washington, DC: US Government Printing Office, 1994), pp. D-24 to D-25. Courtesy of Jeffrey T. Richelson,* The U.S. Intelligence Community.

Community. They claim their "primary mission is to provide all-source intelligence to the US armed forces." "All-source" sounds rather all-encompassing to me, and I suspect it means precisely what it says, although their obvious function is providing intelligence on military matters.

I think the second paragraph is interesting:

> Since the end of the Cold War and Desert Shield/ Storm, DIA has undergone dramatic change. Regional priorities have changed, missions and functions have been realigned, and a strategic plan has been created to reflect new global realities. [Author's note: The missions described next were most, if not all, joint efforts with UN forces. In fact, you may remember the recent incident of the young soldier who refused to wear the UN uniform . . . he had signed up to serve his country, not the United Nations, and he recognized the importance of the implications of doing otherwise.] Crises in places like Somalia, Haiti, Bosnia, Rwanda, Iraq, and North Korea, as well as such global challenges as the proliferation of weapons of mass destruction, terrorism, narcotics trafficking, and monitoring of arms control treaties have increased the scope of demands for intelligence in the post-Cold War world. . . .

On the Internet, the FAS offers aerial photos of two DIA facilities, the Defense Intelligence Analysis Center (DIAC) located at Bolling AFB and the Clarendon site, available at websites (respectively):

(http://www.fas.org/irp/overhead/dia.htm)
(http://www.fas.org/irp/overhead/diava.htm)

Central Imagery Office (CIO) / National Imagery & Mapping Agency (NIMA—eff. 10-1-96)

At the time the intelligence wheel which we have been using was created, it contained the Central Imagery Office (under the auspices of the DoD). However, in keeping with

the "condense and centralize" goals, the National Imagery and Mapping Agency was established in October, 1996, to combine the functions of "eight separate organizations of the Defense and Intelligence communities." That means we have a much larger, more powerful entity than the former CIO. The announcement may be read in full at their website:
(http://164.214.2.59/org/backgrn.html)
Below is an excerpt from that release:

> . . . NIMA will improve support to national and military customers alike. [Author's note: Can the *contrasting* of the term *national* with the term *military* mean anything other than they are engaged in civilian activity, as well?]
>
> NIMA incorporates the Defense Mapping Agency, the Central Imagery Office, and the Defense Dissemination Program Office in their entirety; and the mission and functions of the CIA's National Photographic Interpretation Center. *These organizations are disestablished effective today.* Also included in NIMA are the imagery exploitation, dissemination, and processing elements of the Defense Intelligence Agency, National Reconnaissance Office, and Defense Airborne Reconnaissance Office. [Emphasis added.]

NIMA Logo and Seal

Not to be outdone by the larger agencies (which may not be much larger now, with the exception of the NSA and the CIA), NIMA has its own logo and seal (next page). Following is what they have to say about the meaning of the elements of their seal:

> The NIMA seal's eagle and stars exemplify the principles of freedom our country was founded on and underscore the national security mission of the National Imagery and Mapping Agency. Laurel symbolizes honor and high achievement and the three crossed arrows represent the organization's mission and role in total

NIMA logo and seal. Note again the Masonic / occultic Phoenix / Eagle bird.

military preparedness and defense. Black represents outer space and the globe represents mapping and imaging. The Latin phrase, *Tempestivum Verum Definitum,* stands for Timely, Accurate, and Precise.

The organizational chart for NIMA displayed herein was obtained from their website.
(http://164.214.2.59/org/orgchart.html)
The NIMA headquarters is located in Fairfax, Virginia, with other major facilities in northern Virginia, Washington, DC, Bethesda, Maryland, and St. Louis, Missouri. . ."with support and liaison offices worldwide." It is interesting to note that NIMA has printed a full page of Disclaimer Notices on material obtained from their website, including Disclaimer Notice, Disclaimer of Liability, Disclaimer of Endorsement, and Use of NIMA Seal. It most certainly is no surprise that they are monitoring those who access the information. . .the surprise is that *they admit it!* "Such monitoring may result in the acquisition, recording and analysis of all data being

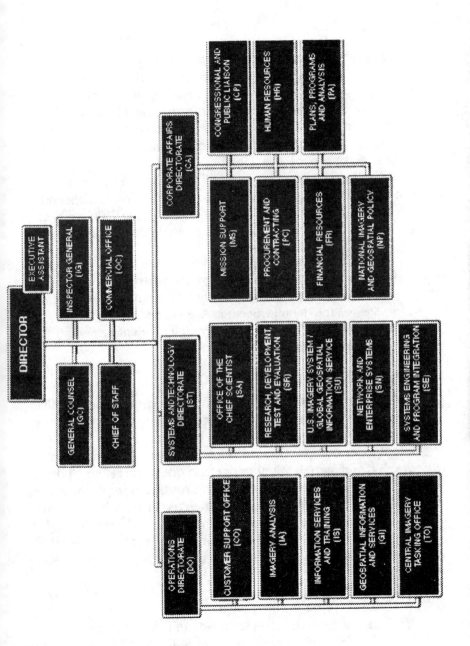

NIMA Organizational Chart

communicated, transmitted, processed or stored in this system. . . . Use of this system *constitutes consent* to such monitoring" [emphasis added]. The other disclaimers apply primarily to the misuse of the information received.

I have included a photo from the Internet picturing the Central Imagery Office (CIO) administration buildings and an aerial photo of the Defense Mapping Agency (DMA) facilities (again, courtesy of the FAS). I have no doubts they are now part of NIMA, since it absorbed and "disestablished" the CIO, and according to Richelson (p. 35), the CIO had been authorized broadly to use other agencies' facilities:

> DOD Directive 5105.26 authorizes the CIO to *make maximum use of facilities and personnel* assigned to the Defense Mapping Agency, the Defense Intelligence Agency, the National Security Agency, and, to the extent authorized by the DCI, the Central Intelligence Agency [emphasis added].

National Reconnaissance Office

According to Richelson, the National Reconnaissance Office (NRO) has a broad range of functions, but primarily they manage satellite reconnaissance programs for the entire US intelligence community. This includes the collection of photographic and signals intelligence and ocean surveillance data. They also are "responsible for the routine operation of the satellites, including maneuvers such as turning them on and off and facing them toward or away from the sun."

As with the other organizations on the wheel, the NRO operates under the direction of the DCI and, as with eight of the thirteen, it is part of the DoD.

Under a shroud of deep secrecy, the NRO was established in 1960. The first public revelation of its existence came in 1973 as the result of an error made in a Senate report. Until 1992 the NRO's very existence was still classified, operating under a cover organization that had been established just for the purpose of hiding the operations of this clandestine group.

CIO Headquarters, Tysons Corner, Virginia.

Defense Mapping Agency headquarters facility.

Aerial photo of the National Reconnaissance Office facility.
© *1995 VARGIS, LLC.* • *All Rights Reserved.*

Close-up of Satellite photo of the new National Reconnaissance Office (NRO). The NRO is the second most secret intelligence agency in the world. NRO maintains all NSA satellites and provides NSA with all global satellite intelligence data. © 1995 VARGIS, LLC. • All Rights Reserved.

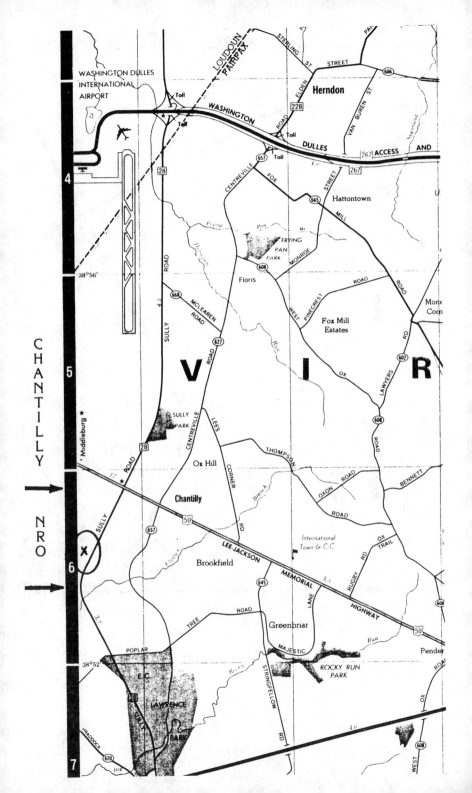

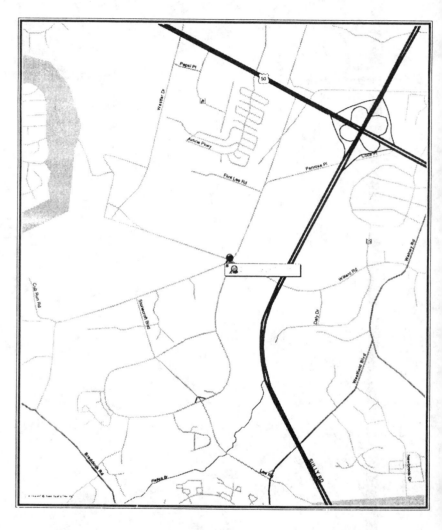

NRO on the local road map.

The NRO headquarters offices are located at 14675 Lee Road, in Chantilly, Virginia. Their other facilities include Onizuka AFB (Sunnyvale, California); White Cloud NOSS Facility Building 59 (Naval Research Laboratory); Crystal City, Virginia; a shared facility (with the CIA Office of Development & Engineering, Reston, Virginia); Defense Communications Electronics Evaluation Testing Activity (D-CEETA—at Ft. Belvoir, Virginia); Aerospace Data Facility (Buckley Air National Guard Base, Denver, Colorado); a temporary facility at Lafayette Business Park, near Chantilly, Virginia; interim facility at Dulles International Airport Center. . .and perhaps even more. As with the other intelligence organizations we have studied, the FAS provides generous maps and aerial photos of all these locations on their website.

Speaking of websites, if you wish to see what the NRO has to say about itself (pages and pages and pages of it), its address is:

(http://www.nro.odci.gov/)

The NRO's annual budget is estimated at roughly $6 billion, and it doesn't seem to be able to account for it very well. So what's a billion or two among friends?! It's only our tax money! Maybe it's my naturally suspicious mind, but I'll bet it's not lost; I'll bet you it is spent in some *secret funding* of some *secret project,* about which as yet we know absolutely nothing. . .one of the "Black" projects of some kind.

The New York Times (January 30, 1996) ran an article by Tim Weiner titled, "A Secret Agency's Secret Budgets Yield 'Lost' Billions, Officials Say." Here is the condensed version of that article.

Do you stash a little cash in various spots of your home—a twenty in your tool chest or maybe a C-note in the bottom of your clothes hamper? "Rainy Day" money. But then the day comes when you need it. . .and you can't remember where you hid it!

If this is you, you'll sympathize with our government's

Figure 2-5. Probable Organization of the National Reconnaissance Office.

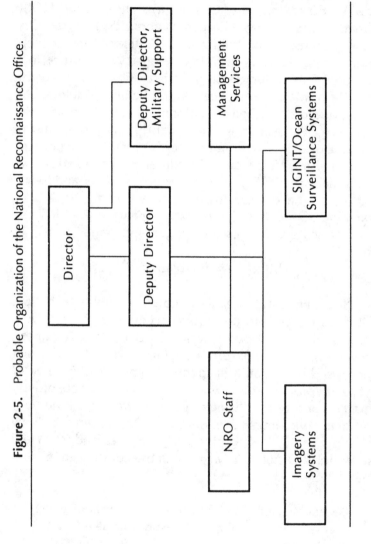

Courtesy of Jeffrey T. Richelson, The U.S. Intelligence Community.

"National Reconnaissance Office." The NRO is an extra-superduper-secretive agency that no one ever heard of. It is so secretive that its very existence was officially denied until 1992, even though its been around 35 years. It manufactures expensive spy satellites for the CIA, the Navy, the IRS, the Republican National Committee, Arnold Schwartznegger, and God knows who else, and is responsible for keeping track of all these satellites, spy missions, and other important stuff.

So, imagine the NRO's embarrassment to discover that it had lost track of more than TWO *BILLION* DOLLARS that Congress had previously appropriated to it. Now, two billion dollars is bigger than a bread basket, so it's not easy to just—poof!—lose it. But it's that "Rainy Day" thing—NRO's top dogs stashed a million here, a hundred million there . . . and next thing you know, no one remembers where it is!

A Senate staffer for the committee that supposedly oversees the NRO dismissed the agency's misplaced billions as "a severe accounting problem." I'll say! He confesses that Congress doesn't really know what the NRO does with the $6 Billion a year it gets of our money. Just last year, for example, the congressional "oversight" committee was shocked to learn that the NRO had built a $300-million headquarters building for itself in the Washington suburbs.

Then the person putting the article on the Internet puts his own postscript on the article: "This is Jim Hightower saying . . . Now *that's* some oversight! If these splurging spooks can build a $300-million headquarters and simply "lose" $2 billion more through the bureaucratic cracks . . . don't you think they have too much of our money?"

Another Internet location
          (http://www.refp.org/Clinton/cc1008.html)

reads:

January 1996: Secret Government
Spy agency 'misplaces' $2 billion of secret budget

The National Reconnaissance Office, an agency that builds spy satellites, informed Congress that it lost track of more than $2 billion of its $28 billion budget. The NRO budget is classified as "top secret." Critics of the agency told *The New York Times* that the money went into a secret "slush fund."

Another site on the Internet provided the following information on the budgets of the major intelligence organizations in the US. This information was leaked from the House Committee in 1994.

Total Spending (5 major org'ns) $28,000,000,000

Stats from open sources guessing breakdown:

CIA—Central Intelligence Agency . . . . . . $ 3,000,000,000
NRO—National Reconnaissance Office . .   7,000,000,000
NSA—National Security Agency   4,000,000,000
TIARA—Tactical Intelligence & Related . . 12,000,000,000
       Activities—Pentagon
DIA—Defense Intelligence Agency   600,000,000

Total Documented $26,600,000,000
Leftover (?) . . . . $ 1,400,000,000

Stated Mission of the NRO

To complete our examination of the NRO and its activities, let's check out its Mission, as it sees it to be. As with all the others, it allegedly wants to provide the best information available to those who want to obtain it, but there was one slight difference in NRO's stated goals: "The NRO's assets collect intelligence to support such functions as indications and warning, monitoring arms control agreements, military operations and exercises, and *monitoring of natural disasters and other environmental issues.*" I'm not exactly sure how "intelligence gathering" has anything to do with natural disasters and other environmental issues, unless it's info for the weather man, or is to support the subversive endeavors of the radical environmentalists who are actively pressing for the one-world government of the New World Order (a much more likely option).

The Federal Bureau of Investigation (FBI)

The next major intelligence-gathering organization in our wheel is not operating under the auspices of the DoD, in fact, I believe there is some question as to whether they consider themselves answerable to anybody! (Technically, they are under the DOJ—Department of Justice.) But, just as the other groups are migrating toward the "condense and centralize" mode, the FBI is doing likewise. They are collecting fingerprints from all over, to be converted into digitized, computer-friendly format, storing criminal and terrorist information, and trading data with the NCIC and Interpol (and ultimately with the NAS, I'm sure). The FBI would be considered an "Indirect—Government" group, as their major function is law enforcement, and their collection of data is for the purpose of supporting their criminal justice programs.

The FBI Headquarters is located in the J. Edgar Hoover Building, 935 Pennsylvania Avenue, NW, Washington, DC 20535-0001, Phone: (202) 324-3000, website:
(http://www.odci.gov/is/usic/fbi.html)

Criminal Justice Information Services (CJIS):
Formerly Known as The National Identification Center

Before we get into the details of the background and stated mission of the FBI, I want to enlighten you about a name change of the largest division of the FBI. The section formerly known as the National Identification Center (NIC) is now known as Criminal Justice Information Services (CJIS).

Their media department furnished the following information about the FBI, and the CJIS in particular:

> The Criminal Justice Information Services (CJIS) is the largest division within the FBI. It was established in February, 1992, as the entity to house **the consolidation** of the FBI's criminal justice information services [here is some more of that consolidation of information].
>
> The CJIS Division is the focal point and central repository for criminal justice information services in the FBI. It serves as a customer-driven organization providing "high tech" identification and information services to local, state, Federal, and international criminal justice communities.
>
> This division is responsible for the day-to-day operations of the Fingerprint Identification Program, the National Crime Information Center (NCIC), and the Uniform Crime Reports (UCR) program which includes the National Incident-Based Reporting System (NIBRS).
>
> The CJIS Division is also responsible for the development of the Integrated Automated Fingerprint Identification System (IAFIS), and for partnering with the FBI's Information Resources Division concerning the development of the **NCIC 2000** System.
>
> The FBI must ensure that these systems, as well as any future systems, **completely integrate** in order to provide the criminal justice community the identification and information services it needs as we move into the 21st century [emphasis added].

Revitalization

The FBI is in the process of updating (they call it "revitalizing") several of its main criminal justice programs. A brief synopsis of the changes follow:

> The revitalization of the current NCIC system, NCIC 2000, will include enhancements to existing NCIC

hardware and software, as well as new functionality. This functionality includes the capability to transmit photograph and fingerprint images between a user's patrol car and the NCIC 2000 computer, where the fingerprint image will be rapidly searched against the database for wanted and/or missing individuals. The CJIS Division is partnering with the Information Resources Division on this project.

NIBRS is the enhancement of the current UCR program, which provides an accounting of the extent and nature of criminal activity. NIBRS is an incident-based reporting system, meaning data is collected on each single crime occurrence and its components. Analysis of these facts can provide vital information about crime and its impact on victims, offenders, property, arrestees, and the U.S. society as a whole.

The IAFIS will consist of several integrated segments including Identification Tasking and Networking (ITN), which will provide for the submission of electronic fingerprint images; the Interstate Identification Index (III) [sometime called "Triple I"], which is the national system for the exchange of criminal history records; the Automated Fingerprint Identification System (AFIS), which provides automated fingerprint comparisons and identifies candidates for fingerprint examiners to use in the identification of criminals; and the Fingerprint Image Conversion Operation (FICO), which represents the conversion of approximately 32 million fingerprint cards to electronic images for IAFIS use.

The CJIS Division has relocated to a new facility at Clarksburg, West Virginia. This is the "first time any government organization has attempted to relocate and revitalize operations simultaneously," according to the FBI media office. This new site (see photo and map) is "**located atop 986 wildlife-filled acres** [Author's note: The FBI's location is approximately the same size as NSA's mammoth facility.], contains more than 500,000 square feet of working area [with] many special features, including a 500-seat auditorium, a 600-seat cafeteria with patio seating, a public reception area and atrium, and large windows with scenic vistas in nearly every office. To accommodate the needs of its employees, the FBI has also constructed a **16,000 square-foot** onsite child development center for children aged three months to twelve years (before and after school program and summer camp). The center will focus on developmentally appropriate activities and encourage parental involvement." [Emphasis added.]

This influx has proven to be quite an economic boon for northern West Virginia, and the community of Clarksburg in particular. "There are currently over 1,900 employees working at the West Virginia complex. When fully operational, a total of 3,500 employees are expected. Approximately three-fourths of the current force were hired from within West Virginia at competitive salaries. It is estimated, in today's dollars, that the CJIS Division's relocation will bring in excess of a **70 million dollar payroll** in the the state of West Virginia," according to the Media Information Guide on the CJIS. [Emphasis added.]

State Road Maps Provide Insight

Far from being set in some secret location, I have obtained three sets of blueprints from the West Virginia Department of Transportation, Division of Highways, for the construction of the "FBI Interchange and Access Road," on I-79, "FBI Access Road No. 1" (the north entrance), and "FBI Access Road No. 2" (the west entrance). The size of blueprints precludes me shrinking them down small enough to incorporate into this book; however, I have reduced sections of the top page of each project, identifying the project, showing the location on a map, and showing the signature block where the project was approved. The physical address is: 1000 Custer Hollow Road, Clarksburg, WV 26306, Phone: (304) 625-2000.

Formerly called the National Identification Center. Now known as Criminal Justice Information Services (CJIS), located in Clarksburg, WV. Extremely rare aerial photo courtesy of the FBI.

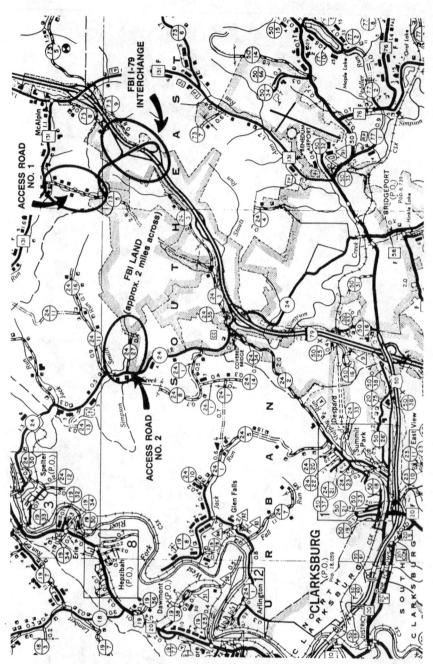

Areas on the above map are marked in accordance with three sets of blueprints received from the West Virginia Department of Transportation Division of Highways.

WEST VIRGINIA
DEPARTMENT OF TRANSPORTATION
DIVISION OF HIGHWAYS

RIGHT OF WAY PLANS

OF

STATE HIGHWAY

FEDERAL PROJECT.NO. HDP-9218(001)
STATE PROJECT NO. X317-79-123.24

ROUTE NO. 1-79

MONONGAHELA *DISTRICT*

HARRISON *COUNTY*

F.B.I. INTERCHANGE AND ACCESS ROAD

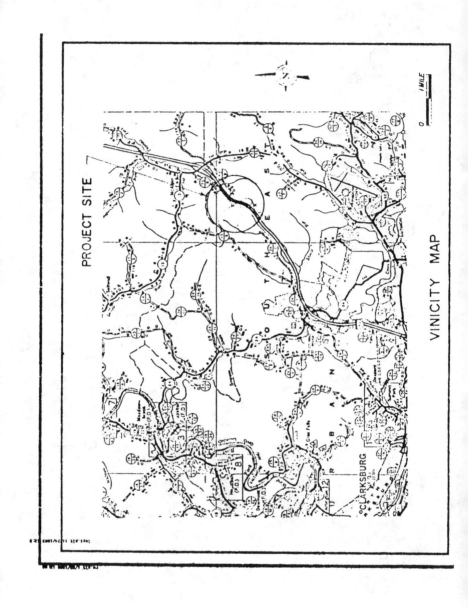

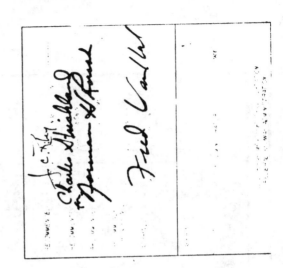

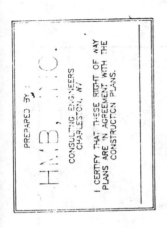

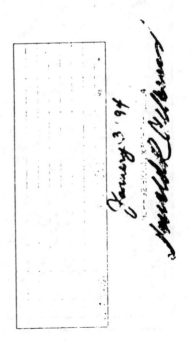

PREPARED BY:

H.M.B., INC.

CONSULTING ENGINEERS
CHARLESTON, WV

I CERTIFY THAT THESE RIGHT OF WAY
PLANS ARE IN AGREEMENT WITH THE
CONSTRUCTION PLANS.

PRINTED

DEC 24 1996

RIGHT OF WAY DIVISION

January 13 '94

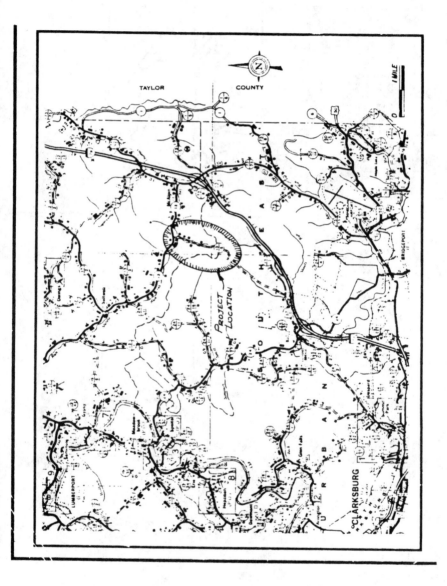

WEST VIRGINIA
DEPARTMENT OF TRANSPORTATION
DIVISION OF HIGHWAYS

RIGHT OF WAY PLANS

OF

STATE HIGHWAY

FEDERAL PROJECT NO.
STATE PROJECT NO.   X317-13/5-1.99, 01

ROUTE NO. 13/5

CLAY DISTRICT

HARRISON COUNTY

RTE. 13/5 STATION 10+00.00 TO STATION 56+75.00 = 4675.00 L.F.   (0.885 MI.)
RTE. 13   STATION 13+00.00 TO STATION 34+00.00 = 2100.00 L.F.   (0.398 MI.)

TOTAL LENGTH = 6775.00 L.F.   (1.283 MI.)

FBI ACCESS ROAD NO.1

KENTUCKY

TAYLOR   COUNTY

are labeled Project X317-13/5-1.99.01, Parcel 9, Tracts 1, 2, and 3.

Norman H. Rough
Registered Professional Engineer # 4698

PRINTED

DEC 24 1996

RIGHT OF WAY DIVISION

RECOMMENDED

RECOMMENDED

RECOMMENDED
CHIEF ENGINEER DEVELOPMENT

RECOMMENDED
FOR APPROVAL

APPROVED
COMMISSIONER OF HIGHWAYS

APPROVED
DIVISION ADMINISTRATOR   DATE

U.S. DEPARTMENT OF TRANSPORTATION
FEDERAL HIGHWAY ADMINISTRATION

END R/W PROJ. X317-13/5-1.99.01
STATION 56+75.00

TO BRIDGEPORT
(FBI COMPLEX)

REVISIONS

I HEREBY CERTIFY THAT THIS IS A CORRECT COPY OF THE
PLANS OF PROJECT X317-13/5-1.99.01

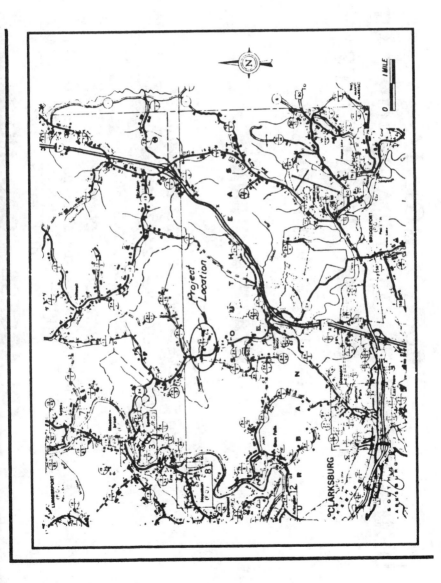

WEST VIRGINIA
DEPARTMENT OF TRANSPORTATION
DIVISION OF HIGHWAYS

RIGHT OF WAY PLANS

OF

STATE HIGHWAY

FEDERAL PROJECT NO.

STATE PROJECT NO.   X317-24/27-0.00, 01

COUNTY ROUTE NO. 24/27 &   24

SIMPSON   DISTRICT

HARRISON   COUNTY

RTE. 24/27 STATION 10+00.00 TO STATION 33+88.00 = 2,388 L.F. (0.45 MI.)
RTE. 24   STATION 92+55.00 TO STATION 105+75.00 = 1,320 L.F. (0.25 MI.)

TOTAL LENGTH = 3,708 L.F. (0.70 MI.)

FBI ACCESS ROAD NO.2

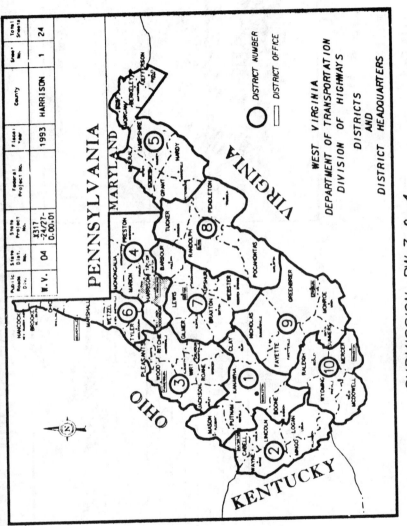

SUBMISSION: RW-3 & 4

PRINTED

DEC 2 4 1996

RIGHT OF WAY DIVISION

RECOMMENDED ....
DIRECTOR RIGHT OF WAY DIVISION

RECOMMENDED ....
DIRECTOR OF DESIGN

RECOMMENDED ....
CHIEF ENGINEER DEVELOPMENT

RECOMMENDED ....
FOR APPROVAL   STATE HIGHWAY ENGINEER

APPROVED ....
COMMISSIONER OF HIGHWAYS

APPROVED ....
DIVISION ADMINISTRATOR   DATE

U.S. DEPARTMENT OF TRANSPORTATION
FEDERAL HIGHWAY ADMINISTRATION

REVISIONS

REVISION NUMBER	SHEET NUMBER						DATE	BY

1-19   9-93

I HEREBY CERTIFY THAT THIS IS A CORRECT COPY OF THE
PLANS OF PROJECT X.3IT-24 (27) 000.01

BUSINESS MANAGER

TO BRIDGEPORT

FBI Fact Sheet

Think of this as the *"Reader's Digest* version" of the stats on the FBI (as of July 31, 1996). I will elaborate a bit more on its investigative programs, after I have furnished this concentrated version of its history and current status.

This abbreviated fact sheet may be found on the Internet at:
(http://www.fbi.gov/general/facts/fact.htm)

Established: An investigative agency under the Department of Justice (DOJ) was formed in 1908; after various changes in name, it became known as the FBI in 1935.

Organization: The FBI is headed by a Director [presently Louis J. Freeh] and Deputy Director. Headquarters is comprised of nine divisions and four offices. The FBI maintains 56 field offices, approximately 400 resident agencies, four specialized field installations, and 23 foreign liaison posts.

Employees (as of 7/31/96): Special Agents, 10,529; Support Personnel, 15,398.

Investigative Programs:
- Applicant Matters
- Civil Rights
- Counterterrorism
- Financial Crimes
- Foreign Counterintelligence
- Organized Crime/Drugs
- Violent Crimes and Major Offenders

Budget: The FBI's total annual funding for all operations, salaries, and expenses is approximately $2.5 billion. [After subsequently receiving a "special allowance" to increase their technology and activites, the figure is now approximately $2.9 billion.]

Mission: To uphold the law through the investigation of violations of federal criminal law; to protect the United States from foreign intelligence and terrorist activities; to provide leadership and law enforcement assistance to federal, state, local, and international agencies; and to perform these responsibilities in a manner that is responsive to the needs of the public and is faithful to the Constitution of the United States.

Training Facility: The FBI Academy is located in Quantico, Virginia. It occupies 385 acres and is approximately 40 miles south of Washington, D.C.

Term of FBI Director: Public Law 94-503, section 203, enacted on October 15, 1976, provides for the appointment of the FBI Director by the President with the advice and consent of the Senate. In addition, the term of an FBI Director was limited to 10 years.

FBI Motto: Fidelity, Bravery, Integrity.

Greater Detail on FBI Activity— Author's Random Comments

Locations: Among the locations mentioned above are included: "The FBI also operates specialized field installation: two Regional Computer Support Centers—one in Pocatello, Idaho, and one at Fort Monmouth, New Jersey—and two Information Technology Centers (ITCs)—one in Butte, Montana, and one at Savannah, Georgia. The ITCs provide information services to support field investigative and administrative operations. In addition, the FBI provides support for the National Drug Intelligence Center (NDIC) in Johnstown, Pennsylvania. [Author's note: Another new database facility created by the Clinton Administration.] The NDIC collects and consolidates drug-trafficking intelligence developed by law enforcement and other official users. The facility is overseen by DOJ [Department of Justice]."

Notice how the terms "collect and consolidate" just keep recurring in this literature.

Investigative Programs: The above named technical installations undoubtedly are used nationally and internationally, based upon their own comments. Here is what is printed, expanding on the "Investigative Programs" mentioned briefly above. Notice the emphasis on "close relations" and "information sharing." It would seem that their primary purpose is to collect, condense, and make available to everybody information about. . .well, just about everything! Poking into the private business of prospective employees, appointees, *et al,* is the business of their Applicant Program. Of course, it is necessary to be sure that we are not hiring spies, but their digging goes much deeper than an individual's politics and criminal history (or the lack thereof). And the abuse of such records is no longer merely speculation—early in 1997, nearly 1,000 such files on members of the opposing party were found mysteriously in the White House . . . definitely a place they were not supposed to be. It has proven to be a well-deserved embarrassment to the elected and appointed officials in the Executive Branch of our government. That situation is still under investigation as of the writing of this book.

Investigative Programs

The FBI's investigative authority is the *broadest of all federal law enforcement agencies.* The FBI therefore has adopted a strategic approach which stresses long-term, complex investigations. The FBI investigative philosophy also emphasizes close relations and information sharing with other federal, state, local, and foreign law enforcement and intelligence agencies. A significant number of FBI investigations are conducted in concert with other law enforcement agencies or as part of joint task forces.

As part of this process, the FBI has divided its investigations into the following programs:

Applicant Program
- Department of Energy and Nuclear Regulatory Commission Applicants
- Department of Justice candidates
- FBI Special Agents and Support Applicants
- U.S. Court candidates
- White House Staff candidates

Civil Rights Program
- Civil Rights Act of 1964
- Discrimination in Housing
- *Equal Credit Opportunity Act*

Counterterrorism Program
- Domestic Terrorism

- Hostage Taking
- Overseas Homicide/Attempted Homicide (U.S. Persons)
- Protection of Foreign Officials and Guests
- Sabotage
- Domestic Security
- Attempted or Actual Bombings
- Nuclear Extortion
- Sedition

Financial Crime Program
- Bank Fraud and Embezzlement
- Environmental Crimes
- Fraud Against the Government
- Corruption of Public Officials
- Health Care Fraud
- Election Law Violations

Foreign Counterintelligence Program [Author's Note: As I see it, this category is redundant. The FBI should be involved in domestic matters of law enforcement. There is more than adequate coverage of foreign intelligence gathering provided by a myriad of other agencies, as I have pointed out.]
- Espionage
- Foreign Counterintelligence Matters

Organized Crime/Drug Program
- Drug Matters
- Racketeer Influenced and Corrupt Organizations Criminal Enterprise Investigations
- Labor Racketeering
- Money Laundering
- Organized Crime/Drug Enforcement Task Force Matters

Violent Crimes and Major Offenders Program
- Fugitives Wanted as a Result of FBI Investigations
- Escaped Federal Prisoners (some instances)
- Probation/Parole Violations (some instances)
- Unlawful Flight to Avoid Prosecution (including

parental kidnaping fugitives)
- Crime on Indian Reservations
- Theft of Government Property
- Interstate Transportation of Stolen Motor Vehicles
- Interstate Transportation of Stolen Property
- Theft from Interstate Shipments
- Assaulting, Kidnaping, or Killing the President, Vice President, or Member of Congress
- Bank Robbery, Burglary, or Larceny
- Crime Aboard Aircraft
- Kidnaping—Extortion
- Sexual Exploitation of Children
- Tampering with Consumer Products
[Emphasis added.]

The FBI's $2.9 Billion Budget

Now, let's give a little more consideration to that $2.5 billion budget (which by now is reported to be $2.9 billion). *Time Magazine,* April 28, 1997, page 28, reports: "For the better part of a generation, both political parties have thrown money and laurels at the FBI for one reason: to stop crime. Under Clinton, while agency after agency saw its budget dwindle, the FBI's jumped 25%, to $2.9 billion. Congress paid for 3,600 new employees, **new computers**, new field offices. Law-and-order-Republicans were there first, but Clinton and the Democrats joined in until there was simply no constituency that didn't see the FBI as the all-purpose answer to voters who routinely listed crime among their top concerns. For a nation whose greatest enemy is suddenly within, the **FBI has become the Pentagon of the post-cold war world.**

"This means, like the well-protected Pentagon of 20 years ago, virtually no congressional oversight. Any lawmaker who raised concerns risked being flayed as soft on crime. But without accountability, several things happen, all of them bad. Money gets wasted [or "lost"—keep reading!]. Officials get sloppy." [Emphasis added.]

Under the picture of Director Freeh appeared the following caption:

Dragging the Agency into the Modern Age

Director Louis Freeh has been trying to change the agency's culture, but his critics charge him with obsessive secrecy, bullheadedness, and micromanagement. His relations with the Clinton White House are also poor.

It would appear that a lot of people are unhappy with the power and authority given to, or assumed by, the FBI. A plot was uncovered to bomb the new CJIS National ID Center (pictured earlier) in Clarksburg, West Virginia. Two reports appeared in the Associated Press, but as with all reports, they reflect the leanings of the individual writing the article. The basic facts are in both articles, but I am including both, as one has considerably more—though condensed—information than the other.

FBI Arrests seven in bombing plot

Seven people connected with a right-wing militia were arrested Friday on charges of plotting to blow up the FBI's national fingerprint record center and two other federal buildings in West Virginia.

Agents began making the arrests after Floyd Raymond Looker, leader of the Mountain Militia, gave blueprints of the FBI complex to an undercover agent in exchange for $50,000, the FBI said. The agent was posing as a middleman for a fictitious international terrorist group.

The blueprints of the new $200 million FBI complex in Clarksburg were obtained by a Clarksburg firefighter who belonged to the militia, the FBI said. The fire department keeps the blueprints in case of a fire.

"There was a plot. It was ended before it could be con-summated," said John P. O'Connor, agent in charge of the FBI's Pittsburgh-based division. "There were never

any explosive devices constructed. There was no immediate threat to our facility."

O'Connor said the militia targeted two other federal
facilities in the state. He declined to identify them.

Law officers confiscated plastic explosives and detona-
tors Friday at five sites in West Virginia, Pennsylvania, and
Ohio. The arrests came after a 16-month investigation.

The fingerprint complex is known as the FBI Criminal
Justice Information Services Division. Opened last year,
it contains fingerprint records that the FBI has collected
from police departments nationwide. The identification
division provides information to state and local police
departments.

The fingerprint center eventually will use computer
programs for converting fingerprints into electronic
images.

Automated criminal record-keeping also will be available for background checks, whether the person is
seeking a job at a day-care center or trying to buy a gun.

The seven defendants, including Looker, were jailed
without bail pending hearings next week. The charges
included conspiring to make bombs, transporting explosives across state lines, and conspiring to place
explosives near the FBI complex.

On October 13, 1996, the *Lubbock Avalanche-Journal*
reported the incident as follows:

Militia was suspicious FBI knew of bomb plot

CLARKSBURG, W.Va (AP)—Leaders of the West Virginia Mountaineer Militia were suspicious that federal
authorities knew of their plans to blow up three federal
buildings.

They even ordered one member to remove his shirt
one day to prove that he wasn't wearing a wire. They
asked on the wrong day, according to court documents.

The member was an informant who had been secretly

recording members conspiring to destroy the FBI's Criminal Justice Information Services Division [CJIS] complex in Clarksburg, about 80 miles south of Pittsburgh, and two other government buildings in West Virginia, the documents say.

The information he provided led to the arrest Friday of seven men linked to the militia on conspiracy charges. They were being held Saturday pending detention hearings.

The informant had gone to the FBI 16 months ago after becoming disenchanted with the group's activities, which included making and testing home-made explosives, U.S. Attorney William D. Wilmoth said Saturday.

At least one militia member, according to the informant, believed the FBI complex contained a clandestine operation that might be a command center when the government turned against the people under the "**new world order**," according to court documents.

Prosecutors do not believe the alleged conspiracy was linked to anti-government groups in other states.

"I don't want it to appear to be some nationwide conspiracy or anything more grave than the charging documents show. As far as we could tell, it was localized," Wilmoth said.

The Criminal Justice Information Services Division, which opened last year [1995], houses fingerprint records the FBI has collected from police departments nationwide. [Emphasis added.]

And from many other sources, as well. Note that the militia was concerned about evidence to be used against us at the time of transition to the New World Order. Although misguided in their plans for violent action, they arrived at the proper conclusion about the New World Order; however, I'm convinced it will be the NSA, rather than the FBI—and I want it clearly understood that **I do not advocate** this type of action as a way to solve our dilemma. While we still have the opportunity to do so, we must pursue all legal means to "correct the course," i.e., make our voices heard at the ballot box, call-in radio programs, local community action programs, staying aware of pending legislation (on all levels—and the implications thereof), with appropriate calls and letters to all elected officials, etc., etc. Aside from that, all that I can advise is to make personal and spiritual preparations for the time that is fast drawing near. You see, no matter how vigilant we are, nor how we vote, nor how much we get involved in attempting to forestall the onslaught of the New World Order . . . ultimately, these attempts will be futile—they are doomed to fail—because the Bible guarantees us in the Book of Revelation that these events, indeed, will occur.

Combating Terrorism

President Clinton, a New World Order man himself, has been given the perfect opportunity to increase and extend the surveillance activities of the government agencies, under the guise of protecting us from terrorism—both inside and outside our borders—because of the unfortunate acts of violent terrorism that occurred during his term in office. They've been wanting this power for a long time, and this provided the perfect excuse.

On August 5, 1996, President Clinton made a speech titled "Combating Terrorism," which, by September 28, 1996, was available on the Internet at this address (6 pages): (http://www.whitehouse.gov/WH/EOP/NSC/factsheets/terror.html) Because of its availability, I won't quote it here in its entirety, but I do want to quote some of it, and list some of the "Record of Accomplishment" about which they brag so proudly. (Whenever they brag about *accomplishments,* you can kiss another freedom or another piece of your privacy "Goodbye.")

> *"In this fight. . . . American Leadership is indispensable.*
> *. . . Make no mistake about it: The bombs that kill and*
> *maim innocent people are not really aimed at them, but*
> *at the spirit of our whole country and the spirit of freedom.*

> *Therefore, the struggle against terrorism involves more than the new security measures I have ordered and the others I am seeking. Ultimately, it requires the confident will of the American people to retain our convictions for freedom and peace and to remain the indispensable force in creating a better world at the dawn of a new century."*

> President Bill Clinton
> The George Washington University
> August 5, 1996

Nonsense! This is an example of Big Brother "double-speak" in the highest form. The "new security measures" he has ordered and the additional ones he is seeking are **all** based upon tightening down on our freedoms and right to privacy. Then he reveals that it will require the "confident will" of the American people to retain freedom and peace to remain the "indispensable force" in the New World Order (the dawn of a new century). Of course, he is requesting that we all *volunteer* to lay down our Constitutional guarantees where these matters are concerned, "for the greater good." And contrary to America being the indispensable force, the New World Order is based on the merging, blending, and disestablishment of individual countries and governments; their powers must be sublimated to the universal authority, not to mention their businesses and wealth. I'm sure they would be happy to confiscate our economy, providing it hasn't been totally demolished in the takeover—a part of the plan to break us down and leave us vulnerable to anyone who comes along offering a solution, no matter how temporary.

The Antichrist/The Beast will be on the scene to furnish that solution "just in the nick of time." Ultimately, during the one-world government (NWO), no one can buy or sell without his approval (mark). More will be discussed later in this book about his role in this period of time.

More Big Brother surveillance is called for by Clinton (likely through the NSA)

President Clinton has made the fight against terrorism a *national security priority*. [NSA?] His past and recent efforts have advanced a concerted strategy to fight terrorism on three fronts: (1) beyond our borders by *working more closely than ever with our friends and allies*[by exchanging information with them—**even our former enemies**—read on]; (2) at home, by *giving law enforcement the most powerful counterterrorism tools available* [tools which could be directed at us at any time that THEY determine US to be the radicals, terrorists, antigovernment, operating contrary to the PUBLIC good, etc., etc.]; and (3) in our airports and airplanes by increasing aviation security. These efforts are part of the President's comprehensive strategy to ensure that Americans enjoy the *safety and security* they deserve and that America enters the 21st century as the greatest force for peace and prosperity on earth. [Emphasis added.]

I am reminded of the scripture telling us that when men cry "peace and safety," sudden destruction will come upon them (I Thessalonians, Chapter 5). Further information in this document reiterates the use of "shared information" in the prevention of international terrorism. I believe that this will be via the Internet or the "Internet II".

Other points of interest include the opening of an "FBI office in **Moscow**, with more soon in Cairo, Islamabad, Tel Aviv, and **Beijing**. The FBI is involved actively in providing counterterrorism training to over forty countries in the international law enforcement community." To support all this, Clinton has called for additional funding so the FBI can grant an increase in "training and assistance programs to foreign nations."

More worldwide joint action has been instigated by the

establishing of the "Group of Seven" (G7) *plus Russia*. Funding for the counterterrorism portion of the FBI's activities has been increased by 40%, and that's above the normal Congressional budget funding. The FBI has created a Counterterrorism Branch that acts as the **center for information collection** [that's all those computers collecting again], analysis, and dissemination [and sharing!] to better combat terrorism at home and abroad.

The International Crime Control Act of 1996 provides, among other things for the "fight against money laundering, so criminals and terrorists have a tougher time financing their activities." Seriously, now, when have you ever known the big-time "criminal element" to be caught without a way around the system? All this Act has done is make the government privy to the banking and business transactions of the independent businessman, especially if cash is involved, and it has turned our bank employees into watchdogs, duly sworn to report any violations, even anything they see that *appears* suspicious . . . they call it "structuring" in an attempt to hide your transactions from Big Brother, and it's definitely illegal. But just remember, your friendly neighborhood teller has been forced into monitoring and reporting your banking business to the IRS and/or others.

" . . . the President has consistently and repeatedly called for additional counterterrorism *tools* that Congress thus far has refused to approve: broader wiretap authority to cover pay phones and hotel phones. . . . " That is self-explanatory —they want greater eavesdropping capabilities. It seems to me they have more than plenty right now!

Next, they discuss greater security measures at airports. The "President ordered the FAA to impose new, tough airport security measures. . . . " This undoubtedly will include profiling on frequent fliers. Clinton established the Aviation Safety and Security Commission, which suggested "deployment of advanced detection technologies, [and] improved screening [profiles] of airline passengers and employees. As of this writing, Delta and United, and American Airlines' SABRE

(**S**emi-**A**utomated **B**usiness **R**esearch **E**nvironment—Reservations) System have linked with the CIA for the purpose of passenger profiling. Other airlines will follow suit shortly.

Much more information about The SABRE Group is available on the Internet. The following three addresses are for an "overview," "history," and "new technology," respectively.

(http://www.sabre.com/corpinfo/overview.htm)
(http://www.sabre.com/corpinfo/history.htm)
(http://www.sabre.com/news/tech__news.htm)

They ask the question, "Who Are We?" and answer:

> The SABRE Group is a world leader in the electronic distribution of travel-related . . . services and is a leading provider of information technology solutions for the travel and transportation industry.

They state as their goal to be the leading provider of such "solutions." They proudly declare the size and power of their computers (and justifiably so; they are number 261 of the top 500 computer facilities in the world). They inform us of the American Airlines contribution to the history and formation of SABRE. They tell us that the old system handled 84,000 calls per day, but today's system can handle over 20 million equivalent calls. "To run this massive reservation system, American Airlines built the world's largest privately-owned computer system in Tulsa, Oklahoma [the central facility]."

Terry Jones, Chief Information Officer of SABRE, answers questions in *Technology News* that are frequently expressed. The one that caught my attention reads:

> **Question:** How do you think security concerns play into the growth of electronic commerce and what has The SABRE Group done to insure customer privacy?

Mr. Jones spent two paragraphs explaining how "safe" it is to make reservations over the Internet using your credit

card, because there are no thieves on the Internet (according
to him). He also reports how they are spending time and
expense to convince the credit card companies of this, as well.
Not surprisingly, he doesn't even address the privacy issue
raised in the above question.

Now, back to our report. In their "Getting Results" section
they are bragging that:

> In the Philippines our intelligence prevented a terrorist
> from bombing multiple U.S. commercial aircraft as they
> crossed the Pacific.
>
> Under the Clinton administration, we have prevented
> major terrorist attacks before they happened. In New
> York City, U.S. law enforcement foiled plots against the
> United Nations and the Holland Tunnel.
>
> Swift Arrests and Prosecutions: Justice Department,
> international, national, and local law enforcement atten-
> tion culminated in the near immediate arrest of Okla-
> homa City bombing suspects and the rapid conviction
> of the World Trade Center bombers, as well as the arrest
> of a suspect in the Unabomber case.
>
> The Challenges Ahead: Continue pushing Congress
> for new legislation to give our law enforcement the
> resources the President asked for initially: increased wire
> tap authority. . . .

In a news release dated January 14, 1997, the FBI Assistant
Director James K. Kallstrom presented a nine-page announcement about electronic surveillance "required" to do the job
they feel they should be able to do. It is a very, very detailed
report. To read it in its entirety, access the Internet at:

(http://www.fbi.gov/pressrel/tele/telephon.htm)

Here are the first two paragraphs of the Introduction which
pretty much sums up what they are after, and why they are
forcing the communications industry to comply.

> Acting on a mandate from Congress, the Federal

Bureau of Investigation today is announcing the amount of telephone system capacity the nation's law enforcement agencies may need for court-approved *electronic surveillance to protect the public from terrorism, violence, drugs, and other grave offenses* and to deal with unexpected crime emergencies through 1998 and beyond.

The Communications Assistance for Law Enforcement Act of 1994 (CALEA) *requires the telephone companies* to ensure that their systems and networks have *both the capability and capacity to accommodate all federal, state, and local law enforcement agencies'* court-approved intercepts in the face of new or changing telephone technology that could *otherwise prevent electronic surveillance* [emphasis added].

Heaven, forbid! Perish the thought that we actually might regain some of the lost privacy on our phone conversations . . . but don't get too excited. The phone companies are being forced—over much protest—to comply with this new order. In fact, the research and development of technology that would permit this on the new fiber optic and/or satellite phone systems is so expensive that the government agreed to foot a large portion of the bill, thanks to us taxpayers, of course!

The other noteworthy part of this report deals with the increase of surveillance and wire tapping. Throughout this news release, Kallstrom keeps bringing up the point that just because they have greater capacity/capability doesn't necessarily mean they will increase their wiretap surveillance. Wasn't it Shakespeare who said, "Me thinks thou dost protest too much!"? It certainly applies here, along with another old adage, "If the shoe fits, etc."

NCIC 2000—"Linking It all Together"

This is the motto of one of the FBI's most active divisions, located in that new facility in Clarksburg, West Virginia. I guess they aren't trying to hide all this merging of databases, etc., as they include it at the top of their letterhead, right under NCIC 2000. Since the 1960's, the NCIC has collected and furnished criminal information to law enforcement agencies. However, with the burgeoning technology and a corresponding increase in requests for assistance, improvements and additions have been installed along the way. NCIC 2000 is a new system being developed to replace the NCIC. NCIC 2000 will perform the existing NCIC functions, augmented with new capabilities. NCIC 2000 will increase capacity, update technology, and add fingerprint and image processing functions. NCIC 2000 will provide increased flexibility to meet future user requirements and will be easier to maintain. New and improved capabilities associated with NCIC 2000 include:

- Addition of image processing (i.e., mugshot, signature, identifying marks)
- Addition of automated single-finger fingerprint matching
- Automation of some NCIC functions that are currently manually performed (e.g., validation, *collection of benefits data*) [That's interesting! The FBI is now involved in benefits data . . . that's your social security, retirement, welfare, etc., which the authorities already have mandated must be by direct deposit . . . no more checks.]
- Access to new databases (e.g., Convict or Person on Supervised Release)
- Addition of linkage fields, providing the ability to associate multiple records with the same criminal or the same crime
- Access to external databases (e.g., the Canadian Police Information Center (CPIC) and the Federal Bureau of Prisons' "SENTRY" database. [Of course, it goes without saying the NSA computers . . . unless they already are so linked together that NSA is no longer considered "external."]

- Automatic collection of statistics for system evaluation
  [From whom? Linked and shared. . .on the Internet
  with anybody who wants to trade!]

There is an extensive amount of information on the Internet
about NCIC 2000. The FBI produces a monthly newsletter
on the Internet keeping information updated on their progress
(they anticipate being fully operational by the fall of
1999—just in time for "2000"). In the following website
address, just change the "v1n1" to the proper volume and
number (e.g., Vol. 2, No. 4, would be "v2n4") if you desire
to peruse the subsequent editions of the newsletter.

(http://www.fbi.gov/2000/2kv1n1.htm)

Vol. 1, No. 3, includes a section called "New Files," which
begins by listing the current files.

Law enforcement officers will have remote access to
the NCIC 2000 system to assist them in performing their
duties and improve their safety. Thirteen files are now
supported by NCIC. They are:

- Person File
- License Plates File
- Foreign Fugitive File
- Violent Felon File
- United States Secret Service Protective File
- Vehicle File
- Violent Gang/Terrorist Members File
- Boat File
- Gun File
- Article File
- Securities File
- ORI File
- Deported Felon File

The new files will be:

- Protection Order File—This file will contain records
  of individuals who should be prevented from. . .

harassment. . . [of] another person, including temporary orders issued by civil or criminal courts.
- Convicted Person on Supervised Release
- Image File—Contains fingerprints, mugshots, signature, and others to identify specialized and generic
images

The FBI reports that the NCIC 2000 will supply external
interfaces to the following five systems (at least for now): Interstate Identification Index (III); Canadian Police Information
Centre (CPIC); Federal Bureau of Prisons (SENTRY); National
Law Enforcement Telecommunications System (NLETS); and
Uniform Crime Report (UCR) National Incident-Based Reporting System (NIBRS).

Under listings for audiovisuals, the NCIC offers training
videos on a variety of subjects: Hate Crimes; NCIC License
Plate and Article File; NCIC Interstate Identification Index and
System Security (known as "Triple I" or "III" in the FBI's
system); and many others.

SAIC (Science Applications International Corporation) was
contracted to design and develop another arm of the
NCIC 2000, called the Interstate Identification Index computer
system (III/Triple I). As the NCIC 2000 does not have the
capability to furnish an on-line criminal history database,
Triple I will support law enforcement agencies nationwide,
via the NCIC 2000. Set-up of this system is estimated at $27.6
million.

Now I want to mention briefly the terms "NLETS" (National
Law Enforcement Telecommunications System) and "OLETS"
(Oklahoma Law Enforcement Telecommunications System).
From here on, it gets very confusing (which makes it so much
easier to put curious people on the wrong trail). I'm just going
to quote what they have printed:

A. Oklahoma Law Enforcement Telecommunications System (O.L.E.T.S):

O.L.E.T.S. is a statewide telecommunications network
for law enforcement agencies that interfaces to the

Oklahoma Department of Public Saftey, the Oklahoma Tax Commission, the National Crime Information Center (NCIC), the National Law Enforcement Telecommunications System (NLETS), and the National Weather Service.

The following information is available for law enforcement use from the Department of Public Safety through the O.L.E.T.S. system:

1. Motor Vehicle Registrations
2. Criminal Records Files
3. Boat Registration Files
4. Drivers License Files

B. National Law Enforcement Telecommunications System (N.L.E.T.S.):

N.L.E.T.S. is accessible via O.L.E.T.S. and provides a switching network for local, state, and federal agencies to exchange information interstate.

Aside from providing a communications network, N.L.E.T.S. also provides information from the National Crime Information Center (NCIC) database files which are managed by the FBI and include:

1. Interstate Identification Index files (III)
2. Out-of-State Vehicle Registrations
3. Stolen Vehicle files
4. Stolen Article files
5. Wanted Persons files
6. Missing Persons files
7. Aircraft Registration files
8. Canadian files
9. Interpol files

The transition to NCIC 2000 will take three years and, as I stated previously, is expected to be complete by the fall of 1999. There are just a couple more items to mention as I wrap up this section on the FBI.

First, I want to repeat the question I raised earlier about why we are spending American taxpayers' money to train

Russians and other foreigners. . .unless they know already that they will be working closely together in the near future, and they want to be sure that everybody is "on the same page," so to speak.

> . . .Representatives of twenty-seven countries from Central and Eastern Europe, Russia, and the newly independent states of the former Soviet Union had expressed interest in sending students to the facility. . . .Academy instructors come from the ranks of the FBI and other federal law enforcement agencies, however, law enforcement agencies from such countries as Canada, the United Kingdom, Germany, Italy, Denmark, Norway, and Sweden have expressed interest in joining the United States in this unprecedented training effort.

The FBI's international activities include participation in working groups with countries such as Italy, Australia, Canada, and Mexico. But the most surprising thing is that the Bureau participates in the **exchange** of mid-level supervisory personnel with police agencies in such countries as Germany, Italy, Australia, and Japan, and in INTERPOL. As if just exchanging information on linked databases on the Internet wasn't bad enough, now we actually are exchanging upper echelon (supervisory) personnel with countries on at least three continents. Just one big happy family. . .world wide!

The final division of the FBI that I will be covering is known as N-CHIP (National Criminal History Improvement Program). According to the May, 1996, edition of *Government Technology Magazine,* the "Justice and Technology" section, N-CHIP was instigated to implement the Brady Background Checks, mandated by the Brady Act, prior to the sale of a handgun. One paragraph reads: "The plan for a nationwide background-check system is to use the Interstate Identification Index (III) as the backbone for **noncriminal-related background checks**. The III now includes criminal records sent by the 30 states participating in the system" [emphasis added]. Their plan is to "build on the existing systems." There is a "Compact" between the states participating in the III. "The compact would open access to necessary databases for **noncriminal queries** by persons authorized to access FBI databases, such as the III." [Emphasis added.]

The Remaining Three Spokes in the Intelligence Wheel

These three are "Indirect" Government agencies, e.g., their basic function is other than intelligence gathering. However, it is interesting to point out that they do enough of it to get themselves included on this intelligence wheel. These are the Department of State, Department of Energy, and Treasury Department—none of them under the authority of the DoD. I will complete this wheel as quickly as possible, now, so that we can move on to other sister (Little Brother?) organizations who gather intelligence indirectly as a means to achieve their goals/missions. . .which for the nongovernment entities is to make a profit.

Department of State—Bureau of Intelligence and Research

The intelligence-gathering arm of the State Department is the Bureau of Intelligence and Research (INR). It is the State Department's primary source for interpretive analysis of global developments. The INR was established in 1946 to provide the Secretary of State with timely, objective assessments, free of policy prescription or preferences. INR's mandate is to tell policymakers what they need to know, not what they want to hear. INR is also the focal point within the State Department for all policy issues and activities involving the Intelligence Community. They are concerned with events and trends that affect both US foreign policy and national security interests.

Department of Energy

Don't make the mistake of assuming that this department is concerned primarily with ecology or environmental issues, i.e., save a whale, or hug a tree (although some of that may fall in their jurisdiction, it more likely falls under the EPA). According to their information on the Internet, they definitely have earned their place in the intelligence community.

> The Department of Energy has a rich heritage of meeting important national goals in the areas of energy, national security, science, and technology. Its mission is to contribute to the welfare of the nation by providing the scientific foundation, technology, policy, and institutional leadership necessary to achieve efficiency in energy use, diversity in energy sources, a more productive and competitive economy, improved environmental quality, and a secure national defense.
>
> The Department's foreign intelligence program is a component of the Intelligence Community. Its missions are: to provide the Department and other US Government policymakers and decisionmakers with timely, accurate, high-impact foreign intelligence analyses; to detect and defeat foreign intelligence services bent on acquiring sensitive information on the Department's programs, facilities, technology, and personnel; to provide technical and analytical support to the Director of Central Intelligence (the DCI), and to make the Department's technical and analytical expertise available to other members of the Intelligence Community.

The Department of Energy can trace its roots in the intelligence community back to 1947, with the formation of the well-known Atomic Energy Commission (AEC). Through a chain of events, the intelligence responsibilities subsequently were transferred, in 1977, to the Department of Energy.

. . . Substantive areas of the Department's intelligence responsibility include nuclear proliferation, nuclear weapons technology, fossil and nuclear energy, and science and technology.

The Treasury Department—Office of Intelligence Support

The final spoke on the wheel is the Treasury Department. Under their jurisdiction fall the activities of the IRS (Internal Revenue Service), FINCEN (Financial Crimes Enforcement Network) and BATF (Bureau of Alcohol, Tobacco, and Fire-arms). I'm sure there are many more, but today I want to address just these three, following a few comments of generic nature on the Treasury Department.

The Office of Intelligence Support was established in 1977. It succeeded the Office of National Security (ONS). The Special Assistant (head of this division) and his staff support the Secretary of the Treasury in his roles as chief economic and financial adviser to the President, *head of the second largest law enforcement department in the federal government,* and the official responsible for the integrity of the country's currency.

FINCEN

The Financial Crimes Enforcement Network has more tentacles than an octopus, with all of them poking somewhere in your financial business. For a complete study on FINCEN, let me refer you to Chapter 11, p. 205, in my previous book, *The Mark of the New World Order.*

I referred earlier to the government making the bank tellers become their personal informants on financial activities of their clients. All that falls under the FINCEN category. From the Treasury Department's info about FINCEN on the Internet, I would like to quote the following:

. . . FinCEN is the nation's central point for broad-based financial intelligence, analysis, and

**information sharing. . . . Its information sharing
network, which includes most federal, as well as
state and local law enforcement agencies** throughout the nation provides increasingly sophisticated analytical tools. . . .

FinCEN's experience in attempting to curtail money
laundering makes it especially sensitive to crimes facili-
tated by the capabilities of advanced information technology. An example of such technology is the emergence
of financial services collectively known as "cyberpay-
ments." FinCEN has a vested interest in understanding
this new technology, to assess the potential for its criminal misuse, and develop policy guidelines which will
help protect the integrity of our financial system. [Em-
phasis added.]

I'll bet they are VERY concerned about cashless electronic
transfers of funds, but wait. . . maybe not as concerned as they
sound. Remember the "back-door key"? Well, they undoubtedly will be the ones carrying it, as it pertains to financial
activities. Without a clipper chip, skip jack, or a "back-door"
key by any other name, they might have reason for concern,
but that won't be the case. They will be sure of it, because
they have to keep those money launderers in line. Yeah, right!

Stanley E. Morris became Director of the Financial Crimes
Enforcement Network in May, 1994. FINCEN administers the
Bank Secrecy Act (BSA), which is the core of Treasury's efforts
to fight money laundering. This is another of those double-
speak situations where it means exactly the opposite of what
it says. Since they actually are doing away with your privacy
at the bank, the name might be more appropriate if it were
the "Bank UNsecrecy Act," as the only purpose of the Act
is to access (reveal) your personal/business confidential
financial banking activities. One report I have indicates that
currency transactions of more than $10,000 must be reported
on a BAS form; however, another place I found says the limit
is now $3,000 for a BAS report. An SAR (Suspicious Activity

Report) may be filed on any amount if there is a reason to suspect you are attempting to hide income; this is considered "structuring" to avoid detection and the filing of a BAS report . . . definitely against the law.

Morris also was responsible for the National Asset Seizure and Forfeiture program—a means of seizing criminals' assets gained through illegal activities.

There is so much on the Internet on FINCEN, you'll be glad they only print the top ten, unless you request to see more (they reported about 30,000 matches for the query). FINCEN's address is: Financial Crimes Enforcement Network, Office of Communications, 2070 Chain Bridge Road, Suite 200, Vienna, Virginia 22182; Phone (703) 905-3770; Fax (703) 905-3885. The new website is: (http://www.ustreas.gov/treasury/bureaus/fincen/infinc.ht)

On March 26, 1996, FINCEN issued amendments to the Funds Transfer rules. The rules were issued under the Bank Secrecy Act (BSA), administered by FINCEN. The second change applies primarily to wire transfers; however, the first change reads as follows:

> The first rule . . . requires banks and non-bank finan-
> cial institutions to collect and retain information about
> transmittals of funds in the amount of $3,000 or more;
> it also requires the verification of the identity of non-
> account holders that are parties to such transmittals of
> funds.

FINCEN is very diligent in closing up the loopholes . . . they change the rules frequently, and each change gives them access to more information, it seems. Now they have gained permission to obtain information from individuals' IRS forms, use them as they deem necessary, and SHARE them with anyone who "needs" them, in all levels of government and law enforcement. As I said above, for the full story on FINCEN, read *The Mark of the New World Order*.

The Bureau of Alcohol, Tobacco, and Firearms (BATF)

Of all the nonmilitary government law enforcement agencies, I believe this is the most aggressive against your average American citizen. (Remember Waco and Ruby Ridge?)

ATF is a bureau of the Treasury Department, with law enforcement, regulatory, and tax collection missions for alcohol, tobacco, explosives, arson, and firearms. John W. Magaw, formerly Director of the US Secret Service, became Director of the BATF effective September 30, 1993, by appointment. On their Internet website:
(http://www.atf.treas.gov/@__ATF/NRT__SRT/nrt__srt.htm) they give some startling statistics concerning their operations since 1979. Although no statistics are given on the number of deaths and injuries caused by terrorists, I have a feeling that the figures wouldn't be very far apart, if you omit any statistics from armed conflicts (wars).

National Response Teams (NRTs)

Presently, ATF maintains four regional NRTs, organized by geographical region, to help Federal, state, and local investigators in overcoming the difficulties inherent in large-scale arson and explosives crime scene investigations. Each team, consisting of special agents, explosives technicians, and forensic scientists, is equipped to respond to major incidents within 24 hours of a request by State or local authorities. Major incidents can easily overwhelm the resources of local law enforcement or fire department personnel. This specialized response capability is the only one of its kind offered by a Federal law enforcement agency.

Since 1979, NRTs have been activated on 304 occasions to incidents that CAUSED 264 DEATHS, 1,923 INJURIES, and $1.8 billion in PROPERTY DAMAGE [emphasis added].

International Response Team (IRT)

Designed around the NRT concept, ATF initiated the IRT to provide assistance to the U.S. State Department in fire and bomb scene investigations on U.S. Government property abroad. Through the IRT, ATF provides technical and forensic assistance to foreign police and fire service agencies. The IRT has responded to numerous foreign arson or explosives-related incidents, including the 1992 and 1994 bombings of the Israeli Embassy and a Jewish community center in Argentina.

The Internal Revenue Service (IRS)

I'm sure none of us needs a technical definition of the IRS, and since this book doesn't deal with earnings, reporting, etc., I will give only a cursory glance at the IRS, as it deals with their contribution in the collecting, storing, and sharing of information. I have classified them as an "Indirect" government intelligence gatherer.

The Martinsburg Chamber of Commerce, of Berkeley County, West Virginia, the site of three IRS facilities, has this listing:

IRS—Martinsburg Computing Center
Gerald A. Rabe, Director
P. O. Box 1208, Stop 100
Martinsburg, WV 25401
Phone: (304) 264-7111   Employment: 267-3152
Product: Tax Administration
Number of Employees: 800
Union: National Treasury Employees

See the map and aerial photo of the Martinsburg facilities.

According to the *Webster's Family Encyclopedia,* 1996-97 edition, "The IRS is the arm of the US Treasury Department that enforces tax laws and collects taxes. Established in 1862,

*Aerial photo of the
Internal Revenue Service (IRS) facility.*

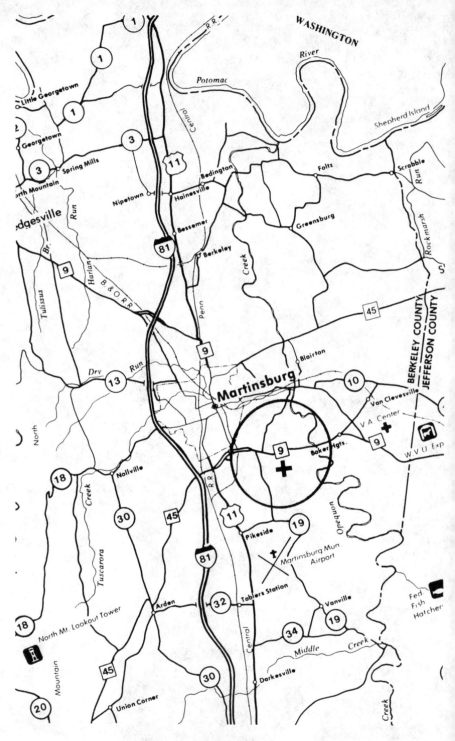

New IRS National Database Center.

the IRS has 8 administrative districts [another reports says there are 9, and yet another says 10—I believe 10 to be the correct number as of the writing of this book], each with its own director, and has facilities for audit, review, and collection."

And even though there appears to be no legal connection, there is a close working relationship and sharing of data with the Social Security Administration, as the IRS collects all the fees levied for this government retirement program. (A little more about the SSA later.)

The biggest complaint about the IRS lately has been their waste of vast resources, with nothing much to show for it. They have been operating on obsolete computers and such since the 1980's, which accounts for some of the problems they are having. A number of articles have been written addressing the problems of the IRS and the amount it is spending compared with the amount of unpaid taxes it is allowing to slip through its fingers.

The April 7, 1997, edition of *TIME* magazine (pp. 58-62), carried an article by Richard Stengel, of Washington, DC, titled "An Overtaxed IRS," with a subtitle accusing: "Its klutzy computer system costs the Federal Government $150 billion a year in uncollected taxes and makes the agency an easy mark for cheats." Here are some excerpts:

> . . . Like the old Soviet Union, grand and powerful on the outside but an antiquated shambles within, the IRS has profound problems with outdated technology and outmoded thinking that have undermined its self-described mission: "To collect the proper amount of tax revenue at the least cost."
>
> The agency better known for turning the thumbscrews on tax miscreants is collecting something like $150 billion a year less than the proper amount, and misspending billions doing it.
>
> . . . Over the past decade it has spent nearly $4 billion in an attempt to bring its computers up to date. But . . . [a] world-class information-systems officer concedes

that the IRS's computers "do not work in the real world."

. . .Tracking down the records of a single taxpayer means getting access to as many as nine different computer systems. [Author's note: Just think how *convenient* it would be to have all the information in just one place, accessible to any agency who thinks they need it!]

. . .With its 106,000 employees, $7 billion annual budget, and 10 regional service centers, each the size of a small city, the **IRS is the second largest federal agency, after the Pentagon.**

. . ."The IRS does not have a modern customer-service capability. . .the sort of thing VISA and American Express do every day."

. . .The IRS had automated its processing system, eventually gathering everything into 10 service centers, with a computer nucleus in West Virginia.

. . .[A call for funding to modernize the IRS was made in the 1980's, but] Congress was spooked by the idea of a more centralized, all-knowing, all-seeing IRS, and said no thanks. The IRS was told simply to replace worn-out machines: nothing new and nothing fancy.

[Congress finally recognized the seriousness of the problems confronting them if the IRS were unable to collect the funds required to keep the government running, so they approved a plan.] All systems would be go by the year 2001, the agency blandly assured Congress. With all the requests and funding, the final price tag for what ultimately became known as the Tax Systems Modernization plan was around $8 billion.

Modernization turned out to be a digital Tower of Babel. Treasury Deputy Secretary Lawrence Summers, charged with looking after the IRS, says, "I think modernization has gone way off track. They tried to build the Taj Mahal."

This is a nation founded on a tax revolt. No one wants a meddlesome Big Brother tax system that can find your odd sock for you, but it ought to be as capable as American Express or Citicorp. [Emphasis added.]

All of this helped to expand the IRS facilities around Martinsburg, West Virignia, for the purpose of a place to put all that computing "stuff." (See marked areas on the aerial photos shown previously.)

This will enable the IRS to do the things they planned, regarding matching and comparing, such as income versus purchases, etc., reported in the *Los Angeles Times,* article of February 12, 1995, titled "On-Line IRS Checks Databases Against Returns," and the *Reno Gazette-Journal* article of March 18, 1995, titled "IRS auditors become gumshoes: IRS takes a closer look: Crackdown slows refunds." In other words, if you are a waiter somewhere reporting $10,000 annual income, but the cross referencing of your records with the Department of Motor Vehicles reveals that you have purchased and registered a new Ferrari, the computer is going to go "tilt," and you can expect a letter, call, or visit from an IRS agent wanting to know about unreported tips or other unreported income that would allow you to purchase such an automobile on that size of income.

Part of the "improvements"—the additional facility in Martinsburg, West Virginia—is located on West Virginia Hwy. 9 in the Liberty Business Park, within a mile of two other IRS-occupied buildings. US Senator Robert Byrd (D-WV) and other distinguished guests cut the ceremonial ribbon for the opening of the US Internal Revenue Service Computing Center Annex. The 63,000-square-foot building, which comes with a $70 million price tag, houses several high-tech IRS functions. About 350 of the 800 people the IRS employs in Berkeley County work there. " 'The IRS wants to **consolidate** all of its computer services from 12 to three,' Byrd said. They will be located in Detroit, Mich., Memphis, Tenn., and Martinsburg." [Emphasis added.]

Even in view of all the so-called "improvements," this may prove *not* to be the IRS's biggest concern. *Business Week,* May 19, 1997, carried an article titled "IRS Reform May Get

Los Angeles Times

SUNDAY, FEBRUARY 12, 1995
COPYRIGHT 1995/THE TIMES MIRROR COMPANY/CC1/478 PAGES

D4   SUNDAY, FEBRUARY 12, 1995 ★   LOS ANGELES TIMES

Your Money

PERSONAL FINANCE / KATHY M. KRISTOF

On-Line IRS Checks Databases Against Returns

If you have a back tax bill with the Internal Revenue Service, watch out.

In the midst of a program called economic reality, the federal tax agency is going on line, searching for signs of noncompliance as well as electronic records of cars, credit and real estate it can seize from delinquent taxpayers.

The purpose of the new plan is to ferret out tax scofflaws who cheat the federal government out of an estimated $120 billion each year—roughly 17% of total receipts.

A cadre of IRS agents with computers and modems now will be searching records filed with the Department of Motor Vehicles, county tax assessor's offices, credit-reporting companies and the U.S. Bureau of the Census in an effort to find people who are underreporting their business sales, overestimating their deductions or trying to hide assets—or themselves—from federal tax collectors, IRS officials say.

While tax officials have been able to request copies of these records in the past, they generally had to do it by foot—hoofing it down to various county offices and standing in line to get the data they needed to determine whether taxpayers were hiding assets. As a result, they tended to check only on taxpayers who appeared fairly likely to be big-money cheats, industry experts say.

Now they are able to get access to these same records in a fraction of the time and from the comfort of their government offices. The bottom line: It's faster and easier to ferret out tax fraud, big and small.

"We will be using information from various [electronic] sources as part of our economic-reality approach," says Frank Keith, an IRS spokesman in Washington. "It is probably the most effective way to uncover unreported income, which is a significant portion of the tax gap."

The new plan, which went into effect late last month, is part of a continuing effort to make tax collection more efficient. In the past

> **'We will be using information from various [electronic] sources as part of our economic-reality approach. It is probably the most effective way to uncover unreported income, which is a significant portion of the tax gap.'**
>
> **FRANK KEITH**
> *IRS spokesman*

several years, the IRS has boosted its computer matching program, making it simple to discover underreported income from employers, bank and brokerage accounts. This takes computer matching a step further, aiming it at tax deductions, such as the personal property taxes most people pay on their cars and business expenses.

In addition, the program will try to help each of the IRS' 64 districts

nationwide find areas where voluntary compliance has gone astray. The IRS will begin compiling a host of demographic information about people in each district. (Districts normally conform to state boundaries, but highly populated states, such as California, have several each.) This information will include currency and banking reports, license information, construction contract information and census data.

For example, the IRS will be looking through census data to determine how many people in a district identified themselves as self-employed and then compare that to the number of tax returns filed with self-employment income, Keith says.

This demographic data has no names attached and will not be used to audit individual returns. Instead it will be used to signal problem areas—such as underreporting of gratuity income or sales figures—and to help districts better focus their audit attention.

The second part of the program is directed at individuals who have delinquent tax bills.

The IRS will get current addresses for taxpayers who have apparently dropped off the rolls by buying them from credit-reporting companies, such as TRW, Trans Union and Equifax. In addition, if the IRS is trying to collect back taxes, it can get your full credit file to determine whether you have enough credit to pay the bill without resorting to a longer-term payment plan.

DMV records will be tapped both to help with collection efforts—to see if you have a car to sell to pay

taxes—and to help determine whether a taxpayer is lying about income or deductions. The IRS will be suspicious, for example, of a waiter who reports $20,000 in total income but drives a new Porsche.

Property records will be used in the same way, IRS officials note.

The combination of electronic checking on income and electronic checking on deductions and assets should make the IRS far more efficient, tax officials say. However, a few credit experts warn that it also puts a burden on individuals who are under IRS scrutiny.

Why?

The records are not always right. And the tax agency does not need to inform you that it is searching these records, nor is it required to allow you to correct records that are in error. The IRS is not the purveyor of the credit, DMV or property information, Keith explains. Consequently, it cannot correct somebody else's database. Nonetheless, having an IRS agent asking about a long-sold car or assuming there is available credit on what is actually a long-canceled card can be a nightmare for both the taxpayer and the auditor, tax accountants say.

If you're under IRS scrutiny, it may behoove you to check your own records for accuracy.

Kathy M. Kristof welcomes your comments and suggestions for columns but regrets that she cannot respond individually to letters and phone calls. Write to Personal Finance, Business Section, Los Angeles Times, Times Mirror Square, Los Angeles, CA 90053, or message kristof@news.latimes.com on the Internet.

SATURDAY, MARCH 18, 1995
RENO GAZETTE-JOURNAL

BUSINESS

STEVE FALCONE, BUSINESS EDITOR
PHONE, 788-6322, FAX, 788-6458

10B

FEDERAL INCOME TAXES
IRS auditors become gumshoes

By Vivian Marino
ASSOCIATED PRESS

From now on when the tax auditor calls, he won't just scrutinize your 1040 form, pay stubs and charity receipts. He might eyeball the car you drive, ask how you catered your child's wedding and check what your rich uncle bequeathed in his will.

Beginning this year, all individuals chosen for Internal Revenue Service audits will not only have their returns investigated but their personal lives examined. Small business owners and professionals will be held up to their peers, as the IRS looks for suspicious inconsistencies or discrepancies.

"It wants to know how someone with a $30,000 income can afford a $400,000 house or drive around in a new Lincoln," said Joseph F. Lane, a former IRS supervisor from Menlo Park, Calif., who now represents clients in tax disputes.

These changes, which the IRS is quietly instituting, are part of a strategy dubbed "Compliance 2000," aimed at getting more people to pay the taxes they owe. Uncollected taxes total at least $127 billion, IRS figures show.

The tax agency's goal is to raise the voluntary compliance rate from the current 83 percent to 90 percent by the year 2001.

But some tax experts, who say they've seen the training manuals the IRS is preparing for its 15,500 auditors, contend that some of the new procedures are too invasive.

"They're trying to turn these auditors, who are basically accountants, into detectives," said Frederick W. Daily, a San Francisco tax attorney and author of "Stand Up To The IRS."

"They are supposed to look for body language . . . They want to know what kind of car you drive . . . whether you have relatives with money, their IRS is getting away from your return and now it's you being put under a microscope."

One section of the new IRS training manuals lists some highly personal areas for auditors to check, said Lane. Among them: weddings of children, cultural background, vacations, address and neighborhood, home furnishings.

Steve Pyrek an IRS spokesman, acknowledged that the agency's "approach to audits will go be-

IRS takes a closer look

The Internal Revenue Service is quietly training its army of auditors to look at more than just your tax return to determine whether you're paying what you owe. IRS training documents now suggest these "Components of Economic Reality," to help determine whether your lifestyle is consistent with your reported income.

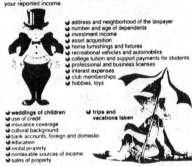

- ♦ address and neighborhood of the taxpayer
- ♦ number and age of dependents
- ♦ investment income
- ♦ asset acquisition
- ♦ home furnishings and fixtures
- ♦ recreational vehicles and automobiles
- ♦ college tuition and support payments for students
- ♦ professional and business licenses
- ♦ interest expenses
- ♦ club memberships
- ♦ hobbies, toys

♦ weddings of children	♦ trips and vacations taken
♦ use of credit	
♦ insurance coverage	
♦ cultural background	
♦ bank accounts, foreign and domestic	
♦ education	
♦ rental property	
♦ nontaxable sources of income	
♦ sales of property	

Who gets audited?

Historically, people with higher incomes face a higher chance of an IRS audit.

5% percentage audited (1993)

total personal income	under $25,000	$25,000-$50,000	$50,000-$100,000	$100,000 and over
	0.68%	0.58%	0.88%	4.03%

Sources: CCH Federal Tax Guide, Riverwoods, Ill.; Lane Brothers, Menlo Park, Calif.

AP/Wm J. Castello, Rick Gladstone

yond the "traditional methods" of merely comparing returns with informational statements like W-2 wage statements and 1099 interest income forms.

"Training efforts have begun this year to give our examiners new techniques," he said. "They'll look at more than just the numbers that are on a return."

The goal of these examiners, Pyrek said, is to determine "economic reality," whether reported income is consistent with the way you live.

While the agency has taken this approach before in going after unreported income, this is the first year such techniques have become standard policy for all audits. Pyrek said training classes began earlier this year and are expected to continue on a regular basis.

For individuals, the new auditing approach means IRS examiners will likely poke into public records, such as state motor vehicle information, to see the type of cars they drive or if they own a boat, or county property tax rolls.

Crackdown slows refunds

WASHINGTON (AP) — The government has issued 17 percent fewer tax refunds than it had by this time last year as a result of an anti-fraud crackdown, the Internal Revenue Service said Friday.

In a report on this year's filing season through last week, the IRS said it had received 46.5 million returns, down 1 percent from 47 million last year.

But the number of returns processed, 36.4 million, is down 11 percent from last year and the number of refunds certified, 22.4 million, is down 17 percent.

Also, the IRS' electronic-return program has been hard-hit by rule changes that make it much more difficult for taxpayers to get refund-anticipation loans. Electronic returns through March 10 totaled 8.8 million, down 23 percent from the same period a year ago.

The IRS is counting on growth in electronic filing to speed the transformation of its antiquated paper-based returns processing system.

However, filings so far this year bear out predictions from tax preparers that electronic filing would fall off after the IRS made it risky for tax banks and finance companies to make refund-anticipation loans.

Lenders have cut back on loans and raised their fees because the IRS stopped issuing speedy notices that a refund is coming soon. The government has cited the loans as an inducement for fraud, particularly under the earned income tax credit program for low-income workers.

The IRS also has delayed about 4 million refunds — both paper and electronic — because Social Security numbers for taxpayers and their dependents are missing or don't match government records and because of more thorough anti-fraud checks by computer.

Lost in the Dust of Battle."

> When it comes to the Internal Revenue Service, the
> Clinton Administration and Congress agree on one thing:
> The agency is in desperate need of an overhaul to
> become more efficient and customer-friendly. But that's
> where the consensus ends. The Treasury Dept. and
> Capitol Hill are heading for a furious struggle over
> whether the Treasury or an independent board should
> run the agency. -
> [Even though it is officially a branch of the Treasury
> department...] the IRS is now semi-independent.

The Treasury Department wants to "rectify" that situation
by taking stronger control from the top; others in Congress
say it is a failed, wasteful system and needs fresh blood with
top management skills to solve its many problems. That is
the basis of the ensuing fight. Rob Portman (R-Ohio) and Bob
Kerry (D-Neb.) (co-chairmen of the bipartisan commission
on this matter) say that the Treasury never has managed the
IRS well, and they have little confidence that strengthening
Treasury's hand would improve matters. "Since Treasury's
commitment to reform shifts with the political winds...[and]
there needs to be much more consistent direction from the
top."

"Under the Kerrey-Portman plan, the nine directors...
would have vast powers." The GOP is pushing for this solution,
however, "horrified Administration officials are lobbying hard
to sink the plan."

One last piece of information about the IRS...in spite of
all the money spent and all their new equipment, they are
desperately trying to get their computers to recognize the
change of the millennium at midnight, December 31, 1999.
Of course, they are not alone; banks and other financial
institutions, as well as others with computers that automatically date everything, are experiencing the same challenge.

But the IRS is concerned that all unpaid taxes at that time instantly will become a century past due (since with the present system, the next date will read January 1, 1900), with all the penalties and interests that the computer is automated to accrue; it seems it could work on refunds the same way and send out a bunch of checks that were not supposed to be issued.

We will say "Goodbye" to the Intelligence Wheel, and as soon as I introduce you to the Canadian version of the NSA, we will be moving on to examine and discuss other direct or indirect intelligence gatherers, government or privately owned.

Canada's Intelligence Community

As I mentioned when discussing New Zealand's intelligence activities, an organization exists called UKUSA. Here is what the Canadian's have to say about it.

> Canadian SIGINT [signals intelligence] activities take place, and can only be understood, in the wider context of the UKUSA SIGINT community, a *secret SIGINT alliance* that traces its origins to the Second World War. The post-war continuation of this intelligence alliance was formalized in 1948 with the signing of the *still-secret UKUSA SIGINT co-operation and information-sharing* agreement between the United Kingdom and the United States.
>
> The member agencies of the UKUSA community include the Communications Security Establishment [CSE—Canada's equivalent to the NSA], the United States National Security Agency (NSA), the United Kingdom's Government Communications Headquarters (GCHQ), Australia's Defence Signals Directorate (DSD), and New Zealand's Government Communications Security Bureau (GCSB). A number of other countries' SIGINT agencies also participate in the UKUSA community, including those of Germany, Japan, Norway, South

Korea, and Turkey. These countries are sometimes described as "Third Party" members of the agreement. In addition, some countries, such as China, host UKUSA SIGINT stations or share SIGINT on a more limited basis. [Emphasis added.]

According to the Internet printout, CSE maintains liaison officers for these various groups, and permanent liaison officers at NSA HQ at Fort Meade, Maryland. The current liaison with the NSA is John Eacrett. There are also NSA and GCHQ liaison officers at CSE HQ.

Communications Security Establishment (CSE)— The Canadian Sister to the NSA

Officially begun on September 1, 1946, it began operations on September 3, 1946, and, as with many of the US agencies, it began as one thing and evolved over the years into the present CSE. The current Chief of CSE is A. Stewart Woolner. The formal mandate (mission) of CSE is a classified document, presumably approved by the Cabinet; it never has been laid out in statute. As with the NSA, the CSE may "intercept signals that begin and end in Canada, that begin in Canada and end abroad, or the reverse."

So, in the process of gathering their "foreign" intelligence data, they are collecting and storing information on Canadian citizens simultaneously. "It would appear, therefore, that CSE's 'foreign intelligence' mandate does permit it to intercept many types of communcations that do involve Canadian participants. In fact, the Department of National Defence has admitted that CSE occasionally intercepts communications that involve or contain information about Canadians:. . . . In addition, the government has confirmed that CSE maintains a data bank, DND/P-PU-040, 'Security and Intelligence Information Files,' that contains 'information concerning [Canadians] identified as potential risks to national security.' "

Once you have started targeting "potential risk" subjects, you then are trying to "catch" somebody, even before a crime has been committed. I know "prevention" is better than "cure," but you are walking a very fine line between caution and stepping all over one's civil rights, privacy, freedoms, etc. And just who and what is to determine which parties should be considered potentially risky? Vocal dissidents? Local militias? You and me (if we disagree with Big Brother's actions)? Canada is not alone here. . .the US is doing precisely the same kind of monitoring, as I mentioned earlier, and are walking the same tightrope where personal liberties are concerned.

Information Technology Security: Government of Canada Public Key Infrastructure

This extremely good report explains all about "Public Key Infrastructure," a vital link in the evolution to becoming a cashless society. I suggest you download it from the Internet, at:

(http://www.cse.dnd.ca/PKI/gocpki_e.htm)

I will quote below some of the parts that address our particular concerns.

> The Government of Canada PKI will allow the federal government to:
> - provide more efficient delivery of services to Canadians
> - provide electronic commerce and confidentality services to public servants
> - better protect privacy of information used in Government business

They define cryptography (encryption and decryption) as the discipline that treats the principles, means, and methods for making plain information unintelligible and reconverting the unintelligible information back into an intelligible form.

> . . .Cryptography has been around for hundreds of years but awareness of it has taken off with the wide use of the computer and open networks (e.g., INTERNET).

> Faster and more complex computers and communica-
> tions systems have pushed the use and development of
> new cryptographic systems, which rely on the use of
> Public Key Cryptography.

Just what is Public Key Cryptography? We are told that
conventional cryptography uses a single mathematical key
for both encryption and decryption, whereas Public Key
Cryptography uses two keys instead of one. One key is kept
private and the other key is made public.

Next they define the digital signature and spell out its
function in the system, then they address the question of the
Public Key Infrastructure.

> A Public Key Infrastructure is a network which makes
> possible secure financial electronic transactions and
> exchanges of sensitive information between relative
> strangers. A PKI will provide confidentiality, authentica-
> tion, integrity, and non-repudiation support to informa-
> tion technology applications and electronic commerce
> transactions. It works partly by establishing a directory
> which will contain each user's Public Key and identifica-
> tion (digital signature).

When they answer the question of where the Government
of Canada PKI fits in, among other things, they tell us this:

> . . .The Government of Canada PKI is the infrastruc-
> ture that integrates other technologies (i.e. Electronic
> Authorization and Authentication, smart cards, etc.) into
> a seamless solution for secure departmental information
> management and electronic commerce, whether internal
> or external to government. It is planned to be operational
> in 1998.

Why do they need the Canada PKI?

Without security, the value of the information highway (Internet) is significantly reduced. Security is a fundamental requirement for applications such as:

- basic electronic commerce (i.e. purchase orders, credit card information, etc.)
- private e-mail
- work flow automation using electronic forms with signatures
- legally binding electronic contracts

Security issues must be addressed before the information highway can begin to be used to its full potential. The Government of Canada PKI will provide solutions to the following issues:

- Privacy—keep information confidential [except from them, of course]
- Access control—only allow selected recipients access to the information [without a doubt, the Big Brother agencies will have access]
- Integrity—assurance that the information has not been altered [although, that would not be difficult if someone had a backdoor key to get in]
- Authentication—proof of the originator of the information
- Non-repudiation—prevents anyone from denying that he/she sent the information [in other words, no more surfing the Net (nor banking, nor purchasing, etc.) in anonymity].

ARPA / DARPA

The acronym ARPA stands for Advanced Research Projects Agency, which is now known as DARPA (DefenseARPA). ARPA/DARPA is a research and development agency engaged in keeping the US on the cutting edge (or even further out there) of new developments in technology and computing.

DARPA's address is: Defense Advanced Research Projects Agency, 3701 North Fairfax Drive, Arlington, VA 22203-1714.

In its Science and Technology section, *The Economist,* September 28, 1996, carried an article on the future of computers, titled "The Weirdest Computer of All." Their subtitle says, "A quantum computer would rely on the surreal behaviour of the very small to work miracles with information. There is new hope that it might someday be more than fantasy."

I want to quote briefly some remarks about DARPA (which I have documented in the previous chapter) concerning its having been underwritten by the NSA, at least in its beginning stages...and perhaps it still is, via some of those Black Projects...it possibly could account for some of that missing $2 billion from their budget that they can't seem to locate at the moment.

> Naturally, building a useful quantum computer would be difficult. Only the very smallest objects behave in a detectably quantum way. This means that the components of such a computer would be very tiny and very delicate. But so great is the theoretical appeal of the machine that America's Defense Advanced Research Projects Agency (DARPA) has just created an Institute for Quantum Information and Computing, and given it $5m to investigate the possibilities.

In 1996 DARPA's budget allegedly was $2.2 billion. One of their goals is to develop, within 10 years, "not obviously absurd, but easily reachable" technologies. First mentioned among the examples of this technology is for spying: "a nearly silent, fast-hovering mechanical 'hummingbird' unmanned surveillance vehicle." Another is the "electronic dog's nose" for sniffing out unexploded ordnance, and I presume drugs in transit. The third item they want to develop is perpetual power sources "fueled in an environmentally sound manner."

There is a long list of programs that have gone on literally for decades. We are interested in the one called ARPANET,

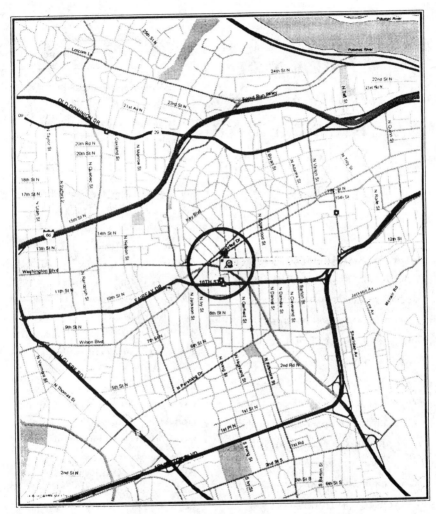

Road map of the ARPA/DARPA location in Arlington, Virginia.

DEFENSE
ADVANCED
RESEARCH
PROJECTS
AGENCY

THE *DEFENSE ADVANCED RESEARCH PROJECTS AGENCY (DARPA)* IS THE CENTRAL RESEARCH AND DEVELOPMENT ORGANIZATION FOR THE DEPARTMENT OF DEFENSE (DoD). IT MANAGES AND DIRECTS SELECTED BASIC AND APPLIED RESEARCH AND DEVELOPMENT PROJECTS FOR DoD, AND PURSUES RESEARCH AND TECHNOLOGY WHERE RISK AND PAYOFF ARE BOTH VERY HIGH AND WHERE SUCCESS MAY PROVIDE DRAMATIC ADVANCES FOR TRADITIONAL MILITARY ROLES AND MISSIONS, AND DUAL USE APPLICATIONS.

Perspective

DARPA's primary responsibility is to help maintain U.S. technological superiority and guard against unforeseen technological advances by potential adversaries.

DARPA focuses on the future. It is responsible to the Department of Defense as a whole and reports directly to its executive management; thus, its organization and operation are unique within the Federal Government. DARPA reaches out beyond the traditional federal laboratory structure to deal directly with the nation's industrial and academic communities. In this sense, DARPA plays a special role in DoD's Research & Development (R&D) investment strategy by acting in large measure as a venture capitalist, but measuring return on investment in terms of products and processes rather than in dollars. DARPA has a continuing history of technological success accomplished by working with world class scientists and engineers.

which after more than 20 years' of DARPA investment has evolved into the Internet. (The NSA was pushing this from the very beginning.)

Strategy Six, of seven, in the list of how to determine which projects take priority, states:

> Predict the future, live in the future, operate in the future. . . . In order to grapple with systems, particularly systems that have a large component of software, the technology community and service, university, and government researchers need to live in a time machine, they need to operate the computer system that seems very innovative and expensive today but will become affordable in the future.

From the five-page report ARPA has on the Internet, I have excerpted a few comments below.

> . . . the ARPA program is shifting focus from stimulating the development of the new scalable computing technology base. . . toward developing the technologies needed to enable a broad base of applications and users, including their extension to a National Information Infrastructure [probably similar to the Canadian PKI].
>
> The current scalable computing technology base is characterized by the first 100 gigaflop class computing systems. . . .
>
> ARPA is the lead DoD agency for advanced technology research and has the leadership responsibility for High Performance Computing (HPC) within DoD. The ARPA HPC Program develops dual use technologies with broad applicability to enable the defense and intelligence communities to build on commercial technologies. . . .
>
> ARPA has no laboratories or centers of its own and executes its programs in close cooperation with the Office of Naval Research, the Air Force Office of Scientific Research, the Army Research Office, Service Laboratories, the National Security Agency [NSA], and other

DoD organizations and Federal agencies. ARPA participates in joint projects . . . [with] the intelligence community. . . .

. . . A joint project with NSA is developing gigabit
network security technology. . . .

DARPA on a Global Scale—The Internet

According to DARPA, "Internet technologies will be developed to enable continued scaling of the networks to every
individual and system needing access."

They report further about their plans to enhance the global
Internet: "Experimental gigabit networks are overlaying and
enhancing the Internet. ARPA's Networking Systems program
develops and evaluates these technologies as foundations for
a global scale, ubiquitous information infrastructure . . . ."

ARPA projects include: "Advanced Internet-based services
will be developed to enable the effective deployment of
distributed Internet-based systems. . . . Mobile and wireless
technologies will enable users and their networks to access
the information infrastructure with the appropriate authentication, privacy, and security. . . . A variety of access tools and
interfaces will be developed to enable interactive access to
the infrastructure."

It is well known that the NSA funds experimental programs
(for lack of better terminology) at many universities and
"think tanks." ARPA also is engaged in that activity. "The
ARPA program, along with NSF, provides the majority of
Federal support to universities in computer and computational
science."

Where Wizards Stay Up Late: The Origins of the Internet

I want to close out this ARPA section with a book review
(*Publishers Weekly,* July 15, 1996) of the above titled book
by Katie Hafner and Matthew Lyon (Simon & Schuster, 320
p., ISBN 0-684-81201-0). The clever title may be so clever
that it misleads one, however, this is an excellent book on

the origins of the Internet. (The name of the reviewer was not furnished.)

Hafner, coauthor of *Cyberpunk*, and Lyon, assistant to the president of the University of Texas, here unveil the Sputnik-era beginnings of the Internet, the groundbreaking scientific work that created it and the often eccentric, brilliant scientists and engineers responsible. Originally funded during the Eisenhower administration by IPTO (Information Processing Techniques Office) within the Defense Department's Advanced Research Projects Agency (ARPA), ARPANET, the Internet's predecessor, was devised as a way to share far-flung U.S. computer resources at a time when computers were wildly expensive, room-sized behemoths unable to communicate with any other. The husband-and-wife writing team profile the computer engineering firm of Bolt, Baranek, and Newman [BBN], which produced the original prototypes for ARPANET, and they profile the men (there were virtually no women) and an alphabet soup of agencies, universities, and software that made the Internet possible. And while the book attempts to debunk the conventional notion that ARPANET was devised primarily as a communications link that could survive nuclear war (essentially it was not), pioneer developers like Paul Baran (who, along with British Scientist Donald Davis, devised the Internet's innovative packet-switching message technology) recognized the importance of an indestructible message medium in an age edgy over the prospects of global nuclear destruction. The book is excellent at enshrining little known but crucial scientists/administrators like Bob Taylor, Larry Roberts, and Joseph Licklider, many of whom laid the groundwork for the computer science industry.

Social Security Administration (SSA)

This is another Indirect/Government intelligence-gathering agency. *Webster's Family Encyclopedia,* 1996-97, says this about the Social Security Act (1935):

> US law that provided guaranteed benefits for retire-ment-aged workers (65 or over), based on income and worker and employer contributions. Part of Pres. Franklin D. Roosevelt's New Deal program, it was, in effect, a pension plan to provide for old age in a nuclear family society. Subsequent amendments provided for depend-ents of deceased workers, disabled and unemployed workers, and health insurance benefits. The Social Security Administration is the agency in charge of the program.

The Treasury Department, under the auspices of the IRS, produces a newsletter with information on both Social Security items of interest, as well as items of interest on the IRS. It is called the *Reporter: A Newsletter for Employers.* The Spring, 1997, edition carries a front-page article titled "Social Security Leads the Nation's Computers into 21st Century." This is the article explaining the problem with the dates and the com-puters. It explained that the computers determine dates based upon two digits. What must be done is alter the computer programs to accept dates with four digits. . . that should solve the problem until about December 31, 9,999 (that's a JOKE, folks!). Here are some excerpts:

> Social Security depends heavily on computer opera-tions. Over 30 million lines of software now in use are date-sensitive. . . . It expects to have its computers converted to the four-digit standard by 1998. Because of its expertise, the President asked the Social Security Administration to lead government agencies in identify-ing strategies to deal with the year 2000 computer systems issue that will affect federal agencies and the

private sector.

The turn of the century poses an enormous challenge for the data processing community in every federal, state, local, public, and private sector business and organization around the world. Unfortunately, there is no universal quick-fix that will solve everyone's problems. The code in every computer system will have to be converted line-by-line. This is very labor-intensive, and very costly.

While each organization must find solutions that meet its unique needs, Social Security leads discussion on cross-cutting aspects of the problem. **These include inter-agency data exchanges**. . . [emphasis added].

For more information, they invite you to check the Internet:
SSA: (http://www.ssa.gov)
IRS: (http://www.irs.ustreas.gov)
The IRS is not the only agency troubled with bureaucratic SNAFU's. The SSA had established "Social Security Online" on the Internet. As of December 16, 1996, they were announcing that they were in their third year on the Web:
(http://www.ssa.gov/)
In this particular issue, they were announcing Internet accessibility to their "PEBES" program. PEBES is an acronym for Personal Earnings and Benefit Estimate Statement. In other words, you may inquire from the SSA (at their website) about what you may expect your retirement income to be, based on your past and future expected earnings. Since most of us are curious about that, they received many inquiries. But because of problems, they pulled the plug on the program within a month (the information is still available by mail if you complete the proper forms). The June, 1997, edition of *Government Technology* carried this article:

Social Security Retires Records Site

WASHINGTON, D.C. (NB) — Bowing to congressional pressure and a raft of negative publicity, the U.S. Social Security Administration immediately shut down access to Social Security Personal Earnings and Benefits Estimate Statements (PEBES) on its World Wide Web site in early April.

The information, which could be accessed from the Social Security Administration's site at (http://www.ssa.gov), had been available online for only a month. According to SSA spokesperson Tom Morgenau, the same information has been available to the public by mail for over 10 years.

Noting that confidence in the agency's ability to protect the privacy "of the sensitive data we maintain on American citizens" had been questioned, SSA Acting Commissioner John J. Callahan said he was suspending the online PEBES service "in order to conduct a rigorous evaluation of the system's security features." [Author's note: Sounds a little backward to me, sort of like closing the barn door after the horse is gone. Why didn't they put such a plan through a rigorous evaluation BEFORE they activated it?]

The shutdown occurred less than 24 hours after U.S. Senate Majority Leader Trent Lott and several other senators sent a letter to Callahan expressing their "serious concern regarding recent reports in the media indicating it may be possible to gain unauthorized access" to confidential PEBES information through the Internet.

"Although we support the Social Security Administration's efforts to make PEBES more readily available," the senators wrote, "we are concerned that PEBES Online may not afford sufficient protections against violations of individual privacy."

They are trying to tighten down unauthorized access by everybody but the guys with the back door key.

As you can see, the SSA is right on the bandwagon with the collecting and sharing of data. Before I close this section on the SSA, I want to tell you that they have available many videos on the various aspects of Social Security, which I would suggest you address their website and obtain, if you have a need for information on specific subjects.

Federal Emergency Management Agency (FEMA)

FEMA is in the "Indirect/Government" category of the intelligence gatherers. It is an independent agency of the federal government, established by one of those notorious Executive Orders, rather than congressional legislation. Based on their stated purposes, you may wonder why I am addressing FEMA in this book. Before I get into documenting my assertions, I'll just tell you "up front." FEMA has been given ultimate control over the country and its citizens, including calling in the military (or probably the UN troops) if FEMA deems it necessary to restore order during a natural or manmade disaster. The President has given this authority.

> Executive Order 12148 establishes the FEMA and delegates most of the President's authority under the Stafford Act to FEMA.

You can just imagine what could result from all this power being in the hands of one organization, if it were decided that YOU were the radical who needed to be brought into line with, say, the New World Order government transition, for example. Furthermore, it is no secret that they are attempting to merge our FEMA with Russia's counterpart (EMERCOM), getting us all ready to live together in harmony. They are setting up the Internet to handle the global communications with a UN organization (for the time being under FEMA) called Global Emergency Management System (GEMS). Now for some background.

Manual for Civil Emergencies

I have excerpted from this manual points of interest about FEMA.

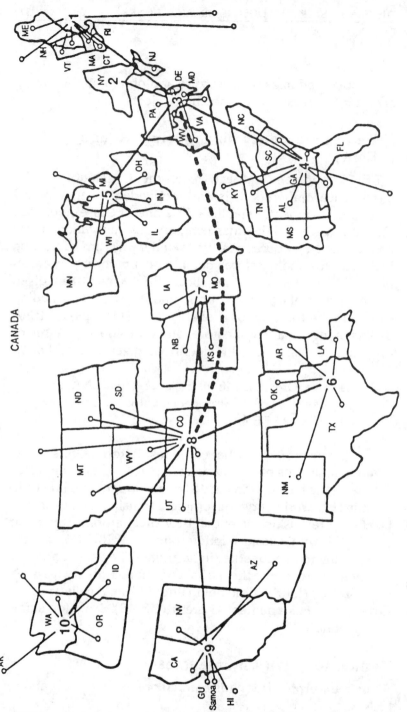

FEMA map depicting states assigned to each of 10 regions.

CONUSAs AND FEMA REGIONS

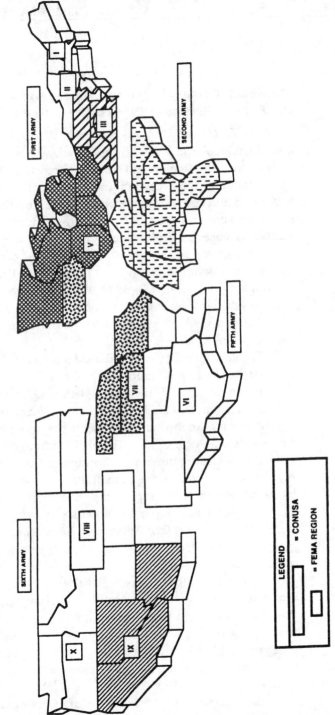

Map depicting the 10 FEMA and Army Reserve regions.

The Federal Emergency Management Agency and the Federal Response Plan (FEMA / FRP)

BACKGROUND: FEMA was created in 1978 to provide a single point of accountability for all Federal emergency preparedness mitigation and response activities. Under the direction of the President, the mission of FEMA is to plan for and coordinate the protection of the civilian population and resources of the Nation [there's that old standby excuse...they're doing it for our own good, which brings me back to that priceless line from The King and I, "Might they not protect me out of all I own?" Undoubtedly!]....The FRP is FEMA's [with the DoD] primary vehicle for response to natural and technological disasters and civil emergencies [riots, uprisings, civil disobedience, et al].

ORGANIZATION: The National Headquarters of FEMA is located at Federal Center Plaza, 500 "C" Street SW, Washington, DC, 20472. The FEMA National Emergency Training Center is located at Emmitsburg, Maryland. It is the home for two institutions that conduct the agency's nationwide training program. The ten FEMA regions are superimposed over the Forces Command Continental Army structure on one map; the other shows the states by name and in which region they are located. Each FEMA region has a Regional Director.

LEGAL AUTHORITIES: Although FEMA relies upon many emergency legal authorities, it operates under two major legal provisions.

a. Robert T. Stafford Disaster Relief and Emergency Assistance Act [The Stafford Act]. Through this Act, the President is granted broad authority to respond with financial assistance when an emergency is declared. By delegation, FEMA is authorized to provide disaster assistance...following Presidentially declared emergencies....

b. The Federal Civil Defense Act of 1950. This Act

vests authority in the President to enhance National
security in the United States by promoting civil defense
*for the protection of life and property from attacks. . . . The
President has delegated to the Director of FEMA responsibility for preparing National plans and programs for civil
defense. . . .*

Other Military Support to FEMA: There is a long history
of military personnel being associated with FEMA and
its predecessor agencies in the area of civil defense and
emergency preparedness. [Emphasis added.]

Under the section titled "Execution" of the FRP, it states
that a Presidential Declaration allows FEMA to activate a part
or all of the response structure and emergency support
functions and *task other Federal Agencies to provide support.
FEMA requests military support through DOMS. . . .*
I have more to share here about FEMA, but for a thorough
study on the power, plans, and dangers of FEMA, refer to my
previous book, *The Mark of the New World Order,* pp. 82ff.
In this book, I want to emphasize their activities to merge
the countries of the world together in a global Internet, and
their link with the UN. The FEMA News Desk
(http://www.fema.gov/fema/wittspch3.htm)
has provided a transcript of the opening remarks for the
United States-Russian Federation Press Conference by James
Lee Witt, Director of FEMA, September 4, 1996. Excerpts
follow:

Good afternoon ladies and gentlemen. I am very
pleased to welcome. . .(EMERCOM of Russia) delegation to FEMA. Today, we have embarked on an important
cooperative initiative between our great nations.

We have heard much about the important work of
EMERCOM of Russia. . . .

Today, we embarked on an historic undertaking—the
first U.S.-Russian Federation Joint Committee meeting
on natural and man-made disaster prevention and

response. This initial meeting is the first step in the implementation of the new Memorandum of Understanding on Cooperation on Natural and Man-made Technological Disaster Prevention and Response, signed by Vice President Gore and Prime Minister Chernomyrdin in Moscow on July 16, 1996.

We have much to learn from each other. . . .

I know we are talking about "sharing information" in this book, but don't you think this is going a little bit too far?

Who is FEMA?

As mentioned earlier, FEMA is an independent federal agency with more than 2,600 full-time employees. They also have nearly 4,000 standby disaster assistance employees who are available to help as needed. **In February, 1996, President Clinton conferred Cabinet status on James Lee Witt, Director of FEMA.**

On June 19, 1996, President Clinton announced the National Arson Prevention Initiative (NAPI) because of a series of arson fires in our nation's houses of worship. NAPI is a cooperative effort **led by FEMA** in partnership with the Department of Housing and Urban Development, Department of Justice, and Department of the Treasury.

FEMA Computer Program Named in Finals for Award

A press release appeared on the Internet on October 31, 1996. It begins like this:

National Information Infrastructure Awards Selects FEMA World Wide Web Site as Semifinalist In Second Annual Competition

WASHINGTON—The National Information Infrastructure (NII) Awards recently announced that the FEMA had been selected as a semifinalist in their annual program. FEMA's Web site (http://www.fema.gov) was one of 190 exceptional information highway projects chosen from the initial pool of 850 entrants.

United Nations Global Emergency Management System (UN / GEMS)

Below are listed some of the GEMS from the UN:

Pan American Health Organization
Relief Web
UNICEF
UN Department of Humanitarian Affairs
World Health Organization

"In addition to these, FEMA's Global Emergency Management Service provides access to a wide variety of emergency management and disaster related web sites."

G-7 "Plus Russia"

Earlier I described to you an organization of seven countries (allies) called G-7 "plus Russia." FEMA, Gemini, and G-7 are linked to promote the advancement of information exchange and enhancement of the Internet between nations. One plan is called Government Online and is engaged in doing just what it says, getting governments online on the Internet. Another one is the GEM program, described above. They have many more projects of interest. You may inquire at their website:

(http://www.ispo.cec.be/g7/projidx.html)

National Communications System (NCS)

As I close out the section on FEMA, I want to make you aware of the National Communications System (NCS), as it is FEMA's equivalent in the communications field, in other words, it has full control of all communications in any form in the event of any "emergency," whether real, imagined, or created!

Its stated mission is: "Lead the planning, coordination and integration of government telecommunications capabilities to ensure access to, and use of critical information services required for effective response in an all hazards environment."

It was created by Presidential Memorandum (I'll bet you guessed that!) by John F. Kennedy, followed in April, 1984, by the signing of Executive Order No. 12472, "Assignment of National Security and Emergency Preparedness Telecommunications Functions (NS/EP)," expanded its mission to include exercising wartime and *nonwartime* emergency telecommunications, and in the coordination of the planning for and provisioning of NS/EP communications for the Federal Government *under all circumstances.*

As an organization, the NCS brings together the assets of 23 Federal departments and agencies to address the full range of NS/EP telecommunications issues. Among the many on the list you will find the CIA, FEMA, and the NSA.

The Multitude of "Indirect" Intelligence Gatherers—Government or Nongovernment

There are any number of entities contributing to the universal database worldwide, putting your personal and business statistics in the hands of those who have no business with access to them. Trading of information is monumental today, not just nationally, but thanks to the development and promotion of the Internet World Wide Web, globally as well. I have selected a number of the more prominent collectors and sellers of information, however, I will mention each with only a brief description of their activities—in many cases they are self-explanatory and in others it only takes a little vision and a small clue to make the connection obvious. In keeping with my previous system, I will label them as either "direct" or "indirect," and "government" or "nongovernment." These are more of the sister organizations of the Big Brother NSA, which have come to be known as "Little Brothers."

National Science Foundation (NSF)—Indirect/ Government

The National Science Foundation is an independent agency of the Federal government that was established in 1950 by an Act of Congress. The agency's mission is to promote the progress of science and engineering.

Well, finally! One of these groups was begun by an Act of Congress. Promoting progress in science and engineering today can be interpreted as promoting computer technology, satellite communication systems, and enhancement of the Internet.

Dr. Neal F. Lane is Director of the NSF. Their mission statement further includes "to secure the national defense"—which establishes a link to the DoD. Then it calls for the NSF to "foster and support the development and use of computers." And like the other agencies, they will "maintain a current register of scientific and technical personnel, and in other ways **provide a central clearinghouse** for the collection, interpretation, and analysis of data..." [emphasis added].

And the NSF is now responsible for running and maintaining the Internet. What does that tell you about linked databases?

National Security Council (NSC)—Indirect/ Government

The National Security Council was established in 1947 and, as other agencies, it has evolved to its present status. It operates in the Executive Office of the President.

NSC describes its function as "the President's principal forum for considering national security and foreign policy matters...." And "The NSC staff serves as an initial point of contact for departments and agencies who wish to bring a national security issue to the President's attention."

Again, with this organization we find current ties with Russia.

Russia/Boris Yeltsin Appoints
Alexander Lebed as National Security Council
Secretary and Presidential National Security Aide,
Sacks Defense Minister Pavel Grachev

MOSCOW, JUNE 18, RIA NOVOSTI NATALIA SAL-
NIKOVA—President Boris Yeltsin of the Russian Federation and Alexander Lebed negotiated here today, with
the head of state signing a decree on appointing Lebed
to the post of National Security Council Secretary and
Presidential National Security Aide.

According to Yeltsin, he has relieved Defense Minister
Pavel Grachev today, appointing Mikhail Kolesnikov in
charge of the Russian Armed Forces' General Staff as
acting Defense Minister.

I just have one question...why the exact same name as
America's National Security Council?

National Telecommunications & Information
Administration (NTIA)—Indirect/Government

It seems strange to define this division of the Department
of Commerce as "indirect," since their major function is to
promote communications technology, which, of course, is
leading to worldwide access to the Internet for education,
business, and other sources of information and activities
(interactive). But the information collected is a byproduct of
their stated goal...not the goal itself.

They are involved heavily in the President's Information
Infrastructure Task Force (a co-op effort by many agencies
and private enterprises).

"NTIA's mission is carried out by the Assistant Secretary
of Commerce for Communication and Information who
administers five major program offices. Through the Secretary
of Commerce, he is the President's principal adviser on telecommunications policy."

US Geological Survey (USGS)—Indirect/ Government

"Welcome to the U.S. Geological Survey, a bureau of the Department of the Interior. USGS is the Nation's largest earth science research and information agency." These are the makers of the maps and takers of the long-distance aerial photos (from space). With the help of new technologies, maps are more accurate and aerial photos more revealing than ever before. They now are using "GPS assisted GIS technology." To interpret that, GPS is the acronym for Global Positioning System, a global satellite-based locator system; GIS stands for Geographical Information Services. This satellite system is now being merged with Russian satellites to complete the link around the world.

USGS's EROS Data Center houses millions of images— aerial photographs, mainly for mapping, and various kinds of satellite images for scientific study.

I believe they also are mapping databases for online "sharing" at the USGS-NOAA, Joint Office for Mapping and Research, 915 National Center, Reston, VA 20192.

They list a whole page of Internet Resources, with World Wide Web Locator Service.

United Nations Crime and Justice Information Network (UNCJIN)—Indirect/Nongovernment

We might debate whether or not the UN is "nongovernment," however, they are not OUR government, at least not yet— even though they may be classified as global government.

> UNCJIN is funded, in part, by the United States Bureau of Justice Statistics. . . .
>
> The United Nations Crime and Justice Information Network was established in 1989 . . . . to establish . . . a global crime prevention and criminal justice information network . . . including a mechanism for *the centralization of inputs* from nongovernmental organizations and scientific institutions.

The goal of UNCJIN is *to establish a world wide network to enhance dissemination and the exchange of information. . . .*

  *. . .*to support the establishment and expansion of computerized national and local criminal justice systems. [Why should a global UN be concerned with local criminal justice?] [Emphasis added.]

Further information may be obtained from UNCJIN at 423 State Street, Albany, NY 12203.

INTERPOL—Indirect/Nongovernment

The *Grolier's Encyclopedia* defines the Interpol this way:

Interpol (International Criminal Police Organization) is a mutual assistance organization of police forces. Founded in 1923, it had a membership of 150 countries in 1990. Day-to-day operations are handled at Interpol headquarters, which was located in Paris until 1989 when the organization moved its headquarters to Lyons, France. Major policy decisions are made at annual meetings of the general assembly of all members.

Each member nation maintains a domestic clearing-house that processes data on international criminals and their activities, especially smuggling, counterfeiting, and trade in narcotics. Members cooperate by detaining suspects within their borders and by providing information on criminals, missing property, and unidentified bodies. Interpol has its own agents, but they may not pass freely from one country to another; arrests and investigations are the responsibility of each country's own police force. Involvement in political, religious, military, or racial matters is strictly prohibited.

The members of Interpol share many things, but probably highest on the list is information. If Interpol has its way, something else we will be sharing is a new office: upon Russian approval, our FBI and Interpol will be setting up a new office in Moscow, Russia, in their efforts to curb the spread of the Russian Mafia. I am convinced that the Russian Mafia is really controlled by the allegedly defunct KGB.

Naturally, the biggest item on their agenda is big computers. Of course, they expect the "Western nations" to foot the bill for these new computers for Russia. ". . . the sooner Russia and the CIS become part of the Interpol network the better." Can you say, "New World Order"? In addition to these communist countries, Red China joined Interpol in 1984.

National Locator & Data—Direct/ Nongovernment

This is one of those profit-making organizations that is in the business of collecting, categorizing, and selling data. Here is their website:

(http://www.iu.net:80/Hodges/)

They claim to have access to 950 million records and are capable of providing information obtained from credit headers, US Postal Service, magazine subscriptions, demographic profiles, nationwide white pages, researchers, Social Security Number records, and public records. Below is a list of Reports & Searches listed at their website:

Commercial Credit Reports
Corporate Records
National Business Kris Cross
Credit Grantor ID Number Lookup
Criminal Histories
Workman Compensation Claims
Public Record Databases (judgments, bankruptcy,
    tax liens)
Motor Vehicle Reports
Real Property Assets
In-Depth Business Background Information
Social Security Number Tracing
Find Social Security Number

Surname Searches
Death Reports
National Kris Cross Plus
Zipcode plus nine neighbors
National Address Identified Update
FAA Records
FAA Tail Number
Registered Voter's Searches
Marriage/Divorce Records Searches
Verify a Stock Broker/Security Dealer's License
Verify a Medical Doctor's License
New York Citizens Profile Reports
Oregon Boat Registrations & Liquor License Search
Texas Boat Registration, Hunting & Fishing License
Florida People Finder
Florida Salt Water Product Licenses
National Trademark Search
Florida Business Data
Florida Accident Reports
Florida Real Estate
Florida Detailed Reports
Florida Professional Regulations
Florida Combined Searches
Florida Sexual Predators
Data Search Services (Hard to find info)
National Dossier
Republic of Panama
Income · Homeownership Demographics

LEXIS-NEXIS—Direct/Nongovernment

This is another huge data-collecting-and-selling company, similar to the one just above, however, it specializes in other types of data collection. "Online services, Information Management Tools Assist Legal, Business, Government Professionals." For example, they provide, on a commercial basis, full-text legal information, in addition to the more customary data.

More than 779,000 active users subscribe to the LEXIS-NEXIS services.

It would appear, however, that too many people were gaining access to too many things they shouldn't, so there have been some changes made.

Service still provides sensitive information
By Rose Aguilar
September 19, 1996

UPDATE—Lexis-Nexis is still providing sensitive personal data on its widely used information service, three months after saying publicly that it had altered the feature in an effort to prevent potential fraud and other abuse, CNET has learned.

Lexis-Nexis had changed its P-TRAK Personal Locator so that users could no longer obtain Social Security numbers simply by entering a name. The company took the action in June, a day after CNET reported that Social Security numbers were widely available on the service.

US Postal Service (USPS)—Indirect/ Nongovernment(?)

One of the largest databases maintained (on every one and every business in the country) is owned by the US Postal Service. Of course, their "need to know" is because everybody moves around so much now, and they have to know where to deliver our mail. So when you turn in your change of address card, it is incorporated into the national database of the USPS, and is accessible to inquiries. The National Customer Support Center is located at 6060 Primacy Parkway, Ste. 201, Memphis, TN 38188-0001, Phone 1-800-238-3150.

See the article reprinted here from the *Spotlight* which provides more details on the plans of the USPS. And of course, this information is available to the NSA if it needs to find you.

A private company, Zip*Data, also sells postal records, categorized in many different ways and furnishing a whole

TECHNOLOGY & LIBERTY

By Clark Matthews

Danger in the Mail

Don't look now, but Uncle Sam has some shiny new shackles with your name on them. Indeed, sources in the U.S. Postal Service recently revealed that they're all set to deliver your very own personalized federal ball and chain directly to your mailbox.

And you read it here first.

If your slave-bracelet comes, don't expect a hefty steel ball and clumsy, clanking chains. Those days are gone. We're closing in on the 21st Century—high-tech restraints are the order of the day.

So instead of a postman straining under the weight of a neighborhood's-worth of iron, you'll see nothing more ominous than a mailbag full of official-looking personalized envelopes.

There will be one for every member of your family. You will find a harmless-looking Smart Card contained in each envelope.

The Smart Card could well be called the "U.S. Card." And if it performs as announced by the Postal Service, it will restrain you as surely as a pair of handcuffs and dispossess you as certainly as a phalanx of marshals with padlocks.

Without the card, you won't be able to own property, receive government benefits, get medical attention, conduct bank or credit-card transactions . . . you name it, and you can't do it. Your life will be completely controlled by the device, if the Clinton administration adopts the Postal Service's proposal.

And, as I wrote two weeks ago, Executive Orders are reported to be drafted to adopt the cards. Without congressional approval.

MEDIA COLLABORATION

Have you heard about the U.S. Card on the TV networks? Or in your local newspaper? I bet you haven't.

It's not exactly a secret, although the national security powers try to obscure its origins by moving the ghastly project around between different government agencies to make it "plausibly deniable."

The computer press has reported on it. The respected industry journal *PC Week* covered the story on its front page—and even tracked down the leads about Clinton's drafted Executive Orders to force the cards

NOW THAT I HAVE FREE ACCESS

TO YOUR BANK RECORDS...

YOUR HOUSE IS NEXT!

NIBBLING AWAY YOUR FREEDOM BIT BY BIT

on Americans. The White House gave *PC Week* a terse "no comment."

And somehow *PC Week* missed one of the most revealing comments made by the U.S. Card's boosters at the Postal Service: They told several people that they were prepared to mail 100 million of the cards in a matter of months.

As alarming and sickening as this prospect seems, you have to marvel at the irony of it all. The Clinton administration, which says it's determined to "break the cycle of dependency" among welfare recipients, is preparing to reduce every American to total dependence—and near-total surveillance—through these infamous cards.

THE U.S. CARD

The U.S. Card, described here two weeks ago, is raising eyebrows throughout the computer community. Frankly, among computer-literate citizens, the U.S. Card is raising more than eyebrows. It's causing people's hair to stand on end.

It is a super Smart Card—a *Tesserea* card, prototyped by the Defense Department and perfected by the distributed-systems experts of the Postal Service, the Treasury Department, the IRS and quite possibly the National Security Agency.

The word *tesserea* is Latin. It means "a piece of a mosaic". It is the name given by ancient Roman conquerors to identity chits they issued to conquered peoples and slaves. It was adopted as the code-name for the Smart Card development project by—apparently—the Defense Messaging Agency. The *Tesserea* cards developed in that program years ago were clearly the precursors of the all-encompassing, mandatory device proposed by the Postal Service and other federal agencies now.

'FRONT END' OF TYRANNY

In computer parlance, the U.S. Card functions as a "front-end". The "back end" of the tyranny will be every bit of personal information about you, wherever in the world the data may be.

This is called "client/server" computer technology, and it has been perfected over many years by both businesses and governments. For all intents and purposes, it works flawlessly. Nearly a million bank cash machines use client/server technology —when was the last time your local bank cash machine made a mistake?

(And was the mistake in your favor? Or the bank's?)

The U.S. Card was proposed as a national identity card and "signature verification" device by the U.S. Postal Service at the "CardTech/SecureTech" conference held in Crystal City, Virginia. The Postal Service's proposal (which was echoed by the IRS—what a coincidence!) calls for the card to "mediate" the information about you in every government database. It will be like a magic key, which opens every government database with information about you.

Of course, without your magic key, you're out in the cold. You won't be able to file tax returns, collect your pensions or social security, conduct bank or credit card transactions or interact with the government in any way.

'MAGIC KEY'

And here's another troubling fact. If federal computer systems are already integrated to this extent—where one card can "unlock" every piece of information about you—then what makes you think you have the only key?

Of course you won't have the only key. And potentially everything you own and all your assets, benefits and entitlements can be "withheld" from you with the push of a few buttons at the Treasury Department, IRS, or who-knows-where.

The Postal Service spokesman who eagerly described the U.S. Card to a "cleared" audience at the CardTech conference said that the databases are ready to be integrated under the card.

To me, that means the databases are integrated now. It can take well over a year to integrate a couple of big databases. If the Postal Service is ready to start mailing 100 million of these cards within months, then the databases are integrated now. They work together—for Big Brother —now. They are being used now.

OVERSEERS WITH MISGIVINGS

The Postal Service took special care to choose a friendly forum to introduce its proposed U.S. Card and the computer systems that make it work. It's no accident they chose the CardTech conference. The CardTech SecureTech confab is hardly an assemby of civil libertarians.

On the contrary—if the globe is becoming a plantation, then most of the CardTech folks want to be the overseers.

The conference is for government and corporate specialists in computer security, personal tracking and surveillance. If Americans are going to be branded or tattooed or implanted with transmitters or otherwise permanently marked and monitored by the government—like slaves in days of old —the folks who attend the CardTech conference generally want to be the ones selling the branding irons.

Even so, people at the conference expressed reservations about the U.S. Card. Not technical reservations, mind you. They know the U.S. Card will work as advertised.

They expressed political reservations.

Those people buy and sell folks' privacy for a living. I guess it's one thing to sell branding irons, but quite another thing to accept a brand yourself. It's up to you. ●

lot more than just your zip code! For them you can call: 1-800-800-MAIL.

Credit Bureaus—Direct/Nongovernment

There are many small and several very large credit bureaus whose business is the collection and sale of personal information on you (usually available to everyone *but* you). Equifax is one such large company, but here I will address only the TRW company, and its sale to the Experian company. Since the purpose and function of a credit bureau is quite evident, I won't bother to describe it. I just want to familiarize you with some of the activities of one of the largest. It's still a case of more merging, bigger and better, etc.

February 7, 1996, it was announced that TRW reportedly was selling its Information Systems & Services Unit for nearly $1 billion. The division—one of the biggest sources of credit reports earns about $604 million in annual revenue. It is important to point out that TRW's Information Systems & Services collects and disseminates a lot more than just credit information.

On November 8, 1996, it is stated, "Experian is the group of information businesses formerly owned by TRW." According to this report, the transaction was valued at more than $1 billion, there are still unnamed investors, and in addition to the above sum, TRW still retains a 20% interest.

Here are some key facts about Experian databases: consumer credit info on more than 190 million individuals; commercial credit info on more than 13 million businesses;

demographic information on 90 million households; demographic information on 14 million business locations; property information on 53.5 million parcels in 35 states.

Apparently Experian feels threatened by fire, earthquakes, tidal waves, *et al* in Orange County, southern California, so they have announced a data center in Allen, Texas, which they claim "is located in a 27-acre technology park north of Dallas —far from potential earthquakes, hurricanes, tidal waves, and flood plains."

A note in passing, Experian has also been reprimanded recently for letting the wrong information get into the wrong hands. They say it has been corrected, but who can say?

Once all this data is purchased by, or traded with the NSA, we will be well on the way to total centralization of data on everybody, especially when you add to that the information on the medical and insurance computers.

Conclusion

The thrust of this whole chapter has been to raise your awareness level of where all this information is going, who is collecting it, and where they are sending it. I want to stress the importance of all this merging and centralizing and sharing, because they are evolving into a much more powerful, consolidated, (eventually) single database.

I will conclude with some quotes from the August 25, 1997, edition of *TIME* magazine, on the cover of which was a picture of an eye peeking through a keyhole, to illustrate the top article, "The Death of Privacy." Also on the cover appeared the copy: "You have no secrets. At the ATM, on the Internet, even walking down the street, people are watching your every move. What can you do about it?"

Invasion of Privacy

Our right to be left alone has disappeared, bit by bit, in Little Brotherly steps.

We're all being watched by computers whenever we visit Websites; by the mere act of "browsing" (it sounds so passive) we're going public in a way that was unimaginable a decade ago. I know this because I'm a watcher, too. When people come to my Website, without ever knowing their names, I can peer over their shoulders, recording what they look at, timing how long they stay on a particular page, following them around Pathfinder's sprawling offerings.

[The] hacker. . .could have threatened my privacy. He could have sabotaged my credit rating. He could have eavesdropped on my telephone conversations or siphoned off my E-mail. He could have called in my mortgage, discontinued my health insurance, or obliterated my Social Security number. Like Sandra Bullock in [the movie] *The Net,* I could have been a digital untouchable, wandering the planet without a connection to the rest of humanity.

. . .As I watched my personal digital hell unfold, it struck me that our privacy—mine and yours—has already disappeared, not in one Big Brotherly blitzkrieg but in Little Brotherly moments, bit by bit.

. . .We register our whereabouts whenever we put a bank card in an ATM machine or drive through an E-Z Pass lane on the highway.

"It's a very schizophrenic time," says Sherry Turkle, professor of sociology at MIT. . . .She believes our culture is undergoing a kind of **mass identity crisis,** trying to hang on to a sense of privacy and intimacy in a **global village** of tens of millions.

We're in the midst of a global interconnection. . . . What would happen if all the information stored on the world's computers were accessible via the Internet to anyone? Who would control it?

Small-scale privacy atrocities take place every day. . . [asked about medical privacies] she rattles off a list of abuses that would make Big Brother blush.

. . .At least a third of all FORTUNE 500 companies regularly review health information before making hiring decisions.

But how did we arrive at this point, where so much about what we do and own and think is an open book?

It all started in the 1950s, when, in order to administer Social Security funds, the U.S. government began entering records on big mainframe computers, using nine-digit identification numbers.

Some "everyday" events that can catch you include: bank machines, prescription drugs, employee ID scanners, browsing on the Web, cellular telephones, credit cards, registering to vote, making a phone call, supermarket scanners, sweepstakes, satellites, electronic tolls, surveillance cameras, mail-order transactions and sending E-mail.

. . . In the old days, information stored in government databases was relatively inaccessible. Now, however, with PCs on every desktop linked to office networks and then to the Internet, data that were once carefully hidden may be only a few keystrokes away. [Emphasis added.]

At the end, the article suggests ways of slowing down this outflow of personal information, but I think it only gives you false hope of a certain amount of privacy. Some of these suggestions may have been helpful if they were started before you were born, but if you have been around a few years you are already hopelessly entangled in the "Web." If you were born just this year, you were assigned a Social Security number even before you were released from the hospital.

The only safe place to have your name written down is in The Lamb's Book of Life. Of course, we are talking about Jesus Christ, the Son of God, who was our sacrificial lamb, dying on the cross for our sin. Scripture says that whosoever shall call on the name of Christ and whosoever believes on Him shall be saved. I hope you all have taken care of that . . . it's the most important business you ever will transact in this lifetime.

The Bottom Line—
The Supercomputer from Hell . . .
Literally

Public speakers—and in particular, preachers—are taught to "tell them what you are going to tell them, then tell them, then tell them what you told them." In book parlance, that could be interpreted, "The Introduction," "The Chapters," and "The Summation." It is a proven technique that helps the listener or reader comprehend and remember a larger portion of the material being presented to them. Being a firm believer in a couple more clichés, i.e., "don't mess with success" and "if it ain't broke don't fix it," I make it a practice to follow that time-proven formula in my books. Therefore, in wrapping up this book, it seems fitting to quote from Revelation 13:15-18; 14:9-11:

> . . .and cause that as many as would not **worship** the image of the beast should be killed. And he [Antichrist] **causeth** all, both small and great, rich and poor, free and bond, to receive a mark **in** their **right hand**, or **in** their foreheads: And that no man might buy or sell, save he that had the **mark**, or the name of the beast, or the number of his name. Here is wisdom. Let him that hath understanding count the number of the beast: for it is the number of a man; and his number is Six hundred threescore and six [**666**]. . . . If any man **worship** the beast and his image, and receive his mark **in** his forehead,

or **in** his **hand,** The same shall drink of the wine of the wrath of God, which is poured out without mixture into the cup of his indignation; and he shall be tormented with fire and brimstone in the presence of the holy angels, and in the presence of the Lamb; And the smoke of their torment ascendeth up for ever and ever; and they have no rest day nor night, who **worship** the beast and his image, and whosoever receiveth the **mark** of his name [emphasis added].

In the preceding chapters, I have gone to great lengths to explain all about the National Security Agency (NSA) and its affiliates in the information-gathering game. I have told you a little bit about the LUCID identification system, bio-metrics, and supercomputers. That is because I firmly believe that the NSA is covertly constructing *the supercomputer from hell!* The reason I added the word *literally* to this chapter title is because even though the hardware, software, and databases are created in the earthly realm, the system (or its successors) ultimately will be used in the spiritual/physical realm. That is, these perfectly innocuous inventions, in and of themselves are just that—innocuous. And please don't jump on the phone or E-mail and lambast the designers and/or producers of this technology. They are sincere gentlemen who have been deceived into believing that they truly are *helping* with progress to make things better for the human condition. Rather than criticizing or offending them, please pray for them that the Holy Spirit would open their eyes.

These technological capabilities, however, placed in the hands of those with ulterior (spiritual) motives, will enable them to proceed with the final stage of our electronic global surveillance and control, as described in the above passage from the Book of Revelation. This system is referred to as The New World Order and has been a goal for world domina-tion since Hitler's day and earlier, and it has been publicized much since President George Bush and Prime Minister Margaret Thatcher were in office.

The Broad Path of "Convenience"

I am convinced the actions of the NSA and its "Little Brothers" are leading us down the broad path of "convenience" toward the ultimate identification. . .the **mark** spoken of in the above biblical reference. *Combine, centralize,* and *share* are some of the buzzwords used by the gatherers of information. Their goal is to have **all** information **in one location** (I believe it will be the NSA), accessible by everybody. The development and purchase of supercomputers by the NSA is making this possible. Their secret funding of research and development projects, university science projects, and other companies has provided them with the "biggest and best" in computer technology.

With the last book I wrote, *The Mark of the New World Order,* we just were beginning to learn about supercomputers and their amazing capabilities, with their *gigabytes* of memory, or as they are called, GFlops (1 billion calculations per second). As knowledge is doubling every 18 months or less, today we have teraflops. . .in fact, we now have a 4-teraflop computer at a laboratory in New Mexico (government purchased, of course)—a teraflop is 1 trillion calculations per second. And now, even that is too slow—can you just imagine what they are doing with all that capability if 4 trillion calculations per second is too slow?!? Now we are learning about "scalable," "massively parallel," and *petaflops*—that's 1 quadrillion calculations per second. With that kind of computing power, you could store everything in your databases and know everything about everything—current to any given time.

Now, of course, what they are selling the world is the efficiency and economy of having all your eggs in one basket, and guarding only that basket. If you can eliminate overlaps and gaps in ID systems (with accompanying statistical data), and if you only have to go to one source, internationally, to find what you need (whether info on terrorists, weapons runners, drug cartels, money launderers, crime families, Russian Mafia, etc.), think how much time you will save (time is money, you know) and how much money you can save if you delete redundant government organizations, doing essentially the same thing, except for their respective departments. Sounds wonderful, doesn't it? That's just what Big Brother wants us to believe.

To avoid an open rebellion and a civil war, the propagators of the New World Order system aren't likely to "kick the sleeping dog." Rather, it is much more effective to lull us into a state of complacency about the long-term implications of what they are doing by giving us one little "convenience" after the next, each progressively more advanced than the previous one . . . desensitizing us, if you will.

This book is a warning to wake up and see what's going on around you. I want to make it clear that these things are merely "technologies," they are not spiritual, nor can they send you to hell. Furthermore, accepting the mark of the beast **is not** something one will do unconsciously. With all their dire implications, neither the MARC card (described in *The Mark of the New World Order*), the national ID card (probably based on the LUCID 2000™ system), the implantable biochip, Big Brother NSA's petaflops supercomputers, nor data fed to NSA by its sister organizations (I call them the "Little Brothers"), are, in fact, **THE** mark (of the beast) to which scripture refers, even though biochip implants seems to be the technology available which most closely matches that described in Revelation 13 (**in** the hand or forehead).

Receiving the mark of the beast is going to be a matter of **worship**, not merely of economics (being permitted to buy or sell). Notice, it does not say you will be *forced* to receive the mark, but you will be *caused* to receive it . . . in other words, by coercion you will **choose** to receive it because of the pressure brought to bear upon you, both economic pressure and peer pressure. Revelation 13:16 clearly specifies that those who reject the mark will be excluded from the world economic order the Antichrist is creating. No one will buy, or sell, or work, or eat, or receive government benefits (i.e., social security, medicare, welfare/food stamps, unemployment, national healthcare, etc.), or transact any business in a global cashless society (probably via the Internet II, or a subsequent version of the World Wide Web) without his mark.

We may not be there yet, but Vice President Al Gore has stated his firm intentions of having us all on the Web by the year 2000, and he has implemented sufficient programs to see that that goal probably will be accomplished, except for the staunchest of holdouts. For example, the government is no longer issuing checks for retirement, benefits, etc. All funds are transferred directly into your bank account by direct deposit. And if anyone wants to hold out for an actual *pay-check*, it won't be issued by the government; it will be issued by some other bank, and you won't receive it until several days after your fellow direct-deposit employees are spending their money.

Although a high-ranking politician made a recommendation that all babies have an implant behind their ear before they leave the maternity ward (and in England one maternity hospital is already putting them into the ID bracelets to prevent kidnapping or mixing up babies), that would defeat the purpose as described in the Book of Revelation, namely, getting everyone to worship the Antichrist (Beast), and, as indicated in the first scripture previously quoted, those who refuse to worship and take the mark will be killed. Therefore, it isn't likely that someone will knock you out and inject an implant into your body.

It is probable that the enforcement of this "worship" (which they undoubtedly will try to pass off as cooperation with the global authorities—i.e., dissenters must be eliminated for the good of the rest of the populace) will fall to the United Nations (UN) troops, just a broader scale of the UN "peace-keeping missions" going on around the globe even today. (By the way, the military intelligence gathered for these joint UN or NATO operations is courtesy of NSA satellites and collection systems scattered around the world...which are now being shared with Russia and other communistic countries.) Just how this enforcement will be carried out is described very plainly in Revelation 20:4:

> . . . and I saw the souls of them that were **beheaded** for the witness of Jesus, and for the word of God, and which **had not worshipped** the beast, **neither had received his** [Antichrist's] **mark upon their foreheads, or in their hands**; . . . [emphasis added].

Before I continue discussing the punishment, I want to point out something else for your consideration. Please notice in both the first scripture quoted and the one just above, there is reference to worshiping *the beast* or *his image*. This has brought much speculation by Christians who stay abreast of the latest technology and its implications in light of biblical prophecy. The consensus seems to be that all of that "petaflops power" is going to be used to scan and track all things from satellites, revealing things in "real time" and enabling the creation of *holographic images* or interactive *virtual reality*. By the means of holographic technology, the image of the beast may be created, and by satellite hookups all over the world, the image may be seen and worshiped. If any organization possesses the capability to pull this off, it is the NSA! Since Satan is not like God, i.e., he is not omnipresent, he must counterfeit that impression by technological means.

A Time to Lose Your Head

No, I didn't make a mistake on this subhead. It is better to lose your head than to lose your eternal soul by selling out to the devil and taking the mark of the beast. But don't kid yourself; it will cost you your head if you are left behind when the Antichrist comes into full power. (Later in this chapter I will document the legislative foundation that has been laid to make beheading—use of the guillotine—an acceptable form of capital punishment in the US.) And should you be able to hide out and avoid the world police force, surviving in the wilderness, the dreadful acts of nature during the Great Tribulation period will be sufficient to destroy most of life on earth. The purpose of my books and sermons is to warn people of how fast we are approaching this coming event, while there is still time for them to receive Jesus Christ as Savior and Lord . . . and I'm truly convinced that the available time is *very, very* short.

Now, back to the punishment—the penalty for rejecting the Antichrist is the loss of one's head—not a very pleasant thought! But as with all things prophesied in the Bible . . . it will come to pass! This is a matter of your eternal destiny, and God created man with a free will—the ability and privilege of making the choice of whom he will serve. Therefore, you can't go to hell by accident, nor can anyone else send you there (by forcibly injecting you with the mark—you still would have to choose to *worship* the beast). It is a decision I strongly advise that you **not** postpone; it is *late* and the time for choices is *now,* before it is *too late.* At the end of this chapter, I have given you full instructions on how to make this choice and seal your eternal destiny with the Lord in heaven, rather than in hell with Satan and his demons. Accept Christ today.

Be Not Deceived!

Many places in the Bible we find the phrase, "I would not have you ignorant." My sentiments exactly! Many other places in scripture, particularly in the words of Jesus, we are admonished, "Take heed that ye be not deceived." This is a primary part of the mission of this ministry—I want to warn you about deceptions lurking out there just waiting to ensnare us.

We find that warning from Jesus in Matthew 24, Mark 13, and Luke 21, *et al.* In Matthew 24, Jesus is educating his disciples about the end times. They were curious: "Tell us, when shall these things be? and what shall be the sign of thy coming, and of the end of the world?" (24:3).

Since Jesus didn't want them "ignorant," He spent nearly the entire chapter of Matthew 24 (and many other places in scripture) telling them (and us) what could be expected to be seen by the generation that was alive upon earth when the "end" arrived. He began His reply by saying, " . . .Take heed that no man deceive you, For many shall come in my name, saying, "I am Christ"; and shall deceive many" [eastern religions and New Age gurus, et al] (24:4,5). Then He tells about all the terrible events leading up to the end. But right in the middle of the chapter, He returns to the warning not to be deceived: "For there shall arise false Christs, and false prophets. . ." (24:24).

How does this tie in with the NSA and the burgeoning technology? Jesus describes other terrible events that will occur and tells us that *even though we won't know the day nor hour* (24:36), *we can know the season* (24:32). And we know the season by recognizing that the events we see happening all around us with greater frequency and intensity are, in fact, fulfillments of Jesus's prophecies in scripture. It is imperative that we understand that Jesus was trying to let us know when the "end times" would arrive. He said, ". . .when ye shall see all these things, know that it is near, even at the doors" (24:33). Then He clinches it by telling us that ". . .this generation [the one that witnesses these events] shall not pass, till **all** these things be fulfilled" (24:34) [emphasis added].

The NSA Didn't Originate the Concept of a New World Order, But It May Help Bring It to Pass!

What is the *real* origin of the New World Order? It is my opinion, being convinced by the evidence I have amassed, that we are that generation of which Christ spoke, and that all things found in Matthew 24 (and other related prophetic books, i.e., Daniel, Ezekiel, Revelation, et al) will be fulfilled in our lifetime. Never—before now—has technology been sufficiently advanced to carry out such a worldwide endeavor . . .which fulfills yet another prophecy: "In the last days knowledge shall increase"—with the implication that it will increase exponentially. And if you don't believe that is happening—when knowledge is doubling every 18 months or less, and Gflops have been left behind by teraflops and the forthcoming petaflops, and the new semiconductors on the drawing board are shrinking from 1/200th the thickness of a human hair (.25 microns) down to 1/1000th the thickness of a hair—then you need to "wake up and smell the coffee, folks!"

Ever since the Tower of Babel (in the Book of Genesis), Satan has been attempting to create a New World Order where people would worship him as the God of this world. Scripture indicates that God, indeed, will permit this to occur at the end of the age. For the past 200 years, specifically subsequent to May 1, 1776, the Luciferians, New Agers, witches, Satanists, socialists/communists, fascists/nazis, liberals, *et al,* all have been using a new term to describe this final form of global enslavement under the Antichrist. The term they have been using is the "New World Order."

It should be obvious by now that there is ample evidence to support my conclusion that this final New World Order is about to occur. Scripture says that the devil will divide the world into 10 kingdoms, and, indeed, that has occurred under the Treaty of Rome, which divided the world into exactly 10 regions, the United States and Canada being region number one of this New World Order occultic world government. (By the way, just a point of information: "Treaties" supercede all other regulations of government, including the Constitution. So when our government signs the papers committing us to a trade treaty, or a disarmament treaty, or an environmental treaty, the terms of that treaty are given precedence over any other national law, and usually are enforced by some arm of the UN.)

Jesus warned us that deception would be rampant during this time—so much so that He specifically warned us even the elect of God would be deceived and believe the lie of this New World Order under the devil, if it were possible. He implied that only the elect *could not* be fooled, and this is why so few today are able to discern the truth of what's occurring. Most people—unfortunately, even most Christians—are blind to what's happening in terms of the prophetic scriptures, as they apply to the times in which we live.

Don't Miss the Signs of His Soon Return

I Thessalonians 5 warns us to beware when people speak

of peace and safety, and indeed, George Bush promised us peace and "security" (safety) when he announced the beginning of the New World Order...then promptly committed the US to fight in the Iraqi war. The Lord tells Christians that they should not be asleep like the rest of the world; rather we should be awake, aware, and watchful regarding these end times events. Unfortunately, most *are* dead asleep or blind to what's happening. The signs of the Lord's second coming—the end of the age, the New World Order under the Antichrist and his 666 economic mark system, and Armageddon—all are apparent so visibly, even in our secular news media, that no one should miss the signs of His soon return.

Pentagon Calls for Armageddon in the Year 2001

Even *The New York Times* indicated in a 1992 article that the Pentagon is planning for a total mobilization for global war in the year 2001.

Many top fundamentalist/evangelicals subscribe to the dispensational belief that there will be a total of 6000 years from Adam until the end of the age, when Christ returns with His believers to fight and win the battle of Armageddon, ushering in the millennium—the 1000-year reign of peace. I, too, subscribe to this belief. Numerous chronological studies have been done throughout the years and are available for your perusal at most Christian bookstores and libraries. These studies indicate that the years 2001-2004 may conclude this 6000-year period.

Can We Trust Our Calendars?

Probably not, but calculating to the best of our ability, and taking into consideration all known calendar errors and changes, etc., somewhere around the year 2004 this age should end. There is a little-known book called *The Epistle of Barnabas*, included in a respected work by Lightfoot entitled *The Apostolic Fathers*. Although no one can attest for certain that this is the same Barnabas who accompanied Paul in the

Book of Acts, it is believed to be true.

In Chapter 15 of the *Epistle of Barnabas,* this 6000-year plan is mentioned specifically as God's total plan from beginning to end. It says that at the conclusion of 6000, the sabbath millennium will begin.

Let me reiterate, *I am not setting dates for either the end of the age or the return of Christ* (although the Bible definitely indicates, in Jesus' own words, that we should be able to see these events and properly infer that the end is near). Neither am I implying that the *Epistle of Barnabas* is some missing part of the Bible. As a matter of fact, there are many other extrabiblical historical books that indicate that "6000 years" holds some special significance, and may indeed witness the conclusion of all human history. Revelation 20 implies this, because it mentions six times that there will be a thousand-year millennium of true peace, under the true God of this world, Jesus Christ, in a true New World Order, of which this present New World Order is merely an evil counterfeit—just as Satan counterfeits other manifestations of God's power.

Matthew 24:36 only restricts us from knowing "the day and hour" of the end, but other scriptures (24:33, *et al*) say we will know when it is very "near, even at the doors," because we will witness the events outlined in Matthew and other prophetic books. So be very clear—I am not saying that I know the day nor the hour nor the specific year, however, I do believe that the 6000-year plan may hold prophetic significance; all signs seem to indicate that things are about to wrap up soon...and we were told to *watch the signs.* It appears that Lucifer's final hour is at hand and the Great Tribulation period is about to begin, being ushered in by the current New World Order troops. It is not overly significant whether it begins in 2000, 2004, or even a little later; the fact remains that we were told to be watchful and aware, so that the Day of the Lord should not overtake us as a thief in the night.

What Makes New Agers Think They Are New?

It is interesting to note, if you browse in any New Age bookstore or acquire any occultic literature, that the New Agers, the Satanists, the Freemasons, the occultists, and the witches (in other words, all of Satan's representatives in whatever form, shape, or title) all are talking about something very significant that they are expecting to occur about the year 2000—a *harmonic convergence* for a New Age which will bring about a global transformation. They indicate in their books and other literature that the *old age* under Christ ends, and the new age under Lucifer begins around that time. This is why New Agers call themselves "New Agers." They are looking forward expectantly to the New Age under Lucifer in the year 2000±.

Other Signs for Which to Watch

One of the signs pointed out by Christ that would signal the advent of the end of the age is worldwide famine. A *Los Angeles Times* article dated January 1, 1993, says: ". . . global food shortage looms by the year 2000." There are just too many "coincidences" occurring during this generation to warn us that some type of major transformation is in the works for the end of this century/millennium. All but the blind (especially the willfully blind) can see it clearly.

President George Bush, a staunch promoter of the New World Order, wanted to insinuate the New World Order into every area of our lives, but in particular the military, defense, and "police action" portion of our nation. In the September 28, 1991, edition of *The Honolulu Advertiser*, in an article titled, "New (safer) world order," Bush's plan for the disarmament of the US, following the end of Desert Storm, is announced:

> . . . the plan outlined by Bush yesterday calls for such weapons to be dismantled and destroyed after they are withdrawn.

Shortly after, in 1994, our fleet of B-52 bombers were hacked into pieces with a "guillotine" and scattered in a B-52 graveyard in the desert southwest. Then the enemy was invited over to inspect the destruction. It makes you wonder on whose side our leaders are . . . on second thought, there is no need for wonder—it is blatantly obvious! Following the publication of the above article, Bush stated that he hoped that this would encourage the Soviets to do likewise. Good luck!

The Old New World Order

In Ecclesiastes, we learn that "there is nothing new under the sun." As I have explained before, the New World Order is really just an Old World Order that Satan has been trying unsuccessfully to foist on mankind since the Tower of Babel and before. I'm sure he must be dancing with glee to realize that it finally will come into existence in the near future; I'm equally sure that he is painfully aware that his time is short and this New World Order is the final stage of his death grip on this earth. When God's New World Order arrives, Jesus will be the King of kings and Lord of lords over this earth and its inhabitants.

Will the United Nations Become the New World Order Global Government?

What about the United Nations? Is it going to evolve into the infrastructure of the New World Order? Only God knows for sure, but based on over seven years of research into this matter, there is no doubt in my mind that it will. At present, it couldn't accomplish that feat because it is still a collection of independently sovereign nations; whereas the New World Order eventually will relegate independent nations to the status of "world states" or "nation states," only operating under the auspices of the head of world government (Antichrist). But I believe that it is the forerunner that is laying the groundwork for the New World Order.

Identity Crisis or Identification Crisis?

It is vital that you understand the difference between your *identification* and your *identity*, because we are in the process of losing both. Your *identification* consists of the biometric and visual methods used to determine if you are the person authorized to access something. Your *identity* is your soul, your personality. . . it is how you feel about yourself inside, i.e., your patriotism, or lack of it, your privacy rights, your right to train up your children in the way you determine, etc.

At the moment, America is suffering an identity crisis—we no longer know whom we can trust and have the feeling things are turned upside-down. Our elected officials are looking out for the New World Order and the UN, instead of us taxpayers who are paying both for their salaries and for all the ludicrous programs they are implementing to undermine our freedoms. Yes, *America is suffering an identity crisis!*

At the same time, America and Americans are suffering an identification crisis, and it's going to get a whole lot worse. We are being identified for everything; and now all those bar codes and magnetic stripes on all those plastic cards we carry in our pockets are to be linked biometrically, that is, to our fingerprint, eyescan, thermal facial scan, DNA, etc. Then they want to take away all those pieces of plastic in exchange for only one piece. . .which, of course, could still be lost or stolen. *Eureka!* We have just the answer. . .a tiny little implant that can't be lost or stolen and can positively identify everyone by just running their hands over the scanner. Once identified, you can access your medical records, bank accounts, job records, insurance and credit history, etc., all from just this one little source.

Winn Schwartau warns us about chaos on the electronic superhighway in his book, *Information Warfare*. Even though his book is distributed by the World Future Society, a New World Order think tank, Schwartau is intellectually honest enough to warn us about the disadvantages of the electronic control of the world in this fascinating and informative book. He addresses the assault on personal privacy, national economic security, industrial espionage, solutions in cyberspace, and much more. I highly recommend you obtain a copy. (I quoted from it extensively in my book, *The Mark of the New World Order.*)

The Noahide Laws—Could These Be the Foundation for Capital Punishment by Decapitation in The New World Order?

Today such forms of punishment are considered barbaric . . . but if God says in scripture that decapitation will be the method of extermination in Antichrist's reign of terror during the Great Tribulation, and if, as I believe, that time is some-where in the not-too-distant future, then we should find some legal foundations in progress to justify this type of capital punishment.

Even though the major thrust of this book has centered around the NSA and its tentacles reaching into all areas of our lives, as well as the crisis of our identity as American citizens and our identification as individuals, I have provided you with enough peripheral information to give you an over-view of what the New World Order actually is, politically, economically, and spiritually. I have attempted to convey from a factual standpoint how God's scripture is being fulfilled in our time. I have told you about electronic enslavement, bio-metrics, smart card identification on a global scale, probably on the Internet II via the LUCID 2000™ system, which it appears ultimately will evolve into use of biochip technology *in our right hands* to totally enslave us. I have given you scrip-tures to tie it all to the fulfillment of Bible prophecy, i.e., you cannot participate in any of the world's actvities without the **mark**, once the Antichrist takes command of the New World Order. And I have told you what will happen if you decline the offer of this Satanic **mark** (probably a biochip). By now you must admit that this is a *spiritual* choice.

Now, the Antichrist isn't likely to do anything predicted by the Bible—at least not intentionally. So we must have some foundation for switching back to this ancient form of execution, if the Bible prophecy is to be fulfilled as written. I believe we now may have such a foundation in place—at least in the US.

During Bush's administration, shortly before the Gulf war, an innocuous-sounding little piece of legislation was signed into law, allegedly to honor an old man on his ninetieth birthday.

H.J. Res. 104 was signed into law as a proclamation to designate March 26, 1991, as "Education Day, U.S.A." Sounds innocent enough, doesn't it? Not so! Written into all the "WHEREAS's" were incorporated a number of references calling for the return to the ethical values of the "Seven Noahide Laws." Now you won't find any call for decapitation in this harmless appearing little document, but beware, that's just a smoke screen. When one begins to dig into the historical documents of the ancient Jewish Talmud with reference to the Noahide Laws, you will find the commandments they consider ethical values, and what they consider justifiable punishment for breaking them . . . guess what, you lose your head!

Now, don't jump to any wild conclusions, because this law has no apparent "teeth" in it yet; the government *did not* call for the establishment of capital punishment by decapitation, but by joint resolution the House and Senate did establish Public Law No. 102-14 in 1991, which calls for the return to the ethics of the Noahide Laws. I don't think it's too much of a stretch to extrapolate this into fulfillment of scripture, once the Antichrist comes to power. Because one of the Noahide Laws concerns blasphemy, Christians who refuse to worship the beast likely could be executed under violation of the blasphemy law, as they will not acknowledge the Antichrist as God.

In the July-August, 1991, issue of *The Gap,* the newsletter published by the Noahide movement, the lead article revealed that there is pressure being applied for world-wide recognition of the seven laws. Professor of International Law Ernest Easterly, at Southern University Law Center, said: "With further recognition by other nations and international courts, **the Seven Noahide Laws should become the cornerstone of a truly civilized international legal order.**" *Read that: New World Order!*

Legislator Tepfer Wants Heads to Roll In Georgia!

The State of Georgia attempted to pass legislation offering decapitation as an alternative to the electric chair for inmates who were about to be executed. They would have us believe that it was for a good and humanitarian purpose—and perhaps it was—but it still would be in place for the use of those without such lofty purposes. One article reads:

Guillotine Proposed as Means of Execution In Georgia

Georgia lawmaker Doug Tepfer (D, 61st Dist.) has proposed a bill to replace the state's electric chair with the guillotine. Tepfer's reasoning? It would allow for death-row inmates as organ donors, he says, since the "blade makes a clean cut and leaves vital organs intact...."

The guillotine, invented by the French Dr. Guillotine, was mainly used in the 18th and 19th century and chops off a person's head. It hasn't been used for decades in any country in the world.

The measure failed to pass the first time around, but I hear they may try it again. Of course, as we witnessed on the *Prime Time Live* program in October, 1997, we always could set up an execution yard in the parking lot of the hospital to be handy to harvest the spare parts, as they were doing in China, where organs for transplants are sold for sizable amounts. The only problem is that no one really knows if these were criminals, or just dissenters. They were made to kneel in the dirt, then soldiers shot them in the back of the head, execution style, so as not to damage any usable body parts. Where communism prevails, anything can happen...which is why I am frantically warning everyone not to trust the communists. We should not be granting them "most favored nation" status in our trade agreements. And as of the second week of October, 1997, the "window of opportunity" for free evangelism in Russia officially was closed. Thank God for the many organizations that seized the moment and bombarded the Russian people with evangelists carrying the message of the gospel—the good news, helping people with clothing and food, and Bibles in their own language, and training nationals to be able to continue their worship and evangelism after Russia kicks out all the foreign groups. The way the law reads is that only the Russian Orthodox Church will be recognized. Any other church must get permission to exist through them. It is believed that persecution will begin soon and drive the church underground. Pray for our persecuted brothers and sisters in Christ throughout the world.

Possible Scenario to Usher in The New World Order

Based on over seven years of research, having read over 300 books, mountains of periodicals and technical product brochures, occultic newsletters, and various New Age and Masonic publications, I feel I have gained an incredibly good understanding into the mindset of Satan's people who wish to bring about this New World Order. I will attempt to convey to you a *possible* scenario that could occur in the next few years to bring about world government under the Antichrist.

I want to make it absolutely clear that I am not prophesying—I do not consider myself a prophet in the biblical sense, however, the knowledge I have accrued during these seven years gives considerable credibility to my conjectures concerning these events.

The Luciferians, who desire a New World Order under the devil, often use a little-known Latin phrase that describes how they intend to bring it all about. That phrase is *ordo ab chao.* *Ordo ab chao* means "order from chaos." In other words, they purposely plan to create more than enough chaos in the world to convince us that we need a New World Order to fix it. The Book of Daniel says that the Antichrist first will come as a peacemaker, and "by peace he shall destroy many." So even though many wars and rumors of wars are occurring around the world presently, it's going to get worse, because the devil has to terrify the world into needing a worldwide peacemaker to bring order out of chaos. As this book goes to press, we are hearing the sabers rattle in Korea, Bosnia, the middle east, and many other places. I believe that in the not-too-distant future both Korea and the middle east will present the Antichrist with the chaos he needs to pull this off. These areas soon could explode into full-blown war—horrifying quagmires—that will call for a complete mobilization of US Armed Forces to help quell the planned disorder. . .under the command of UN officers, of course! There even could be a **limited** nuclear strike, utilizing small atomic weapons. Such a nuclear conflagration—unheard of since World War II—would terrify the world into thinking that it was on the very precipice of Armageddon (even though *actual* Armageddon will be several years after the Antichrist comes to power). The world, then, would need a world government under a charismatic, global leader (the Antichrist) to restore order and create peace from chaos. . .*ordo ab chao.*

In addition to the war chaos scenario presented above, Satan's people also could create an international financial disaster—an economic cataclysm the likes of which the world never has seen—creating havoc around the globe that is unparalleled in history. Worldwide famine and uncontrolled contagious diseases are other forms of chaos. Other possibilities could be created as a result of an information "meltdown," created by terrorists, thieves, government agencies, or others. As Winn Schwartau suggested in *Information Warfare,* an informational "Chernobyl" is inevitable—it's just a matter of where and when. As a result, virtually everyone's wealth will be wiped out over night—not difficult in a cashless society! Banks will close and circumstances will be desperate, even worse than the Great Depression of the 1930's through which our parents lived. People will be reduced to poverty and will be dependent totally upon the government for subsistance. Money, food, medical assistance, and other benefits will be used to make people gratefully submit to the government's plan to resolve this and other global crises.

Dr. Henry Kissinger, a new world order "lieutenant," was quoted several years ago as saying that what the world really needed to make it realize that world government was necessary, was an outside threat of some kind. He postulated that a UFO alien invasion might be such a world-unifying threat. (Again, I hear echoes from the Iron Mountain Report, as well as the NSA's facilities in Roswell, New Mexico, and Pine Gap, Australia.) He [Kissinger] further stated that when confronted by this threat, the people of the world gladly would relinquish their national sovereignty and individual rights to receive protection from the UN-led world government against these "invaders." So, based upon this insight from Mr. Kissinger, I surmise that in addition to war chaos, economic cataclysm, and other disastrous events, such as famine and natural disasters, i.e. floods, hurricanes, earthquakes, volcanic eruptions, meteor bombardment, etc., we also may be confronted with a demonic manifestation in the form of a UFO invasion. New Agers contend that the "aliens" are poised and ready to make intervention into the affairs of mankind at just the right time to "save us from ourselves." And they widely believe that such events may occur near the year 2000.

By this time, advanced technology probably will have moved us forward to the point that our smart cards already will have been replaced by a more positive, unalterable means of permanent identification (biochip implants). But until then, we are being pre-conditioned (desensitized) to accept such technology by means of routine use of biochip identification of animals, as well as an imminent national ID card—probably based on the current military MARC card, using the new LUCID 2000™ system for implementation.

Eventually, as citizens of the world, as well as members of nation-states, we will be required to accept a new system of international identification, the **MARC/MARK of the New World Order**, which likely will be the **mark of the beast** described previously. Since the scripture calls for the mark to be placed either in the right hand or the forehead, it is

significant that we find the following in an article by Donald
R. Richards, CPP, titled "ID Technology Faces the Future,"
which appeared in the April, 1994, edition of *Security Management* magazine, discussing biometric identification methods,
which states:

> Since users are likely to be clothed from head to toe,
> the identification decision must be based on the **hands**
> or the **head**. . . [emphasis added].

The ramifications of accepting this mark, as I outlined in
detail earlier, result in the loss of your eternal soul and eternal
torment in hell (Rev. 14:9-11). The price you will pay for *not*
accepting the mark will be your head. . . literally! Neither of
those choices sounds very appealing to me. It pays to make
your choice prior to this event, while there is still time. . .even
though it may be very short.

Choosing the Right New World Order

The drive toward a New World Order continues. Jesus
predicted a time of terrible judgment, so bad that if God did
not intervene, there would be no flesh left on the earth (Matt.
24:22). Someday Jesus *will* return, and when He does, He *will*
establish His reign on the earth for a thousand years (Rev.
20:6). This will be God's New World Order promised throughout the Bible. The time to choose which New World Order
is for you is **now**, before the time for choices is past. Satan's
counterfeit is near at hand and, according to Joel 3:9-12,
millions will perish during his cruel reign; however, Jesus,
the Savior, invites you to receive His grace and forgiveness
instead, and rejoice in His New World Order forever.

No man can serve two masters; that is a biblical admonition,
but you know it to be true from everyday experience. Two
other scriptures warn us to "choose you this day whom you
will serve" and that "today is the day of salvation." Those
are easy to interpret. . .the choice is ours—don't wait until
it is too late to make it; and today is the only day we have

to accept the Lord's offer of salvation, since none of us have any guarantee of tomorrow.

In spite of New Age propaganda to the contrary, there are really only two choices: The Son of the one true God, The Lord Jesus Christ—or Satan, the fallen angel, the father of lies, the Antichrist, the false god, whose number (according to scripture) is 666. For those who may believe that we don't have any choice in our destiny, I want you to consider what God said in the Old Testament. First we are told in Joshua to "choose you this day whom you will serve. As for me and my house, we will serve the Lord." In another place God said: I set before you this day life and death—choose life! I also urge you to *choose life!* Not only are the rewards "out of this world," but you can escape God's judgment for rejecting His Son.

How Can I Make My Choice and Choose Life?

The Bible promises that all who have received Jesus Christ as their Savior and Lord will be saved from the coming wrath of God on a Christ-rejecting, God-hating world. Yes, you, too, can escape the coming New World Order horror by making Christ your Lord and Savior today. Don't procrastinate, do it now. Worship is a choice. Choose to worship Jesus Christ, not the Antichrist. All it takes on your part is a sincere invitation (it's usually called a prayer), then Jesus does the part He promised. . .He washes you clean by His shed blood, welcomes you into God's family, and becomes your Savior. This is not *religion,* it's a *relationship.* Once you have established the relationship with Jesus by asking Him to become your Savior (an immediate transaction), then proceed to make Him the *Lord* of your life. . .seek to pattern your life after His example, described in the Bible, and seek His direction for your life. He has promised never to leave us nor forsake us. Then tell someone about this new relationship. The Bible says that you must believe in your heart and confess with your mouth—you can think of it as comfirming the transaction.

Personal Preparations

Of course, being spiritually prepared is the most important thing, but you might give consideration to preparing in the natural, as well, i.e., store extra food, acquire some precious metals, etc. because some very precarious times lie ahead of us before the Lord returns for His church.

Jesus said, "Surely I come quickly." To which we respond, **"Even so, come, Lord Jesus."** May God bless you and keep you in the days ahead.

Readers are encouraged to contact Terry Cook
or
Second Coming Ministries, Inc.
for information on other
publications, videos, and speaking engagements.

Terry L. Cook
Second Coming Ministries, Inc.
61535 S. Highway 97, Unit 9, Ste. 288
Bend, OR 97702
Phone (541) 593-9916 / Fax (541) 593-9917